CONTEMPORARY
*B*lack
*B*iography

ISSN-1058-1316

CONTEMPORARY

*B*lack

*B*iography

Profiles from the International Black Community

Volume 70

GALE
CENGAGE Learning

Detroit • New York • San Francisco • New Haven, Conn • Waterville, Maine • London

GALE
CENGAGE Learning

Contemporary Black Biography, Volume 70

Kepos Media, Inc.: Paula Kepos and Derek Jacques, editors

Project Editor: Margaret Mazurkiewicz

Image Research and Acquisitions: Leitha Etheridge-Sims

Editorial Support Services: Nataliya Mikheyeva

Rights and Permissions: Katherine Alverson, Jhanay Williams

Manufacturing: Dorothy Maki, Cynde Bishop

Composition and Prepress: Mary Beth Trimper, Gary Leach

Imaging: Lezlie Light

© 2009 Gale, Cengage Learning

For product information and technology assistance, contact us at **Gale Customer Support, 1-800-877-4253.**
For permission to use material from this text or product, submit all requests online at **www.cengage.com/permissions.**
Further permissions questions can be emailed to **permissionrequest@cengage.com**

Gale
27500 Drake Rd.
Farmington Hills, MI, 48331-3535

ISBN-13: 978-1-4144-3277-9
ISBN-10: 1-4144-3277-1

ISSN 1058-1316

This title is also available as an e-book.
ISBN 13: 978-1-4144-3791-0
ISBN-10: 1-4144-3791-9
Contact your Gale sales representative for ordering information.

Printed in the United States of America
1 2 3 4 5 6 7 12 11 10 09 08

Advisory Board

Contents

Introduction

Contemporary Black Biography provides informative biographical profiles of the important and influential persons of African heritage who form the international black community: men and women who have changed today's world and are shaping tomorrow's. *Contemporary Black Biography* covers persons of various nationalities in a wide variety of fields, including architecture, art, business, dance, education, fashion, film, industry, journalism, law, literature, medicine, music, politics and government, publishing, religion, science and technology, social issues, sports, television, theater, and others. In addition to in-depth coverage of names found in today's headlines, *Contemporary Black Biography* provides coverage of selected individuals from earlier in this century whose influence continues to impact on contemporary life. *Contemporary Black Biography* also provides coverage of important and influential persons who are not yet household names and are therefore likely to be ignored by other biographical reference series. Each volume also includes listee updates on names previously appearing in *CBB*.

Designed for Quick Research and Interesting Reading

- **Attractive page design** incorporates textual subheads, making it easy to find the information you're looking for.

- **Easy-to-locate data sections** provide quick access to vital personal statistics, career information, major awards, and mailing addresses, when available.

- **Informative biographical essays** trace the subject's personal and professional life with the kind of in-depth analysis you need.

- **To further enhance your appreciation** of the subject, most entries include photographic portraits.

- **Sources for additional information** direct the user to selected books, magazines, and newspapers where more information on the individuals can be obtained.

Helpful Indexes Make It Easy to Find the Information You Need

Contemporary Black Biography includes cumulative Nationality, Occupation, Subject, and Name indexes that make it easy to locate entries in a variety of useful ways.

Available in Electronic Formats

Diskette/Magnetic Tape. Contemporary Black Biography is available for licensing on magnetic tape or diskette in a fielded format. Either the complete database or a custom selection of entries may be ordered. The database is available for internal data processing and nonpublishing purposes only. For more information, call (800) 877-GALE.

On-line. Contemporary Black Biography is available online through Mead Data Central's NEXIS Service in the NEXIS, PEOPLE and SPORTS Libraries in the GALBIO file and Gale's Biography Resource Center.

Disclaimer

Contemporary Black Biography uses and lists websites as sources and these websites may become obsolete.

We Welcome Your Suggestions

The editors welcome your comments and suggestions for enhancing and improving *Contemporary Black Biography*. If you would like to suggest persons for inclusion in the series, please submit these names to the editors. Mail comments or suggestions to:

The Editor

Contemporary Black Biography

Gale, Cengage Learning

27500 Drake Rd.

Farmington Hills, MI 48331-3535

Phone: (800) 347-4253

Sani Abacha

1943–1998

Military ruler

Even by the standards of an era during which military coups and dictatorships were the norm in many post-independence African countries, the rule of Nigeria's General Sani Abacha is considered to have been particularly brutal. Responsible for the imprisonment and executions of scores of perceived political opponents, Abacha also was believed to have amassed a fortune from his personal dealings in Nigeria's oil reserves and to have embezzled several billion dollars from the central bank of his own administration, which he placed in accounts overseas. After Abacha's death in 1998, the missing money became the subject of an international lawsuit involving the government of Switzerland—where the bulk of the money was discovered—and Abacha's surviving family members. Further scandal erupted when Abacha's widow's name became associated with a now-infamous Nigerian e-mail scam; while Maryam Abacha was not believed to be directly responsible for the "spam scam," the family's notoriety only increased because of it.

Found Success in Military

Abacha was born on September 20, 1943, in Kano, Kano State, Nigeria. From 1957 to 1962 he was a student, first in the City Senior Primary School of Kano and then in the Provincial Secondary School (later renamed Government College). During the years immediately following its independence, from 1960 to 1966, Nigeria was governed by a civilian regime, the First Republic. In these years Abacha trained for the military and received his first appointment in the Nigerian Army. He attended the Nigerian Military Training College in the northern city of Kaduna from 1962 to 1963 and received his appointment as second lieutenant in 1963. Following was a series of promotions within the Nigerian military.

When the nominally democratic First Republic fell to a military coup in 1966, Abacha received his first significant promotion, from second lieutenant to lieutenant. The military hoped to stem the tide of strikes, work-to-rule actions (a bargaining tactic whereby employees continue to perform the duties of their jobs but refuse to perform any extra duties), demonstrations, and riots by workers and peasants that had erupted across the country in protest against the civilian regime, which had unleashed an unchecked police force against Nigerian citizens and had failed to maintain public services. Meanwhile, individual politicians displayed their enormous wealth arrogantly in the face of abject poverty, massive illiteracy, unemployment, and hunger. The military proved unable, however, to impose order on the nation.

During colonial times Nigeria had been divided into three regions, roughly corresponding to the areas of its largest ethnic groups, specifically the predominantly Muslim Hausa and Fulani peoples of the North, the largely Christian Yoruba people of the West, and the largely Christian Igbo people of the East. In 1967 the East seceded and formed the Biafran Republic; the ensuing civil war, lasting until 1970, caused the deaths of approximately one million people, according to journalist Peter da Costa in *Africa Report*. At the

At a Glance . . .

Born on September 20, 1943, in Kano, Kano State, Nigeria; died on June 8, 1998, in Abuja, Nigeria; married Maryam Jidah, 1965; children: six sons, three daughters. *Religion:* Muslim. *Education:* Provincial Secondary School (now Government College), Kano, Nigeria, 1957–62; Nigerian Military Training College, Kaduna, 1962–63, 1964; MONS Defense Officers' Cadet Training College, Aldershot, United Kingdom, 1963; School of Infantry, Warminster, United Kingdom, 1966, 1971; Command and Staff College, Jaji, Nigeria, 1976; National Institute for Policy and Strategic Studies, Kuru, Jos, Nigeria, 1981; Senior International Defense Course, Monterey, CA, United States, 1982.

Career: Nigerian Army, commissioned second lieutenant, 1963, lieutenant, 1966, captain, 1967, platoon and battalion commander, training department commander, 2nd Infantry Division, major, 1969, lieutenant-colonel, 1972, commanding officer, 2nd Infantry Brigade, colonel, 1975, brigadier, 1980, announced coup, December 31, 1983, appointed general officer commanding, 2nd Mechanized Division, 1984–85, major-general, 1984, announced coup, August 27, 1985; appointed army chief of staff and member, Armed Forces Ruling Council (AFRC), 1985, lieutenant-general, 1987, chairman, Joint Chiefs of Staff, 1989, ministry of defense, 1990, secretary of defense, August 26, 1993; seized head of state in coup, November 17, 1993, and ruled Nigeria, until 1998.

beginning of that war in 1967, Abacha assumed the position of captain; over the next three years he rose in the Nigerian Army from platoon and battalion commander to commander of the training department, 2nd Infantry Division, and to major in 1969. In 1972, soon after the war ended and the boundaries of the nation were restored, Abacha gained the post of lieutenant-colonel. During the next few years, Abacha received subsequent promotions to colonel in 1975 and to brigadier in 1980.

Commensurate with his military positions, Abacha received further training and education in Nigeria, the United Kingdom, and the United States. In the United Kingdom he studied at the MONS Defense Officers' Cadet Training College in Aldershot in 1963, and at the School of Infantry in Warminster in 1966 and 1971. In Nigeria he attended the Command and Staff

College in Jaji in 1976, and the National Institute for Policy and Strategic Studies in Kuru, Jos, in 1981. In 1982 Abacha studied at the Senior International Defense Course in Monterey, California.

Played Key Role in Military Coup

Abacha first entered the national spotlight at 7 a.m. on December 31, 1983, in a broadcast over Radio Nigeria announcing the overthrow of the civilian regime. Citing the "Text of Coup Broadcast to the Nation, 31 December 1983" in their book *The Rise and Fall of Nigeria's Second Republic, 1979–84,* historians Toyin Falola and Julius Ihonvbere quoted Abacha as having stated, "I am referring to the harsh intolerable conditions under which we are now living. Our economy has been hopelessly mismanaged. We have become a debtor and beggar-nation." For these reasons, Abacha said, the armed forces "in discharge of [their] national role as the promoters and protectors of our national interest decided to effect a change in the leadership of the government of the Federal Republic of Nigeria."

After announcing the first coup in what would become an eleven-year-long series of military rulers, Abacha participated centrally in succeeding coups and continued to move ever closer to holding ultimate power himself. With the first coup on December 31, 1983, General Muhammadu Buhari became head of state and Abacha became both a member of the ruling Supreme Military Council (SMC) and a general officer commanding of the Second Mechanised Division in Ibadan, Nigeria. Next, on August 27, 1985, Abacha appeared in camouflage on Nigerian television to announce another coup. Having been promoted to major-general before the coup, afterward he moved up to chief of army staff and became a member of the Armed Forces Ruling Council (AFRC). General Babangida took the absolute lead as Nigeria's first military president, promising an eventual return to civilian rule.

Throughout Babangida's subsequent eight-year rule, Abacha maintained his position through several high-level reorganizations and steadily gained power, concluding finally with the lead of the entire military upon Babangida's departure in August of 1993. Promoted to lieutenant-general in 1987, Abacha survived Babangida's cut in the AFRC from twenty-eight to nineteen members in 1989, and in the same year received another promotion to chairman of the Joint Chiefs of Staff. When Major Gideon Orkar attempted a coup on April 22, 1990, Abacha defended Babangida and announced the crushing of the coup on Radio Nigeria. In September of 1990 Babangida shuffled Abacha out of the chief of army staff position and into the head of the ministry of defense.

In 1993 Abacha survived even the exit of Babangida himself. When Babangida handed over the reins of government on August 26, 1993, to Ernest Shonekan, a civilian appointee, Abacha assumed the lead of the military as defense secretary. Babangida resigned amid a series of strikes and protests sparked by his annulment of the results of the presidential election held June 12, which most likely was won by businessman Moshood Abiola, according to the *New York Times.* Babangida reportedly voided the elections for fear that Abiola, a wealthy Yoruba-speaker from the Southwest who ran on the Social Democrat ticket, would upset the hold on power formerly wielded by military generals from the North. When he declared himself president anyway, Abiola was accused of treason and put in prison, where he died in 1998, one day after Abacha's death.

Deposed President and Seized Power

In an attempt to gain legitimacy for his term as president of the Interim National Government (ING), the civilian president Shonekan freed political prisoners, lifted press restrictions, and dismantled the oil bureaucracy, which had been accused of squandering the nation's substantial oil revenues. Shonekan, however, also imposed a fuel price increase of 600 percent at the urging of the World Bank and the International Monetary Fund (IMF), according to the *New York Times.* That increase precipitated a national general strike. Police fell into clashes with pro-democracy demonstrators across the Southwest while banks, major shops, and factories remained closed for one week. Finally, the Lagos High Court declared the ING an illegal government. In the midst of this civic unrest, on November 17, 1993, Abacha requested Shonekan's resignation and seized control of the state himself.

Abacha initially offered a few concessions to pro-democracy forces, Abiola supporters, and Yoruba contenders for power, but over the course of his first year in power those actions lost their substance. He also immediately dissolved all remnants of democratic structures inherited from Babangida's transition to democracy. Existing political parties, gatherings, the National Electoral Commission, and federal, state, and local governments were all banned and slated for replacement by military commanders. With no political parties allowed and no campaigning admitted, Abacha's calls for a constitutional conference met with abysmally low voter turnout and boycotts from every region except the North.

In Abacha's first year of governance, his attempts to chart a new economic course for Nigeria were unsuccessful. He had turned away from the economic suggestions offered by the IMF to Babangida and reimposed controls on the economy. Nigeria, however, lacked the infrastructure to achieve the exchange and interest rates Abacha mandated, and production costs skyrocketed. In addition, petroleum workers went on strike to protest Abiola's imprisonment and to press for higher wages, leaving the country's industrial outfits with no raw materials for production.

Violated Human Rights

Gradually succumbing to paranoia, Abacha rarely appeared in public, refused to grant interviews or allow the publication of any personal information about himself, and developed a habit of working only at night. According to Howard W. French—writing in the *New York Times* the day after Abacha's death—the leader regularly purged his staff and the military of perceived political opponents, frequently jailing and threatening to execute his trusted former advisers and, at his death, leaving the Nigerian military in a shambles of suspicion and demoralization. Abacha's persistent crackdowns on civil rights created an atmosphere of terror among the civilian population as well. Wole Soyinka, a Nigerian human rights advocate and winner of the 1986 Nobel Prize for literature, was a vocal dissenter of Abacha's policies. Encouraging the international community to take action, he said in the *New York Times:* "It is a regime of infamy and it should be isolated…. This is going to be the worst and most brutal regime that Nigeria ever had. This regime is prepared to kill, torture, and make opponents disappear." A number of organizations pressed for democratic government, including the National Democratic Coalition (Nadeco), the Campaign for Democracy, and the Movement for the Survival of the Ogoni People (MOSOP).

The leader of MOSOP, Nigerian writer Ken Saro-Wiwa, was another highly visible opponent of the Abacha regime. In 1990 Saro-Wiwa launched a massive environmental campaign against the ecological degradation and loss of human life and livelihood in the Niger Delta widely perceived to be caused by international oil companies, most notably Shell and Chevron. Saro-Wiwa accused the Abacha government of instituting genocide against the Ogoni people by refusing to regulate the companies' activities—which included using private police forces to batter and even kill protesters—and profiting handsomely. As the protests in the region continued, the violence increased. Dozens of Ogoni protesters were injured, and Abacha's military government confiscated Saro-Wiwa's passport and arrested him on numerous occasions. According to the Web site Remember Saro-Wiwa, the international community was growing more and more alarmed by events in Nigeria; after a particularly violent clash between protesters and Shell Oil's security force, "Amnesty International … issued an 'Urgent Action' request, concerned about possible extra-judicial executions by the military against Ogoni protestors."

The request proved prophetic. After the mysterious deaths of four pro-government Ogoni leaders in the spring of 1993, Abacha sent troops into the region and had Saro-Wiwa and four others arrested for murder. Witnesses would later tell of mass rape and terrorism committed by Abacha's soldiers against the antigovernment Ogonis. Saro-Wiwa was kept in prison without counsel until 1995, when he and fourteen others were finally given a trial before a military tribunal. Despite international outcry pleading for clemency—even representatives of Shell Oil had written to Abacha asking for leniency—Saro-Wiwa and eight of his codefendants were executed. In response, Western governments instituted sanctions including the suspension of Nigeria's membership in the Commonwealth of Britain, a halt of U.S. military sales to Nigeria by President Bill Clinton, and the recall of ambassadors from the United States, Britain, France, the Netherlands, Austria, Germany, and South Africa. *Time* magazine named Abacha "Thug of the Year." Abacha continued to promise, however, to hand over power to a democratically elected government on October 1, 1998, according to a report in *USA Today,* and to cede power to civilians.

Before he could act on his promises, though, Abacha died of a heart attack on June 8, 1998, allegedly while in the company of Indian prostitutes. Conspiracy theorists maintained that he was in reality killed by the women with a poisoned apple in an elaborate assassination plot. One day later, Abiola died in his prison cell—again, of a supposed heart attack. When news of Abiola's death spread, Nigeria erupted in violent riots centered on ethnic hatred that had been simmering for years. Followers of the would-be president-elect Abiola, who had been a Yoruba, accused the northern Hausa and Fulani tribes, who counted among their numbers Abacha, of assassinating Abiola.

Embezzled Billions

A decade after Abacha's death, his family and associates remained incriminated in several international scandals. Abacha's successor, General Abdulsalami Abubakar, discovered the extent of Abacha's corruption and secured the return of $1 billion to the Nigerian government from the Abacha family, according to the Basel Institute on Governance. Abubakar also restored democratic governance to Nigeria, allowing the country's first free elections in eleven years. Olusegun Obasanjo was elected president in 1999, and his administration continued to press for the money's return.

In 2000 Nigerian authorities appealed to the governments of countries to which the money had been traced—including Lichtenstein, the United Kingdom, the United States, and Luxembourg, but especially Switzerland—for mutual legal assistance in the case. By 2002 the remainder of the funds still had not been restored. Obasanjo's administration forged a deal with the Abachas that would have let the family keep a portion of the money that had thus far been traced and frozen in European accounts. Abacha's son Mohammed—who had just been released from prison in Nigeria for fraud and money laundering—turned down the agreement, however, continuing to claim that all the funds had been legally acquired.

Further judgments by Swiss courts and subsequent appeals by the Abacha clan held up the case for another three years. BBC News reported in February of 2005 that Switzerland had agreed to return $458 million of the money it held frozen to Nigeria, with the caveat that the money be used for the improvement of services and infrastructure. Yet in April of 2007 Sonala Olumhense wrote in Nigeria's *Guardian* newspaper that the transfer of money had not gone smoothly. Olumhense reported that of a total of $700 million returned by the Swiss to Nigeria, $200 million had allegedly been siphoned off before reaching its destination in Nigeria's public works projects. Charges of corruption in the Obasanjo administration arose. Furthermore, Olumhense quoted then-executive chairman of Nigeria's Economic and Financial Crimes Commission, Nuhu Ribadu, as putting the total known amount pilfered by Abacha at $6 billion. "He confirmed that $2 billion has been recovered. 'The rest is still hanging there outside and we're trying to get it,' he said."

Meanwhile, another of Abacha's surviving sons, Abba Sani Abacha, was implicated in criminal activity in April of 2005. Accused of money laundering, embezzlement, and fraud, Abba was extradited to Switzerland from Germany. In 2007 Mohammed Abacha's name resurfaced in legal proceedings concerning the senior Abacha's personal security team—known as the Strike Force—for the 1996 assassination of Kudirat Abiola, a wife of presumed presidential election winner Moshood Abiola and a vocal civil rights advocate in her own right. During the trial a witness identified Mohammed Abacha as having been a key player in the murder.

Sources

Books

Falola, Toyin, and Julius Ihonvbere, *The Rise and Fall of Nigeria's Second Republic, 1979–84,* Zed Books, 1985, pp. 229–30, 254–57.

Osso, Nyaknno, editor, *Who's Who in Nigeria,* Newswatch Communications, 1990, p. 9.

Periodicals

Africa Report, January/February 1994, pp. 47–49; July/August 1994, pp. 62–64; September/October 1994, pp. 38–41.

Detroit News, November 12, 1995, p. 5A.

Guardian (Nigeria), April 2, 2007.

New York Times, November 18, 1993, p. A15; November 20, 1993, p. A5; November 25, 1993, p. A10; June 9, 1998.

Newswatch (Lagos, Nigeria), November 22, 1993, pp. 12–16; November 29, 1993, pp. 15–17.

Time, December 25, 1995, p. 40.

Times of Nigeria, November 28, 2007.

USA Today, October 2, 1995, p. 3A.

West Africa, September 12–18, 1994, p. 1594;

September 19–25, 1994, p. 1627; October 3–9, 1994, p. 1705.

Online

Basel Institute on Governance, "Chronology (draft): Efforts in Switzerland to Recover Assets Looted by Sani Abacha of Nigeria," Intermediate Training Program on Asset Tracing, Recovery and Repatriation, Jakarta, September 2007, http://www.assetrecovery.org/kc/download?node=78488349-a33e-11dc-bf1b-335d0754ba85&service=afs (accessed August 7, 2008).

Basel Institute on Governance, "Sani Abacha," Asset Recovery Knowledge Center, International Center for Asset Recovery, http://www.assetrecovery.org/kc/node/52f770df-a33e-11dc-bf1b-335d0754ba85.html (accessed August 7, 2008).

Foulkes, Imogen, "Nigeria to Receive Abacha Funds," BBC News, February 16, 2005, http://news.bbc.co.uk/2/hi/africa/4271245.stm (accessed August 7, 2008).

"The Life of Ken Saro-Wiwa," Remember Saro-Wiwa, http://www.remembersarowiwa.com/lifeksw.htm (accessed August 7, 2008).

"Swiss Fraud Charge for Abacha Son," BBC News, April 15, 2005, http://news.bbc.co.uk/2/hi/africa/4449587.stm (accessed August 7, 2008).

—Nicholas Patti and Nancy Dziedzic

Moshood Abiola

1937–1998

Business executive, political leader

Abiola, Moshood, photograph. AP Images.

Moshood Abiola's name is near the top of Nigeria's long list of tragic, politically related deaths that have blighted the history of this West African nation since it achieved independence in 1960. A telecommunications tycoon who made a bid for the presidency in 1993 in the first democratic elections held in Nigeria in nearly three decades, Abiola appeared to have won by a landslide but was prevented from taking office. Defying the military rulers—one of several juntas that had ruled the country with a firm hand for nearly thirty years—Abiola rallied his supporters to oust the regime, but he was arrested on charges of treason in 1994. Four years later he died in custody from an apparent heart attack.

Abiola was born in 1937 in Abeokuta, a medium-sized city in the southwestern part of Nigeria. He was the first child born to his parents that survived infancy. The Abiolas were of the Yoruba ethnicity, but were Muslim—this combination was unusual for the area, because southern Nigeria was predominantly Christian and animist. The northern part of the country, by contrast, was dominated by those of Hausa ethnicity who practiced Islam. As a teenager, Abiola attended a high school set up by Baptist missionaries, where his excellent grades earned him a scholarship to the University of Glasgow in Scotland. He left to began his studies in 1960, the same year that Nigeria earned its independence from Britain.

Grew Wealthy from Investments

Returning a few years later with an economics degree and certification as an accountant, Abiola settled in the then-capital, Lagos, where he was hired as the deputy chief accountant at the Lagos University Teaching Hospital in 1965. He went on to a job with the multinational pharmaceutical giant Pfizer two years later, and by 1969 was serving as the comptroller of International Telephone and Telegraph (ITT) of Nigeria. This division of the much larger telecommunications powerhouse ran the country's wire-based communications systems, and the position gave Abiola access to top military officials, with whom he cultivated friendships that would later aid him in his political

At a Glance . . .

Born Moshood Kashimawo Olawale Abiola on August 24, 1937, in Abeokuta, Ogun State, Nigeria; died on July 7, 1998, in Abuja, Nigeria; first wife, Simibiat Atinuke Shoaga, 1960; married second wife, Kudirat Olayinki Adeyemi, 1973 (assassinated, 1996); married third wife, Adebisi Olawunmi Oshin, 1974; married Doyinsola (Doyin) Abiola Aboaba, 1981; children: estimated at sixty, including daughter Hafsat Abiola. *Politics:* Social Democratic Party of Nigeria. *Religion:* Muslim. *Education:* Attended University of Glasgow, Scotland.

Career: Lagos University Teaching Hospital, deputy chief accountant, 1965–67; Pfizer Products Ltd., comptroller, 1967–68; International Telephone and Telegraph (ITT) of Nigeria Ltd., began as comptroller, 1969, became vice president for Africa and Middle East; ITT Nigeria Ltd., chair and chief executive officer, 1972–88; Concord Press of Nigeria Ltd., founder, 1980, and chair; Radio Communications Nigeria, chief executive officer; National Party of Nigeria, chair of Ogun State branch of the party, 1979(?)–83; elected president of Nigeria in June of 1993 as the candidate of the Social Democratic Party (SDP), but never sworn in.

career. In 1972 he was promoted to the posts of chair and chief executive officer of ITT Nigeria, which he held for the next sixteen years.

Abiola's first foray into politics came during Nigeria's so-called Second Republic between 1979 and 1983, when he chaired the Ogun State branch of the National Party of Nigeria. He also founded a small media empire, Concord Press, which effectively functioned as the public-relations arm of his emerging political brand name. Noted Richard Synge in the *Guardian*, "It was in that brief phase of democratic government between 1979 and 1983 that Abiola became a truly public figure, known for his extraordinary generosity in building schools, as much as for his penchant for marrying more than the usual numbers of wives allowed by Islamic custom." Abiola fathered an estimated sixty children in all, including many by women who were not his wives.

Nigeria's troubled, corrupt Second Republic lasted just four years and ended with a military coup on the last day of 1983. Two years later a major general in Nigeria's armed forces came to power—Ibrahim Babangida, whom Abiola had known for some years.

Babangida eventually announced a timeline for the restoration of the democratic political process, and after long delays elections were scheduled for June 12, 1993. In March of 1993 Abiola had been chosen as the presidential candidate of the Social Democratic Party (SDP), a newly created center-left party. His main opponent in the June election was the candidate of the National Republican Convention (NRC) party, Bashir Othma Tofa. On election day Abiola bested Tofa with majority wins in nineteen out of Nigeria's thirty states. Babangida, however, delayed the announcement of the official results. As unrest mounted, news of Abiola's win leaked out anyway via a grassroots political group called Campaign for Democracy. Babangida's transitional government voided the election results, prompting widespread international outcry. Campaign for Democracy urged Nigerians to mount an opposition campaign of civil disobedience, and Abiola took part in the protests.

Jailed for Treason

Babangida stepped down in July of 1993, after having resisted calls to hand over power to Abiola, who was widely perceived to be the legitimate victor. An interim head of government was himself ousted by another military effort led by General Sani Abacha. Unrest continued, and at last on June 11, 1994—the anniversary of the eve of the thwarted election—Abiola asserted he was the rightful president. He then went into hiding, but was located twelve days later, arrested, and charged with sedition. Major rallies were organized in defiance of Abacha's regime and brutal treatment of the lawful winner of the election. Among Abiola's most prominent supporters was Nigerian novelist Wole Soyinka, the first African to win the Nobel Prize in literature, who was forced to leave the country for a time to avoid Abacha's secret police.

Following Abiola's arrest, the civil strife spread to Nigeria's main source of income, its rich oil fields in the north, where a workers' strike that lasted two months was met with a brutal crackdown on all political dissidence. "Within a year it was reported that Abiola was in solitary confinement, and had lost more than six stone [approximately eighty-five pounds]," reported Synge in the *Guardian*. "His physician reported that he had been cut off from the news, that he was no longer aware of the time, or whether it was day or night." His sole contact with family members came in early 1995. As his daughter Hafsat Abiola wrote in *Newsweek*, "My siblings and I were allowed only ten minutes with him. Usually a fit man, he was limping, suffering from a pinched nerve that resulted from being beaten by a soldier. He was disheveled and had lost a great deal of weight. I spent my ten minutes trying to assure him that he had not been forgotten."

Abiola remained jailed, and the situation was at an apparent stalemate, until early June of 1998, when General Abacha died suddenly from a heart attack. His successor was another general, Abdulsalam Abubakar, who reportedly favored a return to democratic rule. Almost immediately scores of political prisoners were released. A few weeks later United Nations Secretary General Kofi Annan visited Abiola, and reported from Nigeria on July 3 that Abubakar's government had agreed to release Abiola in exchange for him giving up his claim to the presidency. Family members believed he would be freed in a matter of days, but on July 7 he collapsed in front of a delegation of high-ranking U.S. diplomats who had come to visit him. Abubakar permitted an independent autopsy by foreign physicians, and the cause of death was ruled to be a heart attack. His family members, supporters, and even Soyinka voiced their doubts nevertheless. "They either poisoned him or killed him from neglect," Hafsat Abiola told journalists Obi Nwakanma and Marcus Mabry in *Newsweek.* "Either way, they killed him."

Abiola's death was a terrible setback for Nigerians, the majority of whom had anticipated a long-awaited return to democracy with the successful business mogul at the helm of the nation. News of the loss prompted widespread rioting, and crowds in Lagos, shouting "Won fiku sere! O won fiku sere!" ("They play with death! Oh, they play with death!"), were fired upon by government forces, according to Nwakanma and Mabry's report. Elections were held once again in 1999, but they were viewed as fraudulent by international observers, as were elections in 2003 and 2007.

Sources

Periodicals

Guardian (London), July 8, 1998, p. 16; July 10, 1998, p. 2.
New York Times, October 15, 1998.
Newsweek, June 22, 1998, p. 40; July 20, 1998, p. 37.
Time, July 20, 1998, p. 30.
Times (London), July 9, 1998, p. 25.

—Carol Brennan

Uwem Akpan

1971—

Roman catholic priest, writer

Uwem Akpan's debut collection of short stories, *Say You're One of Them,* was hailed by critics as a searing fictional portrayal of Africa's most desperate citizens—its children. The Nigerian writer, who is also a Roman Catholic priest, was lauded for giving voice to the most neglected and unlucky among the millions on the continent whose lives are little more than a daily battle for survival. "Hand-wringing journalists have described the misery of Africa's urban poor, but Akpan also captures the humor and fleeting grace that make the degradation infinitely more painful to read about," noted Jennifer Reese in *Entertainment Weekly* about Akpan's 2008 debut.

Born in 1971, Akpan hails from Ikot Akpan Eda in southern Nigeria, a center of the West African raffia trade. Both of his parents were teachers, and he was one of four sons who grew up speaking both English and Annang, the tongue of his family's ethnic affiliation. Like many households in the southern region of Nigeria, Akpan's household was a Christian one, and his own grandfather had been an influential figure whose conversion to Roman Catholicism decades earlier had prompted many others in their community to follow suit.

Ordained Jesuit Priest

In 1990, at the age of nineteen, Akpan entered a Jesuit seminary in preparation to become a priest. (The Jesuits, more formally known as the Society of Jesus, are a Roman Catholic order founded by St. Ignatius of Loyola in 1534.) Over the next several years Akpan trained for the priesthood and studied theology in both Nairobi, Kenya, and at Creighton University in Omaha, Nebraska. He also spent time at Gonzaga University in Spokane, Washington, where he studied philosophy. He was ordained a Jesuit priest in 2003.

Akpan's career as a writer was also well under way by that point. While still in college he had written some nonfiction pieces for the *Guardian,* a Nigerian newspaper. In 1998, when he submitted an article once again, it was rejected. He noticed, however, that the paper's Saturday section offered some fiction for readers. "So I decided to give it a try," he recalled in an interview with Cressida Leyshon that appeared in the online edition of the *New Yorker.* "It worked. So I started writing furiously for them. The quality of my stories was not very good, but I could raise the readers' adrenaline."

Akpan began to consider working toward a graduate degree in creative writing. As he told Charles McGrath in the *New York Times,* "I understood the major part of the puzzle—that there had to be suspense in a story. But pacing, dialogue, characterization—I still had a lot to learn about fiction. But I kept pushing. I would go away from a story and then come back again." He applied to, and was accepted by, the respected writing program at the University of Michigan. As the program's director, Eileen Pollack, told McGrath, admissions personnel were initially wary about his background as a Roman Catholic cleric—after all, students in creative-writing seminars often debate topics ranging from illicit drug use to alternative sexual relationships.

At a Glance . . .

Born Uwem Celestine Akpan in 1971 in Ikot Akpan Eda, Akwa Ibom State, Nigeria; son of two teachers. *Religion:* Roman Catholic. *Education:* Studied theology at Creighton University; studied philosophy at Gonzaga University; University of Michigan, MFA, 2006.

Career: Contributor to the *Guardian* (Nigeria), 1990s; ordained Roman Catholic priest of the Society of Jesus (Jesuit) order, 2003; teacher of languages at a Zimbabwean seminary, 2006—.

Addresses: *Home*—Zimbabwe. *Office*—c/o Little, Brown & Co., 1271 Avenue of the Americas, New York, NY 10020.

But as Pollack and others soon discovered, "It turned out he had had more experience of the dark side of the world than all the other students put together."

Amazed at Endurance of Forsaken Children

One of the dozens of stories that Akpan worked on simultaneously was "An Ex-Mas Feast," which won a terrific honor in 2005 when the *New Yorker* included it in its annual debut-fiction issue. Akpan's story is set in Nairobi and follows a day or two in the lives of a family whose "home" is a makeshift shanty covered by a piece of tarpaulin. The narrator is Jigana, the family's eight-year-old son, whose prized possession is a school uniform still in its package. His older sister, Maisha, is twelve and already a prostitute whose earnings have paid for the uniform and also support the family. Their mother quiets Jigana, his ten-year-old sister Naema, and a set of two-year-old twins by offering them tubes of toxic glue to sniff to quell their hunger. Jigana takes the family's youngest, an infant, with him to beg on the streets; Baba, his father, is a pickpocket. The family's hopes are pinned on Maisha earning enough to pay Jigana's school fees for the coming session. "This Ex-mas we were not too desperate for food," Jigana relates in the tale. "In addition to the money that begging with Baby had brought us, Baba had managed to steal some wrapped gifts from a party given ... by an N.G.O. [nongovernmental organization], whose organizers were so stingy that they served fruit juice like shots of hard liquor. He had dashed to another charity party and traded in the useless gifts—plastic cutlery, picture frames, paperweights, insecticides—for three cups of rice and zebra intestines, which a tourist hotel had donated."

Asked about the inspiration for "An Ex-Mas Feast," Akpan recounted that he first encountered youth like Jigana and Maisha when he moved to Nairobi, whose streets teemed with homeless adolescents and children begging, stealing, and prostituting themselves. "I'd never seen anything like it before," he told Leyshon in the *New Yorker* interview. He recounted that he would sometimes follow them, but from a safe distance, his interactions with them initially limited because he was not fluent in Kiswahili. "I wasn't thinking of writing then. I was just fascinated and amazed at the endurance I saw in them—how they moved as a group, how they sniffed glue, how they robbed people, how the rest of society regarded them."

Akpan earned his master of fine arts in creative writing from the University of Michigan in 2006, and moved to Zimbabwe to teach languages at a Jesuit seminary there. He completed four more short stories, each set in a different African nation, for his debut collection, *Say You're One of Them,* which was published by Little, Brown, in 2008. "An Ex-Mas Feast," the *New Yorker* story, was also included. In "Fattening for Gabon," a brother and sister from Benin are being raised by their uncle and enjoy rich meals in his household, but only to ensure a good price on the auction block, for he plans to sell them into a sex-slavery ring. The title of Akpan's collection is taken from the story "My Parents' Bedroom," in which nine-year-old Monique, who is the child of an affluent interethnic marriage in Rwanda, witnesses the brutal death of her mother at the hands of her father during that country's horrific 1994 genocidal war. "Say you're one of them" are her mother's last words to her.

Commended for Humanizing the Poor

Akpan's debut earned a slew of accolades. "Akpan never lets us forget that the resilient youngsters caught up in these extraordinary circumstances are filled with their own hopes and dreams," wrote Patrik Henry Bass in *Essence.* Reviewing *Say You're One of Them* in the *Sunday Times,* David Grylls recalled that the author was also a priest and asserted that "it is scarcely surprising that religious imagery pervades these stories, which interweave themes of martyrdom, betrayal and the threat to innocence. But they are never dogmatic or didactic. On the contrary they indict blind partisanship, whether racial, religious or political." Tremendously difficult emotional terrain is the landscape in which Akpan writes, noted Reese in *Entertainment Weekly,* "but the blazing humanity of the characters and the brilliance of Akpan's artistry make this one of the year's most exhilarating reads."

Akpan's literary debut earned some attention because of his dual vocations of priest and writer, but he did not consider them as mutually exclusive. "Since it is not something I can put away, my faith is important to me," he reflected in the *New Yorker* interview. "I hope I am able to reveal the compassion of God in the faces of the people I write about. I think fiction has a way of doing this without being doctrinaire about it."

Selected writings

Say You're One of Them (short stories), Little, Brown, 2008.

Sources

Books

Akpan, Uwem, *Say You're One of Them,* Little, Brown, 2008.

Periodicals

America, November 2, 1996, p. 22.
Entertainment Weekly, June 13, 2008, p. 72.
Essence, June 2008, p. 82.
New York Times, July 3, 2008, p. E1.
Toronto Star, July 13, 2008, p. ID05.
Sunday Times (London), June 22, 2008, p. 47.

Online

Akpan, Uwem, "An Ex-Mas Feast," NewYorker.com, http://www.newyorker.com/archive/2005/06/13/050613fi_fiction1?currentPage=all (accessed August 14, 2008).
Leyshon, Cressida, "Between Two Continents," New Yorker.com, June 13, 2005, http://www.newyorker.com/archive/2005/06/13/050613on_onlineonly01 (accessed August 14, 2008).

—Carol Brennan

Karen Bass

1953—

Politician

Bass, Karen, photograph. AP Images.

In 2008 Karen Bass became the first African-American woman in U.S. history to serve as speaker of a state legislature. While as Speaker of the California State Assembly she wielded considerable power in the political life of America's most populous state, Bass was especially known for her consensus-building skills. In her first speech as speaker, the Democratic lawmaker from Los Angeles cited California's already difficult economic circumstances and pledged to work with Republican lawmakers to solve a looming crisis. "The weight of history is not just on my shoulders," she said. "As we all move forward, it should be with the understanding that a society will be judged on the way it cares for its people."

The daughter of a postal worker and a hair salon owner, Bass was born in 1953 and grew up in the Venice/Fairfax neighborhood of Los Angeles. As a young woman, she earned a bachelor's degree in health sciences from California State University at Dominguez Hills, then completed a physician-assistant training program at the University of Southern California School of Medicine. She practiced and was a clinical instructor at the Los Angeles County/University of Southern California Medical Center, one of the nation's busiest trauma centers.

During the 1980s Bass saw firsthand the devastation that illegal drugs like crack cocaine had brought to her community. Emergency-room visits for drug overdoses were common, but there was also a spike in violent crime—especially among juveniles—that spoke of turf wars over the lucrative drug trade. "Back then, the prevailing view was to throw the book at anyone having to do with drug trafficking," Bass recalled in an interview with Howard Fine in the *Los Angeles Business Journal.* "I became convinced that was all backwards, that we really had to focus on changing public policy to give inner city youth more job opportunities and better education opportunities so that they wouldn't have to resort to the drug trade."

Removed Liquor Stores from Neighborhoods

Bass organized a conference in 1990 to help lead her community forward, and subsequently founded a non-profit group called the Community Coalition; she even-

basically treated as demons," she said in the *Los Angeles Business Journal* interview. The federal bill, however, had come with a clause that allowed states to revise the five-year limits. "So we launched a campaign to get the state to allow people who had made good faith efforts to find work to keep their food stamps and welfare checks," Bass told Fine.

By 2003 Bass had begun to consider a run for a seat on the Los Angeles city council, but her father became ill and she shelved the idea. As she noted in her first speech as California Speaker of the House, he "never wanted me to run for office—because he was afraid I'd be hurt. But yet he was the one who introduced me to politics, watching the civil rights movement on the nightly news and trying to help me understand the concept of legal segregation in the South where he was from—he instilled in me the passion to fight for justice and equality."

Led Foster-Care Reform Effort

Bass's community work had brought her a number of well-connected friends and acquaintances, and a few of them—including Antonio Villaraigosa, the Los Angeles city council member who went on to become mayor of the city in 2005—suggested she run for the 47th state congressional district seat in the California State Assembly. She agreed, and won her first bid for public office in the 2004 election, representing some 423,000 residents in a district that included the neighborhoods of West Los Angeles, Westwood, the Crenshaw District, Culver City, Cheviot Hills, Leimert Park, Baldwin Hills, Windsor Hills, Ladera Heights, Little Ethiopia, and parts of Koreatown and South Los Angeles. When she was sworn into office for the 2005–06 legislative session in Sacramento, the state capital, she was the only African-American woman then serving in the state house.

As a state lawmaker, Bass distinguished herself as an advocate for families, children, and health-care issues. She chaired a Select Committee on Foster Care, which held public hearings and invited former foster children, longtime foster parents, social workers, and other participants in the state's foster-care system to recount their own, often painful, experiences with administrators and the courts. Bass led the effort to reform the system, which included $82 million in new appropriations to better serve children in foster care and their host families. She also pushed for and won legislation that strengthened health-insurance coverage for California children.

Bass also served as the Democratic majority whip for the 2005–06 California State Assembly legislative session, and as vice chair of its Black Caucus. During the 2007–08 legislative session, the Speaker of the Assembly, Fabian Núñez, named her majority floor leader. With Núñez's term in the Assembly set to expire in

tually left her medical work to run it on a full-time basis. The Coalition's mission was to combat drug-related problems and poor police-community relations in Los Angeles, and it had several notable achievements. In 1992, for example, in the wake of the devastating Los Angeles riots, Bass's group mounted a successful campaign to prevent liquor stores from reopening in some of the most impoverished neighborhoods. The figures were impressive: Two hundred had burned down during the civil disturbances, but just fifty reopened thanks to the Coalition's work with state and local liquor-licensing authorities.

The most daunting challenge for Bass and the Community Coalition came in the mid-1990s, when new federal laws ended the government-benefit system known as Aid to Families with Dependent Children (AFDC) and replaced it with Temporary Assistance for Needy Families (TANF). The new legislation was dubbed "workfare" in the press, because it forced recipients either to find a job or to be enrolled in a job-training program in order to continue receiving benefits. TANF's most significant revision, however, was a five-year limit on benefits. Community activists like Bass sounded alarms, noting that capping already meager aid checks and food stamps for mothers with young children would bring immense hardship to urban communities like Los Angeles. "These people were

2008, Bass emerged as the front runner in the competition for the powerful post of Speaker. Backed by her fellow Democrats in the Assembly, who praised her skill in courting bipartisan support, Bass was elected in February of 2008 and sworn in as Speaker in May as the first African-American woman ever to serve in the post. Her duties as Speaker included guiding bills through the legislative process and making committee assignments; as Speaker of the Assembly, Bass was the second-most influential politician in the state after the Republican governor, Arnold Schwarzenegger.

Bass's further political endeavors include participating in the presidential campaign of Illinois Senator Barack Obama. She served as California state co-chair of Obama for President, and headed the group California African Americans for Obama.

Referring in her first speech as Speaker of the Assembly to the loss of her daughter, Emilia Wright, and son-in-law, Michael Wright, in an automobile accident in October of 2006, Bass reflected: "I have experienced the best of your hearts—and I'm not sure I can fully express how much that has meant to me. So many of us have faced personal tragedies and losses—we have stood with each other—we have embraced each other—and helped each other through the bad times.... If we could only harness the power of our common humanity, I don't think there's anything we couldn't do for the people of this state."

Sources

Periodicals

Daily News (Los Angeles), February 29, 2008, p. A3.
Jet, March 24, 2008, p. 16.
Los Angeles Business Journal, April 18, 2005, p. 24.
Sacramento Bee, February 28, 2008; February 29, 2008.
San Francisco Chronicle, May 14, 2008, p. B3.

Online

"Swearing In Address of Assembly Speaker Karen Bass," California State Assembly Democratic Caucus, http://democrats.assembly.ca.gov/members/a47/press/20080513AD47PR01.htm (accessed August 20, 2008).

—Carol Brennan

Kathleen Battle

1948—

Singer

Battle, Kathleen, photograph. Kevin Kane/WireImage.

In the 1980s soprano Kathleen Battle became one of the opera world's most celebrated performers, achieving the level of fame previously accorded to such sopranos as Beverly Sills, Maria Callas, and Birgit Nilsson. Battle, however, was one of the few African-American women ever to rank among the top tier of devotedly followed—and richly compensated—female performers who appeared at the Metropolitan Opera in New York, Covent Garden in London, and La Scala in Milan. Her specialty was the *soubrette,* or servant, role. These youngish, often flirtatious female characters usually did not sing the showstopper arias, but they and their songs were always popular with audiences. In the early years of her career, "Battle projected freshness, innocence and a certain ecstatic quality that was difficult to define but was almost unanimously agreed upon," Tim Page noted in *Opera News.* "Pianist Gerald Moore once wrote that Elisabeth Schumann sang with a smile; Battle, at her best, sang with a delighted shiver."

In 1994, however, Battle was unceremoniously released from her contract with the Metropolitan Opera for what its management termed "unprofessional" actions, a move that sent shock waves through classical-music circles. "Divas are expected to be difficult," wrote Michael Walsh in an article chronicling the dismissal for *Time.* "Opera lore is rife with tales of their devouring egos and overweening eccentricities." Battle never again appeared in an opera production, although she continued a career as a recitalist and recording artist.

Battle's rise to fame was part of her appeal. Born in 1948, she was the daughter of Grady Battle, an Alabama-born steelworker, and his wife, Ollie Layne Battle, who balanced her role of wife and mother of seven with volunteer work at the African Methodist Episcopal church in Portsmouth, Ohio, a town on the river border with Kentucky. Battle was the youngest in the family and attended segregated schools until the age of twelve. "I learned to sing listening to my father," she told Bernard Holland, whose profile of the singer appeared in the *New York Times Magazine* in 1985. "He was a singer in a gospel quartet. My sister taught me how to read music, but I'm really not sure where she learned."

At a Glance . . .

Born Kathleen Deanne Battle on August 13, 1948, in Portsmouth, OH; daughter of Grady (a steelworker) and Ollie Layne (a volunteer) Battle. *Religion:* African Methodist Episcopal. *Education:* University of Cincinnati College–Conservatory of Music, bachelor's degree, 1970, master's degree, 1971.

Career: Music teacher in the Cincinnati, OH, public schools, late 1960s–early 1970s; opera singer and recitalist, 1972—; recording artist, 1984—.

Awards: Grammy Award for best classical vocal soloist performance, 1986, for *Kathleen Battle Sings Mozart*, 1987, for *Salzburg Recital*, and 1992, for *Kathleen Battle at Carnegie Hall*; Grammy Award for best opera recording, 1987, for *Richard Strauss: Ariadne Auf Naxos*, and 1993, for *Handel: Semele*.

Addresses: *Agent*—Ronald A. Wilford, Columbia Artists Management Inc., 1790 Broadway, New York, NY 10019-1412.

Launched to Stardom by a Labor Dispute

Battle's music teacher at Portsmouth High School encouraged her to apply to the University of Cincinnati College–Conservatory of Music, the top music school in the area and one of the best training grounds for performers in the United States. She earned a bachelor's degree in music education and, while teaching music in the Cincinnati public schools in the late 1960s, received a master's degree in performance. Her professional break came in 1972 when the musicians of the Cincinnati Symphony went on strike and the company held an open audition for singers. Conductor Thomas Schippers was so taken with Battle's talent that he hired her as a soloist for the symphony's engagement at the Festival di Due Monde in Spoleto, Italy, later that year. Wearing a dress she sewed at home, Battle made her debut singing Johannes Brahms's *Ein Deutsches Requiem* to acclaim. Once back in Cincinnati she began to appear regularly with the symphony.

In the autumn of 1975 Battle made her New York debut on Broadway, in the title role of Scott Joplin's *Treemonisha*, for which she received favorable reviews. That led to appearances the following season at the New York City Opera, where she was cast as Susanna, the future bride, in Wolfgang Amadeus Mozart's *Le Nozze di Figaro*. It became one of her signature roles.

After that, Ohio connections aided her career trajectory: A Cincinnati native, James Levine, had heard Battle sing in 1973, and when he was named music director of the Metropolitan Opera in 1976, he hired Battle for the following season. She sang the role of the shepherd in Richard Wagner's *Tannhäuser*. Donal Henahan in the *New York Times* wrote that "Battle, a Met newcomer, gave a piping quality to her Shepherd's song."

During the next few years Levine, who was one of her most ardent fans—he occasionally blew kisses at her from his podium during performances—cast her in several productions, including Mozart's *Die Entführung aus dem Serail* in 1980 and *Cosi Fan Tutte* in 1982. In 1985 she made her Covent Garden debut in a Strauss opera, *Ariadne auf Naxos*, as Zerbinetta, receiving enthusiastic reviews from London critics.

In 1988 Battle performed with Luciano Pavarotti, inarguably opera's most famous living voice at the time, on an occasion that some music critics cite as the peak of her stage career: The two appeared in Gaetano Donizetti's *L'Elisir d'Amore* at one of the free summer concerts in New York's Central Park. "Battle is one of the few sopranos capable of upstaging Mr. Pavarotti's Nemorino," asserted critic Allan Kozinn in the *New York Times*, "and she did just that with an Adina sung with such ravishing sweetness that no suspension of disbelief was required for one to understand why Nemorino is immediately smitten with her."

In 1992 she performed a song cycle, *Honey and Rue*, at Carnegie Hall. The writer Toni Morrison composed the sextet of prose poems, which were then set to music by conductor-composer André Previn. The songs became part of Battle's standard recital repertoire at such events as the Tanglewood Festival in Massachusetts.

Dismissed by the Met

While she was receiving accolades for her singing, Battle was gaining a reputation for being tempestuous during rehearsals and demanding of support staff. In 1993, after she walked out of a rehearsal for Strauss's *Der Rosenkavalier*, the general manager of the Metropolitan Opera, Joseph Volpe, replaced Battle with her understudy. Almost a year to the day later, in the midst of rehearsals for Donizetti's *La Fille du Regiment*, the Met announced that it had released Battle from her contract—"an extraordinary statement from an institution that usually maintains an air of patrician diplomacy," according to a *New York Times* article by Kozinn. The article included a brief interview with Volpe, who claimed that "Battle's unprofessional actions during rehearsals for the revival of 'La Fille du

Regiment' were profoundly detrimental to the artistic collaboration among all the cast members, which is such an essential component of the rehearsal process." Kozinn's report also included a statement from Battle, released through her management company. "I was not told by anyone at the Met about any unprofessional actions," it read. "To my knowledge, we were working out all of the artistic problems in the rehearsals, and I don't know the reason behind this unexpected dismissal."

Some of Battle's fans and other observers raised the issue of race in discussions about Battle's dismissal. In his article for *Time,* Walsh acknowledged that backstage at the Met the soprano had been referred to in racially charged language. But he also noted that "sources inside and outside the Met agree" that the cause for her dismissal was her behavior during rehearsals, especially the way she treated fellow performers. He explained that Battle's "diva" quirks were far from uncommon, and that opera singers—whose voices are their instruments, which are trickier and even more temperamental than the rarest seventeenth-century violin—could be uncompromising during rehearsals or nerve-wracked prior to performances. Many great artists "are difficult in their search for perfection in their craft," Peter Gelb, a Sony executive who had worked with Battle on several occasions, told Walsh. "The role of the Met is to support great talents. Nothing a producer does comes close to the challenge and difficulty great artists face when they go onstage." Still, Walsh reported, "The cast of *The Daughter of the Regiment* applauded when it was told during rehearsal that Battle had been fired."

Battle never again appeared in an opera production, although she continued to be in demand as a recitalist. In 1997, for example, she sang to some eight hundred admirers in the Metropolitan Museum of Art's Temple of Dendur. She also appeared on several sold-out occasions at Carnegie Hall. In 2008 she sang "The Lord's Prayer" at the White House in honor of the first visit to the United States by Pope Benedict XVI.

Recorded Frequently

Battle's recordings were well received and earned several Grammy Awards, presented by the National Academy of Recording Arts and Sciences. A 1984 RCA issue of Brahms's *Ein Deutsches Requiem,* which she sang with Levine conducting the Chicago Symphony, was often cited as one of the year's best

classical recordings. Sir Georg Solti, another conducting legend, recorded Battle and Pavarotti in Giuseppi Verdi's *Un Ballo in Maschera* a year later. One of her best-known recordings, *So Many Stars* (1995), is a collection of folk songs, African-American spirituals, and lullabies recorded with such notables as jazz great Grover Washington Jr. In 2002 Sony Classical released *Classic Kathleen Battle: A Portrait,* which included some of her career highlights plus four new songs, two of which were spirituals sung a cappella. Writing in *Opera News,* Judith Malafronte commended the songs as "very beautifully sung and compellingly shaped.... The appeal of this CD is not in the nonsensical program, it's in the singer. She makes you listen and follow along. And that's why she's a star."

Selected discography

Brahms: Ein Deutsches Requiem, Chicago Symphony, RCA, 1984.
Verdi: Un Ballo in Maschera, Decca, 1985.
Kathleen Battle and James Levine: Salzburg Recital, Deutsche Grammophon, 1987.
Strauss: Ariadne auf Naxos, Deutsche Grammophon, 1987.
A Carnegie Hall Christmas Concert, Sony, 1992.
Kathleen Battle at Carnegie Hall, Deutsche Grammophon, 1992.
Verdi: Don Carlo, Sony, 1993.
Handel: Semele, Deutsche Grammophon, 1993.
Kathleen Battle: So Many Stars, Sony, 1995.
Kathleen Battle: French Opera Arias, Deutsche Grammophon, 1996.
Kathleen Battle: Grace, Sony, 1997.
Classic Kathleen Battle: A Portrait, Sony Classical, 2002.
The Best of Kathleen Battle, Deutsche Grammophon, 2004.

Sources

Periodicals

New York Times, December 24, 1977, p. 12; June 22, 1988; February 8, 1994.
New York Times Magazine, November 17, 1985.
Opera News, April 2, 1994, p. 16; August 2002, p. 58.
Time, February 21, 1994, p. 60.

—Carol Brennan

Beyoncé

1981—

Singer, actor

Beyoncé, photograph. Kevin Mazur/WireImage.

Pop singer Beyoncé made her name as part of the superstar R&B-pop trio Destiny's Child, but has emerged as a singular talent in her own right. A veteran performer before her pre-teens, Beyoncé was rehearsing while her schoolmates were goofing around. The payoff came with a string of Grammy and *Billboard* awards, number-one singles, and platinum-selling records with the group, including "No, No, No," *The Writing's on the Wall,* "Bills, Bills, Bills," "Bugaboo," "Jumpin' Jumpin'," "Say My Name," and *Survivor.* Destiny's Child, which eventually became the best-selling girl group of all time, formally disbanded in 2005, but Beyoncé's star continues to rise. In addition to her stellar singing career, she has starred in several feature films and finds time on the side—and makes big dollars in the process—to serve as pitchperson for a number of high-profile brands, including L'Oreal, Pepsi, and Tommy Hilfiger.

Beyoncé Giselle Knowles was born in Houston, Texas, on September 4, 1981, to Mathew and Tina Knowles. A quiet girl, Beyoncé shocked her parents when she took the stage at a school talent show and belted out a version of John Lennon's "Imagine." "I wanted to be a performer," Beyoncé told the *Chicago Tribune.* "I was a shy girl until I was performing." She has cited her influences as Michael Jackson, Janet Jackson, Whitney Houston, and Sheila E. She had collected a roomful of talent competition trophies before it dawned on her parents that their little girl could really have what it takes to become successful in music. The Knowleses were very different from the stereotypical overbearing stage parents; they only encouraged their daughter to have fun. They soon began taking her performances more seriously, however, and working with her on her dance moves and singing stylings, with her mother designing her costumes. Mathew Knowles, previously a successful salesman, became manager of Destiny's Child. Tina Knowles worked in a bank for years and later opened her own successful hair salon, before becoming the group's stylist and clothing designer.

Driven to Pop Stardom

Beyoncé's work ethic was strong, even as a girl. She dedicated herself to a regimen of dance and vocal classes. Her parents never made her practice or attend

At a Glance . . .

Born Beyoncé Giselle Knowles on September 4, 1981, in Houston, TX; daughter of Mathew (a salesman and manager) and Tina (a stylist and designer) Knowles; married Jay-Z (a singer), 2008.

Career: Formed singing group Destiny's Child in Houston, TX, c. 1990; signed with Columbia Records, 1996; began acting career, 2001; launched solo singing career, 2003.

Awards: Best R&B/Soul or Rap New Artist Award, Lady of Soul Awards, 1998; Favorite Group: Urban/Hip-Hop Award, Artist Direct Awards, 2000; Artist of the Year, Artist of the Year: Duo or Group, Hot 100 Singles Artist of the Year, and Hot 100 Singles Artist of the Year: Duo or Group Awards, all *Billboard* Music Awards, 2000; Grammy Awards for best R&B song and best R&B performance by a group or duo, both 2001; Sammy Davis Jr. Award, Entertainer of the Year, Soul Train Awards, 2001 and 2007; Songwriter of the Year Award, American Society of Composers, Artists, and Performers, 2002; MTV Video Music Awards for best female video and best choreography in a video, both 2003; People's Choice Award for best female musical performer (corecipient), 2004; Grammy Awards for best R&B song, best rap/sung collaboration, best female R&B performance, best contemporary R&B album, and best R&B performance by a duo or group with vocals, all 2004; Radio Music Award, Top 40 Artist of the Year, 2004; BET Award for best female R&B artist, 2004; Grammy Award for best R&B performance by a duo with vocals, 2006; MTV Video Award for best R&B video, 2006; Grammy Award for best contemporary R&B album, 2007; BET Awards for best video and best R&B female artist, both 2007; International Artist Award, American Music Awards, 2007.

Addresses: *Office*—Columbia Records, 550 Madison Ave., New York, NY 10022-3211.

Things got more serious in 1990, when Beyoncé, still a young child, went up against fifty other girls to audition for a new female singing group called Girl's Tyme. With an ever-changing lineup—about one hundred girls were in and out of the group—Beyoncé made the cut and performed at banquets and other Houston events. Kelly Rowland joined Girl's Tyme around 1991, and she and Beyoncé became friends. Rowland and her mother—a nanny and single parent—struggled financially and moved often, until the Knowleses took Kelly in, giving her a more stable home. After Kelly moved in, she and Beyoncé were like sisters. Girl's Tyme appeared on the TV talent show *Star Search* in 1992.

Six members of Girl's Tyme rehearsed for months before appearing on *Star Search.* They were all about twelve years old at the time, and thought the show was going to be their big break. They were crushed when they lost, but maintained frozen smiles in front of the cameras, before crying uncontrollably once they got backstage. "We almost went crazy from crying," Beyoncé wrote in *Soul Survivors.* "A lot was riding on that performance." It was at that point that Mathew Knowles decided to become the girls' manager, "because he couldn't stand to hear me bawling anymore," Beyoncé wrote. After the loss the girls decided to call it quits—they were done with show business. Mathew convinced them to reconsider their hasty decision.

After the demise of Girl's Tyme, the group reorganized several times, with different lineups and new names, including Somethin' Fresh, Borderline, Cliché, the Dolls, and Destiny. At this point a quartet, the group was asked to record "Killing Time" for the *Men in Black* movie soundtrack in 1997, and were forced to stick with the name Destiny's Child. The lineup consisted of Beyoncé, Rowland, LeToya Luckett, and LaTavia Roberson. The girls were tight-lipped about the group; it was some time before even Beyoncé's childhood sweetheart knew she was a performer. They felt that their music was very personal, and that it was nobody's business but their own.

Redoubled Their Efforts

Mathew Knowles eventually quit his sales job to manage the group, and invested the family's money in helping his daughter succeed. The strain of being a husband, father, and manager took its toll on the family, and Beyoncé's parents separated briefly when she was fourteen years old. Tina moved with Beyoncé, her little sister Solange, and Rowland into a small apartment. Her parents eventually reunited. "The stability and support my parents provided when we were growing up at home has a lot to do with why Kelly and I are still around today," Beyoncé wrote in *Soul Survivors.*

It took six years for Destiny's Child to secure a recording contract, and it was a tough road. One of the most

class, but they were always clear with her about the payoff of hard work. "I thought of rehearsing as fun," Beyoncé wrote later in 2002's *Soul Survivors: The Official Autobiography of Destiny's Child.* "It was my time to create dance routines and vocal arrangements. It seemed like playtime."

difficult things for Beyoncé, then still just a girl, was the strict diet regimen she had to follow. While Rowland and Roberson were wiry and could eat as they pleased, Beyoncé and Luckett were forced to eat nonfat foods and to abstain from fattening junk food. "It's a shame that a kid would have to worry about her weight," Beyoncé wrote in *Soul Survivors,* "but I was trying to get a record deal and that was a reality."

Mathew Beyoncé worked hard to raise record company interest in his girls. They traveled to Los Angeles, San Francisco, and Oakland, California, regularly to perform in talent showcases, and lived in San Francisco for a couple of months to record their demo tape. Finally, when Beyoncé was about fourteen years old, Destiny's Child signed with Silent Partner Productions, an Elektra imprint. The four girls moved to Atlanta, where Silent Partner was based. They continued their academic studies with a tutor in the mornings, and spent the rest of the day in the recording studio. The deal with Elektra was short-lived—just a "little taste of a career," Beyoncé wrote in *Soul Survivors.* The group was dropped, but rallied and redoubled their efforts to get signed. Not long after the Elektra debacle, the group landed a contract with Columbia Records in 1996.

Waited Anxiously for Debut Album

Destiny's Child's self-titled first album took two years to finish, with hot hip-hop producer Wyclef Jean at the helm. It was during this time that Columbia hired a team of stylists to spruce up the girls' looks, to a disastrous and trendy result. Tina Knowles stepped in and became their official stylist and costume designer at this point. Not only did the girls know and trust Tina, but she also knew their personalities better, and was able to design stylish clothes that both flattered them and reflected their personal style.

The first single from *Destiny's Child,* "No, No, No," sold more than three million copies and pushed the album to gold certification for record sales. The album's great flaw, however, was that it did not present a singular style for the group. Listeners were confused about whether the group was straight R&B or hip-hop. Beyoncé stopped attending high school a few months into her ninth-grade year to record, rehearse, and tour. She continued her education with tutors until finishing her high school requirements in 2000.

The group's follow-up album, *The Writing's on the Wall,* was released in 1999 and made the serious impact that their debut had not. It featured a string of number-one hits, including "Bills, Bills, Bills," "Bugaboo," and "Jumpin' Jumpin'," which was Beyoncé's first serious attempt at writing and producing. Fueled by the hit single "Say My Name," the album went on to sell more than ten million copies.

1999 was a very tumultuous year for Beyoncé. Both Luckett and Roberson left Destiny's Child, leaving a swirl of rumors and litigation in their wake. The media pitted them against Rowland and Beyoncé, and turned it into a no-holds-barred drama. Beyoncé remained mum on the subject other than to say that egos, emotions, competition, and money were at the root of their problems. "Once Destiny's Child started to get successful, that's when we found out who our friends really were," Beyoncé wrote in *Soul Survivors.* "Our whole world changed, and that makes friendship way more complicated. Sometimes I still get mad about it, and sometimes it hurts, but it's now to the point where it's ridiculous," she told *Ebony.* "All I want to do is go into the studio, write my music, do my movies and perform. I'm not trying to hurt anybody, or offend anybody."

Drew Attention with Controversy

If there was an upside to the split, it was media attention. The media had overlooked Destiny's Child before, but with scandal and drama attached, the group became a hot commodity. "Destiny's Child was always very talented," Beyoncé told *Newsweek,* "but I think the thing we were lacking was controversy. I think in order for your group to be successful your story has to be interesting. Our story was very squeaky clean, so I thank God for the controversy. I'm happy because it helps me sell records." They appeared on numerous magazine covers, and record sales soared. Because they were in the public eye, however, they needed to replace Luckett and Roberson swiftly, before the split upset their growing popularity. Michelle Williams and Farrah Franklin rounded out the quartet in early 2000, and Destiny's Child was back on track. Franklin left the group five months later during a publicity tour. Destiny's Child hit the stage as a threesome at an Australian concert soon after, and never looked back. They toured with such hit acts as Christina Aguilera and TLC.

After the media blitz about yet another Destiny's Child lineup change died down, Beyoncé set to work on *Survivor,* the group's third album, which she both produced and cowrote. Beyoncé penned the album's title track after a wise-cracking morning DJ quipped harshly that being a member of Destiny's Child was like being on the reality-TV show *Survivor.* She wrote "Happy Face" about the face she has to put on when she gets down. "There are so many people out there who want to be in my shoes," she wrote in *Soul Survivors.* "Of course, they don't realize my shoes are uncomfortable and they give me blisters—but I can't complain. People think I live in an MTV Barbie World, but I don't. I am by no means a living doll."

Beyoncé wrote the song "Independent Women Part I" even before the director of the film *Charlie's Angels* asked the girls to contribute to the movie's soundtrack. The song salutes hard-working women who provide for themselves rather than depending on others. It broke records worldwide and was one of the biggest-selling singles in history. Beyoncé was nominated for a Grammy Award in 2000 for writing the song. "It seems that the songs I write because of extreme anger, happiness, or sadness become the biggest hits," Beyoncé wrote in *Soul Survivors.* "I guess that's because a lot of other people can relate to them. For me the studio is where I got to get stuff off my chest.... It's my therapy." Out of five Grammy nominations in 2000, Destiny's Child, at the 2001 Grammy ceremonies, took home two awards—one for best R&B song for "Say My Name," and one for best R&B performance by a duo or group.

Hit Big Screen as Foxxy Cleopatra

2001 was a banner year for Beyoncé. Destiny's Child not only won two Grammy awards but earned five *Billboard* awards as well, taking home the award for artist of the year for the second year in a row. The day after the *Billboard* awards show, however, the press was reporting the group was through. The media pounced on a remark Beyoncé made about needing a break from four years of nonstop touring, recording, and promoting Destiny's Child, twisting it into headlines that the group was breaking up. Destiny's Child did not break up, but the girls did take a break. Williams and Rowland each released a solo album, and Beyoncé began developing an acting career and working on her own solo album.

Beyoncé made her acting debut as Carmen in the MTV production of *Carmen: The Hip-Hopera* to favorable reviews in 2001. Her major Hollywood break came with *Austin Powers in Goldmember,* starring comedian Mike Myers. In it, Beyoncé played Meyers's sexy sidekick, secret agent Foxxy Cleopatra, who was a composite of the black action-film heroines of the 1970s. She also performed the film's theme song, "Hey Goldmember." As the film's producer, John Lyons, told *Jet,* Beyoncé "can do anything and have this amazing career in both music and film. If she wants it."

Dangerously in Love, Beyoncé' debut solo album, appeared in June of 2003 and went multiplatinum, launching her into the elite ranks of the entertainment industry. The album, its singles, and its videos won her two MTV Music Awards in 2003 and five Grammies the following year. She had become a superstar in her own right, continuing her acting career, dating hip-hop king Jay-Z, and signing a licensing agreement in early 2005 with the Tarrant Apparel Group for the clothing line she and her mother had created, The House of Dereon. In 2004 Destiny's Child defied critics who speculated they would break up by releasing a new album, *Destiny Fulfilled.* Beyoncé also recorded duets with Stevie Wonder and Slim Thug, winning a Grammy for the former and an MTV Video Music Award for the latter in 2006. Destiny's Child formally disbanded in 2005, but by then Beyoncé was poised to move forward as a solo act.

Accelerated Movie Career

In 2006 Beyoncé starred in *The Pink Panther,* released in February. Her second solo album, *B'Day,* hit stores that September, and the album earned her another Grammy in 2007, for best contemporary R&B album. Toward the end of 2006 she starred alongside Eddie Murphy and Jamie Foxx in the movie version of the musical *Dreamgirls,* playing the lead singer of the Dreamettes, a fictional 1960s pop vocal group resembling the Supremes.

With *Dreamgirls* in theaters and songs from *B'Day,* on the airwaves, Beyoncé was the undisputed queen of R&B by 2007. More awards followed later that year. In June she received two BET Awards—best video for "Irreplaceable" and best R&B female artist. In November she was given the Best International Artist Award at the American Music Awards, making her the first African American woman to be so honored.

Even before a new album was scheduled to release at the end of 2008, Beyonce's name found the headlines earlier in the year. In March she was tapped to star in an upcoming motion picture about the life of legendary singer Etta James. A month later, following much speculation and rumormongering, it was revealed that she and longtime beau Jay-Z had gotten married, a story that made the cover of *People Weekly.* But controversy was never far behind. That summer, celebrity gossip Web site TMZ posted a story claiming that Beyonce's skin tone had been lightened in a widely run L'Oreal ad that had appeared in several major fashion magazines. L'Oreal denied the claim, but the matter had brought criticism from many corners of the blogosphere. This was not, however, the kind of scandal capable of derailing a career as supercharged as that of Beyoncé.

Selected works

Albums with Destiny's Child

Destiny's Child, Columbia, 1998.
The Writing's on the Wall, Columbia, 1999.
Survivor, Columbia, 2001.
8 Days of Christmas, Columbia, 2001.
Destiny Fulfilled, Columbia, 2004.

Albums as solo artist

Dangerously In Love, Columbia, 2003.
B'Day, Columbia, 2006.

Albums as contributor

Men in Black, 1997.
Why Do Fools Fall in Love?, 1999.
Life, 1999.
Romeo Must Die, 2000.
Charlie's Angels, 2000.

Films

Carmen: The Hip-Hopera, 2001.
Austin Powers in Goldmember, 2002.
The Fighting Temptations, 2003.
The Pink Panther, 2006.
Dreamgirls, 2006.

Sources

Books

Knowles, Beyoncé, Kelly Rowland, and Michelle Williams, with James Patrick Herman, *Soul Survivors: The Official Autobiography of Destiny's Child,* HarperCollins, 2002.

Periodicals

Associated Press, August 7, 2008.
Chicago Tribune, July 23, 2002.
Ebony, July 2002, p. 36.
Jet, August 12, 2002, p. 58; March 10, 2008, p. 38.
Newsweek, May 21, 2001, p. 54.
New York Times, February 23, 2001, p. E25.

People, December 25, 2000–January 1, 2001, p. 130; May 7, 2001, p. 39; April 21, 2008, p. 60.
Time, January 15, 2001, p. 128.
USA Today, May 1, 2001, p. D1; April 18, 2002, p. D2.

Online

"Beyonce Knowles Biography," Biography.com, http://www.biography.com/search/article.do?id=9542479 (accessed August 13, 2008).
"Beyonce Knowles' Biography," FOXNews.com, April 15, 2008, http://www.foxnews.com/story/0,2933,204978,00.html?sPage=fnc/entertainment/beyonce (accessed August 13, 2008).
Leahey, Andrew, "Beyoncé: Biography,"*allmusic,* http://www.allmusic.com/cg/amg.dll?p=amg&sql=11:axfuxq8jld6e~T1 (accessed August 13, 2008).
"Celebrity Central: Beyoncé Knowles," People.com, http://www.people.com/people/beyonce_knowles/biography/0,,20004431_10,00.html (accessed August 13, 2008).
Official Beyoncé Web site, http://www.beyonceonline.com (accessed August 13, 2008).

—Brenna Sanchez and Bob Jacobson

Edward Boyd

1914–2007

Marketing executive

From the late 1940s to the early 1950s, Edward Boyd served as a marketing executive with beverage maker Pepsi-Cola and created the first national advertising campaigns aimed at African-American consumers. His tenure at the company was short, but historic. "By offering black America more respect and attention than any major corporation had before," wrote Jocelyn Y. Stewart in the *Los Angeles Times,* "Boyd and his team achieved their goal of driving up Pepsi's sales, pioneered what is now known as niche or target marketing, and helped break the color barrier in corporate America."

Boyd was born in 1914 in Riverside, California, where he grew up in a family of four children. His father was a barber, originally from Toledo, Ohio, while his mother, Emma Barrett Boyd, was descended from one of the few thousand blacks who came to California during the gold rush of the late 1840s. As a teenager, Boyd was a talented singer and harbored an ambition to become an opera star. After graduating from Riverside High School in 1932, he trained for a time with a local opera company, but eventually entered the University of California at Los Angeles with the hope of a career in the U.S. Foreign Service. The diplomatic service, however, was virtually closed to African Americans at the time, and after graduating in 1938 Boyd tried his luck in Hollywood. His roles were few, and he quickly tired of being typecast in the limited parts that studios were then offering to African Americans.

Joined Pepsi-Cola

Boyd found a job with his union, the Screen Actors Guild, and went on to work for the U.S. Civil Service Commission in San Francisco during World War II; he was reportedly the first African American to work at San Francisco's city hall in a professional capacity. He became an expert on housing issues and discrimination, and went on to work as a housing specialist for the National Urban League. In 1947 he was hired by Pepsi-Cola as an assistant sales manager.

Boyd was the protégé of Pepsi's president, Walter S. Mack, who theorized that Pepsi might surpass its biggest competitor, Coca-Cola, in some markets by making an effort to increase sales among African Americans. Mack had tried to put together a sales team for this task back in 1940, but the effort was disbanded when the United States entered World War II. In 1947 Mack hired Boyd to create a national advertising campaign, and Boyd concocted a scheme that was brilliantly simple: He came up with print ads that showed middle-class African Americans enjoying the soft drink. One of the early ads featured a young boy named Ron Brown, who would later become U.S. Secretary of Commerce during the Clinton administration; Brown reaches for a can of Pepsi while his mother looks down, smiling. The ads were the first time that blacks were shown in a national advertising campaign and not depicted as servants, or worse. "We'd been caricatured and stereotyped," Boyd was quoted as saying about the breakthrough in Stewart's *Los Ange-*

At a Glance . . .

Born Edward Francis Boyd on June 27, 1914, in Riverside, CA; died after complications from a stroke, on April 30, 2007, in Los Angeles, CA; son of Robert J. (a barber) and Emma (a real estate entrepreneur; maiden name, Barrett) Boyd; married Edith Jones, 1944; children: Timothy, Rebecca Boyd-Driver, Brandon, Edward Jr. *Education:* University of California–Los Angeles, bachelor's degree, 1938.

Career: Actor in Hollywood films, late 1930s; worked for the Screen Actors Guild; U.S. Civil Service Commission, housing relocation specialist, 1942–45; National Urban League, housing specialist, 1945(?)–47; Pepsi-Cola, assistant sales manager, 1947–51; worked later for the advertising agency Sherman & Marquette Inc., and for the pharmaceutical giant Wyeth International; founded his own market research firm, Resources Management Ltd., in Washington, DC; mission chief for the relief agency CARE; raised alpacas in upstate New York.

les Times article. "The advertisement represented us as normal Americans."

Another campaign that Boyd created at Pepsi depicted notable African Americans, such as Nobel Peace Prize–winner Ralph Bunche. In the era before multicultural education and Black History Month, the posters were immensely popular in the community and were ordered by schools and youth groups as inspirational materials. Pepsi also targeted young consumers with an ad campaign that showed students at historically black colleges. "Boyd hired some of the first black advertising models, flooded black papers with ads and added new sophistication and prominence to the ads already being published in magazines like *Ebony*," asserted writer Douglas Martin in the *New York Times*. "He created the first point-of-purchase displays aimed at minorities. His program also included having celebrities like Duke Ellington and Lionel Hampton give 'shout-outs' for Pepsi from the stage."

Encountered Racism at All Levels

Boyd also headed a twelve-person, college-educated sales force to promote Pepsi products across the country, but they were paid less than their white counterparts at the company. He traveled with the team to schools, church groups, and meetings of various black professionals to increase brand awareness in the African-American community, and their

efforts took them into parts of the Deep South that were still bound by strict segregation laws. There, they stayed in blacks-only hotels and were forced to sit in segregated compartments on buses and trains, but Boyd said the most unpleasant racist moment of his Pepsi career came at New York City's Waldorf-Astoria Hotel in 1949, when Mack addressed complaints during a meeting of the company's influential regional bottlers. Some of the bottlers voiced concerns that the company was focusing too much on black consumers, and Mack agreed with some of their points and made the comment that he, too, did not want Pepsi to become known as the African-American soft drink—though he used a racial epithet.

Boyd recalled that moment when he appeared on PBS's *Tavis Smiley Show* in February of 2007. "I had one of my team members sitting beside me, which was unusual because all of our team was instructed never to sit together," he told Smiley. "I was totally shocked. I was amazed. And I knew immediately that I had to do something to show that I did not accept this. That I was appalled by it. In fact, insulted by it. And so I told the [sales associate] that was next to me, who was on my team, please don't follow me, I have to leave. And I got up and … crossed in front of people to the aisle, to the next aisle, and walked out of the Waldorf-Astoria Hotel grand ballroom."

Mack left Pepsi in 1951 after a management shakeup, and Boyd soon followed after his team was disbanded. Despite his successful track record, he was unable to find another corporate marketing job, and over the next three decades held a variety of positions. He worked for an advertising agency and for Wyeth International when it began an effort to sell its infant formula in African countries; for a time he ran his own market-research firm, Resources Management Ltd. CARE, the international humanitarian relief agency, hired him as a mission chief, which took him to Africa and the Middle East, and he also participated in a leadership training program for teens at the Society of Ethical Culture of New York City. A married father of four, Boyd divided his retirement years between an apartment in New York City and a 120-acre alpaca farm in upstate New York. His earlier achievements with Pepsi were forgotten until *Wall Street Journal* writer Stephanie Capparell wrote about his time at the company in her 2007 book *The Real Pepsi Challenge: The Inspirational Story of Breaking the Color Barrier in American Business*.

Capparell interviewed Boyd extensively for her book, and they appeared together on *The Tavis Smiley Show* to promote it. Several weeks later Boyd suffered a stroke and never fully recovered. He died in Los Angeles at the age of ninety-two on April 30, 2007. One of Mack's successors in the Pepsi boardroom, Donald Kendall, told the writer of Boyd's obituary in the *San Francisco Chronicle* that Boyd's achievement at Pepsi was akin to that of Jackie Robinson, who became the first African-American player in Major League Baseball in 1947. "Robinson may have made more headlines, but what Ed did—integrating the managerial ranks of corporate America—was equally groundbreaking," Kendall told Janine DeFao. "Long before most companies came to see the power and potential of the black consumer, Ed put doors where previously only walls existed."

Sources

Books

Capparell, Stephanie, *The Real Pepsi Challenge: The Inspirational Story of Breaking the Color Barrier in American Business,* Free Press, 2007.

Periodicals

Los Angeles Times, May 5, 2007, p. B8.
New York Times, May 6, 2007.
New York Times Magazine, December 30, 2007.
Press-Enterprise (Riverside, CA), May 5, 2007.
San Francisco Chronicle, May 5, 2007, p. B6.

Other

"Edward Boyd," *The Tavis Smiley Show,* PBS, February 27, 2007, http://www.pbs.org/kcet/tavissmiley/archive/200702/20070227_boyd.html (accessed August 21, 2008).

—Carol Brennan

Donna Brazile

1959—

Political strategist, commentator, educator

Brazile, Donna, photograph. Paul J. Richards/AFP/Getty Images.

In the fall of 1999 Vice President Al Gore named veteran Democratic Party organizer Donna Brazile as his campaign manager for the 2000 presidential campaign. She became the first African-American woman to achieve such a prestigious—and difficult—position in national party politics. Brazile, however, had long been a fixture in Democratic circles, known for her formidable grassroots organizing skills. In 1987 the *Wall Street Journal* named her one of "the powers that (might) be" in national politics in the year 2000. The *Journal*'s prediction proved uncannily accurate. "I'm obsessed with the thought of making things happen.... Ultimately, I do it because I'm scared," confessed Brazile about her career choice to *Washington Post* reporter Donna Britt. "I don't ever, ever, ever want to be poor again. And the best way to insure that won't happen is to organize, to fight for our lives." Since the 2000 election, which Gore lost in controversial fashion to George W. Bush, Brazile has remained one of the nation's top political strategists and a towering figure in Democratic circles.

Brazile was born in a New Orleans charity hospital on December 15, 1959, and grew up in nearby Kenner, Louisiana. Her father, Lionel, was a Korean War veteran who, at various points in his life, had been run over by a truck, suffered a broken back, and even had a heart attack while riding on a city bus. On that occasion he simply got off and checked himself into a hospital. There were nine children in the Brazile family, and their father's income as a janitor was not always sufficient, so he often moonlighted or worked double shifts. Brazile's mother also worked, as a domestic servant, and the children's grandmother lived with them as well. Brazile used to read the morning paper to her grandmother, which helped foster her interest in politics.

Became a Youthful Activist

Brazile has often stressed that she grew up in an impoverished household, and remembering the hardships of her youth inspired her to become active in politics. "There still are poor people," Brazile told Robin Givhan in the *Washington Post* about her long commitment to Democratic politics. "There still are people struggling to live off $5.15 an hour." Federal minimum-wage laws, civil-rights bills, affirmative action

At a Glance . . .

Born on December 15, 1959, in New Orleans, LA; daughter of a Lionel (a janitor) and Jean (a domestic worker) Brazile. *Politics:* Democrat. *Religion:* Roman Catholic. *Education:* Earned degree in industrial psychology from Louisiana State University.

Career: National Student Education Fund, Washington, DC, lobbyist, early 1980s; 20th Anniversary March on Washington, national director, 1983; worked for the Rev. Jesse Jackson's presidential campaign, and for the Mondale-Ferraro Democratic ticket, both 1984; Gephardt for President, national field director, 1987; Michael Dukakis for President campaign, national field director, 1988; affiliated with Community for Creative Non-Violence (an advocate group for the homeless), Washington, DC, 1989; chief of staff for Eleanor Holmes Norton (delegate from the District of Columbia in the U.S. House of Representatives), 1990–99; head of Voter/Campaign Assessment Program for the Democratic Congressional Campaign Committee, 1998; Al Gore for President 2000 Campaign, began as deputy campaign manager and national political director, May of 1999, became campaign manager, October of 1999; Institute of Politics, Harvard University, fellow, 2001; Brazile and Associates, LLC, founder and managing director, 2002—; Georgetown University women's studies program, lecturer; CNN political commentator.

Memberships: National Political Congress of Black Women, cofounder, first executive director; Democratic National Committee's Voting Rights Institute, chair.

Awards: Named one of 100 Most Powerful Women in Washington, DC, by *Washington Magazine;* named one of 50 Most Powerful Women in America by *Essence.*

Addresses: *Office*—Brazile & Associates LLC, 1001 G St. NW, Ste. 1001, Washington, DC 20001.

In Brazile's childhood neighborhood, there were no playground facilities. At the age of nine Brazile learned that a candidate for city council was promising to have one built. She volunteered for the campaign and passed out leaflets in her neighborhood. The candidate won the election and Brazile's neighborhood received a new playground. She later organized the first female baseball team in her community.

In 1975 Brazile's grandmother suffered a stroke and became disabled. She still lived with the family, and Brazile and her sisters helped take care of her. Brazile would forever associate the smell of roses—her grandmother's favorite scent—with a premonition of death. In 1976, although she was not yet old enough to vote, she volunteered for the Democratic presidential campaign of Georgia governor Jimmy Carter. Brazile stuffed envelopes at her local headquarters for the Carter-Mondale ticket.

Became a DC Lobbyist

Brazile financed her college education at Louisiana State University with student loans and financial aid. After earning a degree in industrial psychology, she found work as a lobbyist for the National Student Education Fund in Washington, DC. From there she was hired by Coretta Scott King to work on the planning and reenactment of Martin Luther King Jr.'s famous 1963 civil rights march on the nation's capital. Brazile's work for the King foundation coincided with the successful drive to make the slain civil-rights leader's birthday a national holiday.

In 1984 Brazile became involved with the Rev. Jesse Jackson's presidential campaign, serving as mobilization director, and she also worked with the Rainbow Coalition. The same year, Brazile worked on Walter Mondale's unsuccessful campaign for the White House. In 1987 she was hired as national field director for Dick Gephardt, a Missouri senator making a bid for the Democratic Party nomination. Brazile made history by becoming the first African American to hold such a post for a mainstream white candidate. "She has the ability to walk into a room of Southern white male politicians and get results," a colleague in the Gephardt campaign office told the *Wall Street Journal.* When Gephardt won the Iowa caucuses early in 1988, Brazile's organizational skills were cited as a primary reason for the victory.

Endured Dukakis Debacle

When Massachusetts governor Michael Dukakis defeated Gephardt for the Democratic presidential nomination in the summer of 1988, Brazile was hired by his campaign organization for the same post that she had held on Gephardt's senior staff—organizing the "field," which involved marshaling votes by setting up and running efficient, dedicated local efforts, such as phone

programs, Medicare, Head Start preschool funding, and numerous other pieces of social legislation have all originated with Democratic legislators and were signed into law by Democratic presidents.

banks. Republican front-runner George H. W. Bush, however, waged a bitter, divisive campaign against Dukakis that reached its lowest point with the airing of a notorious television campaign ad featuring the face of an angry-looking African-American male. The man in the ad was Willie Horton, a Massachusetts resident who was convicted of a crime and then released from prison on a furlough that had been signed by Dukakis. Following his release from prison, Horton committed rape and murder. The campaign ad was both offensive and effective, and many African-American leaders strongly protested. For her part, Brazile was incensed that the Dukakis staff had failed to effectively counter the attack.

Dukakis's campaign was also hindered by the fact that Dukakis rarely campaigned in African-American neighborhoods. Strategies and statements released from the Dukakis camp alienated Brazile and other prominent African Americans within the Democratic Party. Brazile grew increasingly dismayed, and even endured racism herself on one occasion. As Brazile recounted to Britt, a midwestern farmer walked up to her during a campaign stop and announced, "You're a Willie Horton n——." Not one to shrink from a fight, she strongly chastised the farmer before heading back to the campaign bus.

The tension between the Bush and Dukakis camps continued to build. One day, while speaking with reporters, Brazile mentioned the oft-repeated rumors that Bush had committed adultery. She urged the reporters to investigate the charges against the Republican candidate. Later, Brazile publicly denounced the Bush campaign's racist tactics, and denounced him as a philanderer. Realizing that the frustrations of her job had sparked her inflammatory words, she submitted her resignation. The campaign manager to whom Brazile's resignation was submitted, Susan Estrich, told Givhan in the *Washington Post* interview that she herself had joked with Brazile that "if I could have figured out a way to get fired, I'd have done it, too." Dukakis went on to lose the election after fielding one of the most poorly organized presidential campaigns in history.

Encountered More Hardship

Following her resignation from the Dukakis campaign, Brazile found herself without a job. She was also certain that her career in politics was over. To make matters worse, her mother was admitted to a charity hospital. "I kept telling myself, 'She's okay, she's okay,'" Brazile said in the *Post* interview with Britt in 1989. "This was the most intense period of my life. I was trying to figure out, 'What did I say?' I needed time to become a human being again, to withdraw. Then I smelled the roses and I froze." Brazile's mother died soon after at the age of fifty-three. Brazile used her last paycheck from the Dukakis campaign to pay for the funeral costs.

During her late twenties Brazile reevaluated her life. She gave up smoking and red meat, began exercising, and quickly shed forty-five pounds. She contemplated attending law school, and landed a new job in Washington as an associate for Mitch Snyder, a well-known advocate for the homeless. For almost a year Brazile lived at Snyder's Community for Creative Non-Violence, the shelter where her office was located. Under Brazile's direction, the Community for Creative Non-Violence coordinated Washington, DC's Housing Now! march in the fall of 1989.

In 1990 Brazile became chief of staff for Eleanor Holmes Norton, who represents the District of Columbia as a nonvoting member of the U.S. House of Representatives, a job she held for the next several years. She also continued working within the Democratic Party. In 1996 Brazile served as local director for the District of Columbia during the Clinton/Gore presidential campaign. During the 1998 midterm elections she ran the Voter/Campaign Assessment Program, an effort organized by the Democratic Congressional Campaign Committee to bring more African Americans to the polls. The program was a great success, and a solid number of Democratic candidates were elected to Congress that year.

Received a Historic Promotion

Brazile began working for the Gore for President campaign in the spring of 1999 when its offices were still on K Street, also called "Lobbyists' Row," in the heart of Washington, DC. Initially she served as Gore's national political director and deputy campaign manager. In October of 1999 Brazile was late for a staff meeting at which Gore was scheduled to make an important announcement. When the elevator doors opened, her colleagues accosted her, telling her that Gore wanted to meet with her privately. She assumed she was about to be fired again. Gore, however, offered her a promotion to campaign manager. By accepting the position, Brazile became the first African-American woman to head a presidential campaign.

"She is the heart of grassroots activism and political leadership and she'll be a great leader for our national campaign," Gore said in announcing the appointment, which also coincided with the revelation that his campaign headquarters would relocate to his home state of Tennessee. "Her more than twenty years of experience in local and national campaigns across the country is a terrific benefit to our effort. I look forward to working with her in her new capacity and I know she will fight hard to bring this campaign closer to the working families of America," Gore remarked. Upon learning of Brazile's promotion, the press was quick to point out that Brazile had been fired from the Dukakis campaign several years earlier. As Katharine E. Seelye wrote in the *New York Times,* however, "Gore's appointment of her indicates he has little concern about it [the 1988 firing over the George Bush fracas]. As one aide back in

Washington sarcastically put it: 'Spreading rumors? Holy smokes! In this town?'"

The appointment of Brazile as campaign manager sent the message that Gore—unlike some of his predecessors—realized that what is termed "the black vote" does not automatically go to the Democratic candidate. "Brazile has been important in shoring up Gore's support among the Democrats' traditional constituencies," noted James Bennet in the *New York Times,* referring to the working poor, African Americans, and organized labor.

Brazile was also charged with the task of cutting campaign spending. One of her first duties as campaign manager was "an examination of what she called 'Goreworld,'" explained Bennet in the *New York Times,* "the results of which revolted her. Consultants were getting paid as much as $15,000 monthly; paid advisers were rendering opinions on what kind of paper the headquarters should use." Brazile immediately slashed the salaries of some staffers, a move that was based, in part, on the fact that living costs in Tennessee were much lower than in the District of Columbia.

Tackled a Tough Job

The principal focus of Brazile's job was to develop strategies that would help Gore win the White House. To help accomplish this task, she worked closely with campaign chairman Tony Coelho and Gore 2000 media advisers Carter Eskew and Bob Shrum. In the *New York Times* report, Bennet explained the nature of the job of Brazile, who had sketched for the reporter a triangle diagram: three phrases on each point read "proven leader," "principled fighter," and "experience that matters." She then explained to Bennet that every statement made by Gore or his campaign staff, in the effort to win voters, needed to touch upon those points. "Every conversation—no matter how it starts off—it's got to go into this box," she told Bennet.

During her first months on the job in Nashville, Brazile continued to commute back and forth to the Washington, DC, area to teach a class, "African American Participation in American Politics," at University of Maryland's College Park campus. Throughout the campaign, Brazile contended that the current state of political campaigns, with their reliance on polls and highly paid consultants, was ineffective in bringing together voters on the issues. She believed it was all about grassroots organizing, and the candidates' commitment to their principles. "I put my energy, voice and spirit into fighting for anybody who wants to speak their voice," she told Givhan. "I don't care what the right wing, the left wing or the chicken wing has to say."

Became Top Political Commentator

Gore lost the 2000 presidential election to George W.

Bush in one of the closest races in history, the outcome hinging on a Supreme Court decision regarding the handling of ballots cast in Florida. While the 2000 election was a defeat for Brazile, it did nothing to slow the ascent of her political stardom. In the wake of the election she accepted a lecturer position at Harvard, and later another at Georgetown. During the 2002 midterm election season, she traveled to more than half of the states to help train Democratic activists. After the elections she worked for a period of time for Senator Mary Landrieu, a Democrat from Louisiana, as a media consultant and organizer. She founded her own consulting firm, Brazile & Associates, which trains people in grassroots advocacy and other political tactics such as media relations and legislative outreach. In 2004 she enjoyed the publication of her book, *Cooking with Grease: Stirring the Pots in American Politics,* in which she recounted the story of her rise from poor Louisiana girl to the very pinnacle of American power.

Brazile also began appearing regularly on several of the most popular political television talk shows. She is a weekly contributor and political commentator on CNN's *American Morning* and *Inside Politics.* She is also a regular on MSNBC's *Hardball* and Fox's *Hannity and Colmes.* The 2008 Democratic presidential primary put Brazile in an interesting position: Should she support the potential first woman president or the potential first Black president? As a highly visible member of the party machinery, she opted to endorse neither candidate before the nomination was decided. But that did not stop her from making her voice heard loud and clear throughout the campaign. She was particularly harsh in her criticism of the media on its handling of both race and gender matters. Election outcomes aside, Brazile's voice will likely be a prominent one in the Democratic chorus for years to come.

Selected works

Books

Cooking with Grease: Stirring the Pots in American Politics, Simon & Schuster, 2004.

Sources

Periodicals

Black Enterprise, February 1996, p. 22.
Essence, August 2004, p. 216.
Ms., Spring 2008.
National Review, February 7, 2000, pp. 17–18.
New York Times, October 7, 1999; October 11, 1999; January 7, 2000.
New York Times Magazine, December 12, 1999; January 23, 2000.
St. Petersburg Times (St. Petersburg, FL), June 27, 2004, p. 4P.
U.S. News & World Report, October 15, 2007, p. 16.

Wall Street Journal, December 4, 1987.
Washington Post, October 7, 1989, p. C1; November 16, 1999, p. C1.

Online

"About," Brazile & Associates LLC: Official Web site of Donna Brazile, http://www.donnabrazile.com/page.cfm?id=2 (accessed August 7, 2008).

Acosta, Jim, "Democrats Dreading a Drawn-Out, Costly Battle for Nomination," CNNPolitics, February 8, 2008, http://www.cnn.com/2008/POLITICS/02/07/dem.delegates/ (accessed August 7, 2008).

"Donna Brazile Cuts Loose on 2008 Campaign," PoliticsWest (*Denver Post*), February 29, 2008, http://www.politicswest.com/node/20993 (accessed August 7, 2008).

"Sister Surge! Black Women and Politics: What We Want & How We're Going to Get It," Brazile & Associates LLC: Official Web site of Donna Brazile, http://donnabrazile.com/viewNews.cfm?id=117 (accessed August 7, 2008).

Other

"Brazile: I'll Quit DNC Position over Superdelegates," *News & Notes,* National Public Radio, February 11, 2008, http://www.npr.org/templates/story/story.php?storyId=18882087&sc=emaf (accessed August 7, 2008).

—Carol Brennan and Bob Jacobson

George Butler Jr.

1931–2008

Record-company executive, music producer

George Butler Jr. was one of the highest-ranking African Americans in the music business during the mid-1980s. A producer and record-company executive, he is credited with discovering both trumpeter Wynton Marsalis and pianist Harry Connick Jr. Among his other notable achievements was luring jazz legend Miles Davis out of a self-imposed retirement. In *Jet* Marsalis noted that "Butler worked very hard to help create quality music and strongly believed in music education.... He had eclectic tastes and embraced a philosophy that accommodated all different types of people and styles of music."

George Tucker Butler Jr. was born on September 2, 1931, and grew up in the Beatties Ford Road area of Charlotte, North Carolina. His musical education began with piano lessons at a young age, but he was known to skip an appointment at the teacher's house to join a baseball game in progress, according to his sister, Jacqueline Butler Hairston, in the*Charlotte Observer.* "He'd shout back, 'Don't you dare tell Mama and Daddy!'" she recalled. "He was my older brother, so I never did." At West Charlotte High School Butler was star of the basketball team, and he continued to play the sport when he entered Howard University in 1949 as a piano major. In the mid 1950s he moved to New York City, where he earned a master's degree in music education at Columbia University.

Signed Marsalis, Connick Jr. at Columbia

In 1972 the chief of United Artist Records hired Butler to head Blue Note Records, the jazz label, which United Artists had acquired in a merger. "At a time when jazz was rapidly losing its audience," Ben Ratliff wrote in the *New York Times,* Butler "strove to fight the trend by arranging for many jazz-pop crossover projects, including albums by Earl Klugh, Donald Byrd, Ronnie Laws and Bobbi Humphrey." Butler served as producer for several Blue Note releases, among them Byrd's *Ethiopian Nights* in 1971 and Laws's *Pressure Sensitive* in 1975.

In 1978 Butler was lured away from Blue Note by CBS Records, which offered him a slot as an artists and repertoire (A&R) executive with Columbia Records, the oldest label in the history of recorded music. His first notable signing was Wynton Marsalis, an eighteen-year-old from New Orleans, who would become one of the most honored jazz artists of his generation. Butler discovered Marsalis playing trumpet in a bar. He subsequently signed Marsalis's brother, Branford, a saxophonist, as well. Their father, Ellis, was a respected New Orleans musician and teacher, whose students included Harry Connick Jr., a piano prodigy who performed on his first jazz recordings at age ten. Butler signed the twelve-year-old Connick in 1979. The three musicians became part of a movement dubbed the Young Lions of jazz, described by Ratliff as "young musicians playing hard bop or traditional styles with polished technique."

Butler's most notable achievement as a record-label executive, however, was urging jazz trumpeter Miles Davis to come out of retirement and record again.

Davis was at the forefront of several new strains of jazz starting just after World War II. By the mid-1970s, however, his groundbreaking foray into funk had been blighted by failing health and a heroin habit. He retreated entirely from performing and recording. According to most reports, Davis rarely left his New York City town house during those years except to buy drugs on the street. In an interview with George Cole for the book *The Last Miles: The Music of Miles Davis, 1980–1991,* Butler said he was surprised to learn that Davis was still signed to Columbia Records. "I decided to call him and introduce myself and just let him know that he had a friend," Butler told Cole. "I knew that a number of people from Columbia had tried getting Miles to record again and failed. I thought I would visit him and talk about three things that interested him most—cars, boxing, and clothes. I didn't have a great deal of knowledge about these subjects, but I pretended I knew more than I did. I knew I was not going to talk to Miles about music."

Coaxed Davis out of Retirement

Butler visited Davis almost every weekday morning for a nine-month stretch, often just watching television with him. Finally, Davis hinted that he had been working on some new material, but when he tried to play it for Butler, it became clear that Davis's piano had just a few working keys. Butler asked the head of Columbia Records for approval to spend $100,000 on a piano as a birthday present for Davis. When the delivery company turned up at Davis's town house, the reclusive performer refused to answer the door. The company called Butler, who contacted a mutual friend and neighbor to persuade Davis to allow the deliverymen in. The friend "told me that when Miles saw the piano, there were tears in his eyes," Butler told Cole. Davis, however, was also famously abrupt on the telephone, and Butler also noted in *The Last Miles* that

"Miles called and said 'Thanks George,' and slammed the phone down before I could say, 'You're welcome.'"

The careful wooing of Davis resulted in *The Man with the Horn,* produced by Butler and released in 1981 to lukewarm reviews. It represented a significant step for the music pioneer, however; Davis was able to wean himself off prescription and illegal drugs, which reignited his creativity and led to important work. Davis eventually left Columbia, however, because he thought Butler and the record company were grooming Marsalis to be his replacement. Davis made some of his displeasure public. In an interview with Nick Kent in the British magazine *The Face,* Davis said of Butler: "I can't stand a black man who wants to be bourgeois! That's a pitiful condition to be in."

When Columbia became part of Sony in the 1980s, Butler was promoted to senior vice president and executive producer. At the time, he was one of the highest-ranking African-American executives in the record business. One of his last notable finds was jazz vocalist Nnenna Freelon; he served as executive producer for her first three albums in the early 1990s. He retired a few years later and settled in the San Francisco Bay area community of Hayward, where his sister, Jacqueline, lived. He was diagnosed with Alzheimer's disease in 2005.

Suffered Alzheimer's in Retirement

Butler was living in a retirement facility, Casa Sandoval, when he went missing for thirty-six hours in January of 2008. "According to police, Butler told the staff at Casa Sandoval that he planned to go back to his home in New York City," wrote Jason Sweeney in the *Daily Review.* "At 9:20 a.m. Tuesday, he walked through a hallway door, went down a stairwell and then exited via a building door. Video surveillance captured Butler leaving Casa Sandoval through a west exit, according to police." Alarms on the doors had been temporarily disconnected because the facility was being renovated. Using a handheld thermal-imaging device, authorities located Butler in a ravine along San Lorenzo Creek, where he had become entangled in bushes. The weather was typical for northern California in January—cold, windy, and rainy, and Butler had been mired there for at least ten hours. "The incident made headlines in the Bay Area," noted a report on AllAboutJazz.com, "and marked a sad episode in the life of a man once considered one of the most influential figures in jazz."

Butler died three months later, on April 9, at a care facility in Castro Valley, California. In a memorial on the Web site The Key Influencer, the record industry executive Vernon Slaughter wrote: "It's sheer irony that a disease that literally makes you forget who you are would take from us a man who accomplished so very many unforgettable things."

Selected works

Producer

Elvin Jones, *Mr. Jones,* Blue Note, 1969.
Horace Silver, *In Pursuit of the 27th Man,* Blue Note, 1970.
Bobbi Humphrey, *Bobbi Humphrey's Best,* Blue Note, 1971.
Donald Byrd, *Ethiopian Nights,* Blue Note, 1971.
Bobby Hutcherson, *Live at Montreaux,* Blue Note, 1973.
Shirley Bassey, *Nobody Does It Like Me,* United Artists, 1974.
Ronnie Laws, *Pressure Sensitive,* Blue Note, 1975.
(Various artists) *Blue Note Live at the Roxy,* Blue Note, 1977.
(Various artists) *Arnold Schwarzenegger's Total Body Workout,* Columbia, 1983.
Branford Marsalis, *Scenes in the City,* Columbia, 1983.
Wynton Marsalis Septet, *In This House, on This Morning,* Columbia, 1992.

Executive producer

Max Roach, *M'Boom,* Columbia/Legacy, 1979.
Miles Davis, *The Man with the Horn,* Columbia, 1981.
Wynton Marsalis, *Wynton Marsalis,* Columbia, 1981.
Miles Davis, *You're Under Arrest,* Columbia, 1985.
Grover Washington Jr., *A House Full of Love (Music from "The Cosby Show"),* Columbia, 1986.
Harry Connick Jr., *Harry Connick Jr.,* Columbia, 1987.
Harry Connick Jr., *20,* Columbia, 1988.
Branford Marsalis, *Trio Jeepy,* Columbia, 1988.
Ramsey Lewis, *Urban Renewal,* Columbia, 1989.
Harry Connick Jr., *We Are in Love,* Columbia, 1990.
Nancy Wilson, *With My Lover Beside Me,* Columbia, 1991.
Nnenna Freelon, *Nnenna Freelon,* Columbia, 1992.
Nnenna Freelon, *Heritage,* Columbia, 1993.
Lou Donaldson, *Sentimental Journey,* Columbia, 1994.
Nnenna Freelon, *Listen,* Columbia, 1994.

Sources

Books

Cole, George, *The Last Miles: The Music of Miles Davis, 1980–1991,* University of Michigan Press, 2005, pp. 36–38.
Kent, Nick, "Lightening Up with the Prince of Darkness: Miles Davis Approaches Sixty," in *The Dark Stuff: Selected Writings on Rock Music, 1972–1995,* Da Capo Press, 1995, p. 274.

Periodicals

Charlotte Observer (Charlotte, NC), April 17, 2008.
Daily Review (Hayward, CA), January 12, 2008.
Jet, May 5, 2008.
New York Times, May 20, 1990, p. 34; April 20, 2008, p. A30.

Online

AllAboutJazz.com, http://www.allaboutjazz.com/php/news.php?id=18108 (accessed September 21, 2008).
Andrews, James, "Celebrating the Life of George Butler," The Key Influencer, April 15, 2008, http://thekeyinfluencer.wordpress.com/2008/04/15/georgebutler/ (accessed September 21, 2008).

—Carol Brennan

Louis Butler

1952—

Judge

Louis Butler is a well-known Wisconsin judge who served from 2004 to 2008 as one of seven justices—and the first African American—on that state's supreme court. His appointment to that post by Governor Jim Doyle followed several decades of experience in a variety of courtroom roles, including public defender, municipal court judge, and circuit court judge. He came to national prominence in the spring of 2008, when state law required him to run for election in order to retain his seat on the supreme court bench. After a bitter campaign that drew national media coverage and provoked intense debate about campaign ethics and negative advertising, Butler lost by a narrow margin to challenger Michael Gableman.

Born Louis Bennett Butler Jr. on February 15, 1952, in Chicago, Illinois, he grew up on that city's predominately African-American South Side. After graduating from South Shore High School in 1969, Butler attended Lawrence University in Appleton, Wisconsin, receiving a bachelor's degree from that institution in 1973. He then entered law school at the University of Wisconsin–Madison, which granted him a law degree in 1977. After passing the bar exam required of all attorneys, he took a job in the Wisconsin State Public Defenders Office. As an assistant public defender, a post he held from 1979 to 1992, he represented criminal-case defendants who were unable or unwilling to hire a private lawyer. After several years of handling cases until the end of the defendant's first trial, he moved on to the appellate division, where he worked with defendants who wanted to appeal their initial convictions. It was in this latter role, in 1988, that he

argued a case (*McCoy v. Court of Appeals of Wisconsin, District 1*) before the U.S. Supreme Court. While he lost the decision, he gained the distinction of being the first public defender from Wisconsin ever to appear before the nation's highest court.

Butler's growing reputation as a skilled and energetic attorney brought him to the attention of Milwaukee's city council, which appointed him to a judgeship in the local municipal court in 1992. There he heard a variety of relatively minor, nonjury cases, including traffic tickets and ordinance violations. Ten years later, in 2002, he won election to the Milwaukee County Circuit Court, where he presided over more serious civil and criminal cases, almost all of which required juries. He remained at the circuit court for two years before being appointed by Governor Jim Doyle to the seven-member Wisconsin Supreme Court in 2004.

Butler's performance in these roles is difficult to assess, because most of the publicly available information is colored by the political rhetoric, both positive and negative, that surrounded a notoriously bitter election campaign in the spring of 2008. According to the official Wisconsin Court System Web site, "Vacancies [on the supreme court] are filled by gubernatorial appointment and the appointee is required to stand for election to a full 10-year term the following spring." It was this unusual feature of state law that necessitated the campaign, though it was delayed until 2008 because of a provision limiting justices to running one at a time.

Challenging Butler for his seat was Michael J. Gableman, a circuit court judge from rural Burnett County. Although judicial elections in Wisconsin are supposed to be nonpartisan, there were strong political overtones to the campaign from the beginning. Democrats generally favored Butler, who was appointed by a Democrat (Doyle); Republicans, meanwhile, tended to favor Gableman, who initially reached the circuit court through an appointment by Doyle's predecessor, Republican Scott McCallum. In a mixed appointment-and-election system such as Wisconsin's, keeping judicial elections free of party politics has never been easy. The 2008 campaign proved particularly difficult in this regard, however, and there were increasing calls—from newspapers, academics, and ordinary voters—to overhaul the system.

Particularly troubling to many observers was the aggressive tone of the advertising on both sides. Total campaign expenditures reached $5 million, an extraordinary amount in light of Wisconsin's relatively small size and the traditionally low profile of most judicial elections. Much of the advertising was funded by special-interest groups unhappy with Butler's decisions in several high-profile cases. Manufacturers, in particular, were unhappy with a decision Butler wrote in *Thomas v. Mallet* (2005), a product-liability case involving lead paint. John Fund of the *Wall Street Journal* called Butler's decision in that case "infamous," arguing that it created a "guilty-until-proven-innocent approach to product liability."

While there were special-interest groups aligned on both sides of the campaign, those working on Gableman's behalf were more visible, in part, perhaps, because Butler publicly disavowed the negative advertising such groups often use. Because negative ads—those that focus not on the favored candidate's accomplishments, but on an opponent's alleged failures or weaknesses—are ordinarily most effective against incumbents, it is perhaps only to be expected that Butler would object to them. There is no question, however, that many voters were made uncomfortable by the tone of Gableman's attacks, particularly a television ad that seemed to emphasize Butler's race. The ad featured an image of Butler alongside one of Reuben Lee Mitchell, an African-American man convicted of raping an eleven-year-old child. As these images appeared on the screen, an announcer remarked, "Butler found a loophole. Mitchell went on to molest another child. Can Wisconsin families feel safe with Louis Butler on the Supreme Court?" Butler quickly rebutted the ad's implication that he had compromised public safety by engineering Mitchell's early release from prison, noting that, while he had represented the defendant before several appeals courts, Mitchell had a legal right to such representation under the U.S. Constitution. Furthermore, Butler and others pointed out, the appeals were unsuccessful; even if they had been granted, however, Mitchell would have won only the right to a new trial, not automatic release. As it was, he served his full term before going on to commit another crime.

The issues raised by Gableman's ad drew national media attention, which in turn heightened an already tense atmosphere. Particularly unsettling to many was the ad's suggestion that, in the words of Adam Liptak in the *New York Times,* "the only black justice on the state Supreme Court had helped free a black rapist." Butler himself called such tactics "race-baiting," telling Liptak that voters "should not be making decisions based on ads filled with lies, deception, falsehood, and race-baiting."

On April 1, 2008, by a margin of 51 to 49 percent, Wisconsin voters chose Gableman over Butler. Butler's term as justice for the Wisconsin Supreme Court expired on July 31, 2008. As of that time, he had made public few details regarding his plans for the future.

Sources

Periodicals

New York Times, May 25, 2008.
Wisconsin Law Journal, August 11, 2008.

Online

"Bio: Justice Louis Butler," http://www.louisbutler. com/more/index.cfm?Fuseaction=more_33371 (accessed July 17, 2008).
"Court System Overview," Wisconsin Court System, http://wicourts.gov/about/organization/overview.

htm (accessed July 19, 2008).
Fund, John, "Wisconsin's Judicial Revolution," *Wall Street Journal Online,* April 5, 2008, http://online. wsj.com/public/article_print/SB12073597578259 1721.html (accessed July 17, 2008).
"Interactive Chats: Louis Butler," *Milwaukee Journal Sentinel Online,* March 21, 2008, http://www. jsonline.com/story/index.aspx?id=730750 (accessed July 17, 2008).
"Justice Louis B. Butler Jr.," http://www.wicourts.gov /about/judges/supreme/butler.htm (accessed July 17, 2008).

—R. Anthony Kugler

Cee-Lo

1974—

Singer-songwriter, rapper

Cee-Lo, photograph. Jonathan Wood/Getty Images.

In the summer of 2006, "Crazy," the infectious pop tune by duo Gnarls Barkley, seemed to be on everyone's lips—and on their iPods. The song, the first single from the album *St. Elsewhere,* was a breakthrough hit for Gnarls Barkley, a collaboration between rap musician Cee-Lo and producer Danger Mouse. Though "Crazy" put him on the charts in a big way, Cee-Lo was no novice to the music business—he had already been recording for some fifteen years, first as a member of the "Dirty South" rap group Goodie Mob and then as a solo artist. Over the course of his career, Cee-Lo has defied easy categorization, deftly mixing musical styles in unexpected ways to create a sound that is uniquely his own. What he will do next is anyone's guess.

Cee-Lo, who has also gone by the name of Cee-Lo Green, was born Thomas DeCarlo Callaway on May 30, 1974, in Atlanta, Georgia. His father, a Baptist minister, died when Cee-Lo was just two years old, and he was raised in a large household that included his mother, sister, uncles, cousins, grandmother, and great grandmother. Though his mother was also an ordained minister, she never had her own congregation and instead sold Amway products to pay the bills. Cee-Lo displayed an early gift and passion for music, often playing the family's heirloom grand piano and singing gospel music in church. An aunt who sang at a local restaurant encouraged him to pursue his talent.

Nevertheless, Cee-Lo was certainly no choir boy. By junior high, he was working as a gang enforcer and committing petty theft. Although he attended Benjamin E. Mays High School in Atlanta for a while, after several arrests he was sent to a military academy. Soon he dropped out of school altogether to pursue a career in music.

When Cee-Lo was sixteen years old, he and his family suffered a devastating loss when his mother was involved in a car accident that left her a quadriplegic; she would die two years later, sending Cee-Lo into a deep depression. The experience had a profound impact on his music: He told *Rolling Stone* magazine in 2001, "From that point on, I had no shame incorporating my feelings about God or the world into my music."

In 1991 Cee-Lo hooked up with three high school friends—Khujo (Willie Knight), Big Gipp (Cameron

At a Glance . . .

Born Thomas DeCarlo Callaway on May 30, 1974, in Atlanta, GA; married Christina Shanta Johnson, March 18, 2000 (divorced 2005); children: Kingston; Sierra and Kalah (stepdaughters).

Career: Recording artist, 1991—; has performed and recorded as a solo artist and as a member of the groups Goodie Mob, Dungeon Family, and Gnarls Barkley.

Awards: Grammy awards, best urban/alternative performance and best alternative music album, both 2007; BET Award for Best Group (Gnarls Barkley), 2007.

Addresses: *Office*—Atlantic Records, 1290 Avenue of the Americas, 28th Fl., New York, NY 10104.

Gipp), and T-Mo (Robert Barrett)—to form the group Goodie Mob. The quartet first appeared on the 1994 album *Southernplayalisticadillacmuzik* by fellow Atlanta rap musicians OutKast (André 3000, one-half of OutKast, was a childhood friend of Cee-Lo's). The following year, Goodie Mob released their own debut, *Soul Food* (1995), which went gold within weeks of its release. They followed up three years later with *Still Standing* (1998).

From the beginning, Goodie Mob wanted to transcend the thuggish style and message of gangsta rap, believing that they could be a positive force in hip-hop music. They pioneered the Dirty South sound, a style of rap music marked by buoyant, club-friendly beats and lyrical depth. Goodie Mob's first two albums were lauded for their "live instrumentation, their organic, bluesy vibe and their smart, unusually soulful lyrics," as noted by *Rolling Stone* in 2001.

Despite the critical acclaim, *Still Standing* did not sell as well as had been expected, and the group hastily released a third record, *World Party,* in 1999. Although the album went platinum, Cee-Lo described it as the "greatest disappointment in my career" in his 2001 interview with *Rolling Stone.* "I hated that album," he said, "It didn't fall in line with anything I wanted to be remembered for." He soon split with the group to pursue a solo deal with Arista Records. The record company had recently experienced success with OutKast's album *Stankonia* and with such "neo-soul" artists as Alicia Keyes, Jill Scott, and Macy Gray, and saw Cee-Lo as a natural fit for the label.

But Cee-Lo's first solo work, *Cee-Lo Green and His Perfect Imperfections* (2002), was unlike anything that

anyone else was doing at the time or anything that Cee-Lo himself had ever produced. His music defied categorization, blending elements of rap, funk, gospel, rock, and soul and even featuring metal guitar and banjo riffs. The song "Gettin' Grown" earned Cee-Lo his first Grammy nomination for best urban/alternative performance in 2003, and the record went to number two on *Billboard* magazine's charts. In 2004 he released a second solo album, *Cee-Lo Green ... Is the Soul Machine,* which produced the radio hits "I'll Be Around" (produced by Timbaland), "The One" (produced by Jazze Pha), and "Let's Stay Together" (produced by the Neptunes).

Cee-Lo's third incarnation, in 2006, would bring his greatest commercial success yet. That year he teamed up with Los Angeles–based disc jockey and producer Danger Mouse (Brian Burton), whom he had first met in 1998 while playing a Goodie Mob show at the University of Georgia. The two clicked, and they soon formed the duo Gnarls Barkley, releasing *St. Elsewhere* in 2006. The album's first single, "Crazy," was a runaway hit in the United Kingdom, debuting at number one on the pop chart based on download sales alone. It stayed at the top for nine weeks, a run not seen since Queen's *Bohemian Rhapsody* in 1975. In the United States the song reached number two on the *Billboard* Hot 100 and number seven on the modern rock chart, scoring airplay across formats and appealing to an incredibly wide audience.

Craig Kallman, chief executive officer of Atlantic Records Group, commented to *Rolling Stone* in 2006, "You don't see a lot of records that have such a broad spectrum of connection to people—young and old. There's something for everybody." Cee-Lo and Danger Mouse were equally surprised by the album's popularity. Danger Mouse told *Rolling Stone* in the 2006 interview that "this record wasn't deliberate on either one of our parts. We didn't worry about who would listen to it or what station would play it. We were just trying to impress each other."

In addition to "Crazy," *St. Elsewhere* featured other lyrics that testified to Cee-Lo's darker side: "The Boogie Monster," about paranoia; "Who Cares?" about schizophrenia; and "Just a Thought," a meditation on suicide.

At the 2007 Grammy Awards ceremony, Cee-Lo took home honors for best urban/alternative performance for "Crazy" and best alternative music album for *St. Elsewhere.* Gnarls Barkley also garnered the award for best group from BET in 2007. The duo released their sophomore album, *The Odd Couple,* in 2008.

Selected discography

Albums with Goodie Mob

Soul Food, La Face, 1995.

Still Standing, La Face, 1998.
World Party, La Face, 1999.

Solo albums

Cee-Lo Green and His Perfect Imperfections, Arista, 2002.
Cee-Lo Green ... Is the Soul Machine, Arista, 2004.

Albums with Gnarls Barkley

St. Elsewhere, Atlantic, 2006.
The Odd Couple, Atlantic, 2008.

Other Albums

(With Dungeon Family) *Even in Darkness,* Arista, 2001.
Closet Freak: The Best of Cee-Lo Green and the Soul Machine, 2006.

Sources

Books

Palmer, Tamara, *Country Fried Soul: Adventures in Dirty South Hip-Hop,* Backbeat Books, 2005.

Periodicals

New York Times, June 18, 2006; April 6, 2008.
Rolling Stone, March 14, 2001; August 24, 2006, p. 82.

Online

"Cee-Lo," VH1, http://www.vh1.com/artists/az/cee_lo/bio.jhtml (accessed July 15, 2008).
Official Cee-Lo MySpace Page, http://www.myspace.com/ceelogreen.

—Deborah A. Ring

Alice Coltrane

1937–2007

Musician, spiritual leader

Coltrane, Alice, photograph. Michael Ochs Archives/Getty Images.

Though perhaps best known as the wife and bandmate of the saxophone great John Coltrane, Alice Coltrane was a major jazz artist in her own right. One of the first female instrumentalists to emerge in the male-dominated jazz world of the 1950s and 1960s, Coltrane soon became known for her innovative incorporation of harp scales and other unusual sounds, as well as for the strong spiritual or mystical element present in almost all her work. A skilled businessperson, she won widespread praise for her astute management of her husband's financial and artistic assets following his death in 1967. Much of her later life was devoted to the ashram, or Hindu study center, she founded near her home in Woodland Hills, California, outside Los Angeles.

The daughter of Solon and Anne McLeod, Coltrane was born Alice McLeod in Detroit, Michigan, on August 27, 1937. Music filled the McLeods' working-class household. Anne McLeod played piano and sang in her church choir, and Alice's elder half-brother, Ernie Farrow, was a talented bass player who began playing jazz professionally in the late 1940s. Alice herself began piano lessons at the age of seven, studying Beethoven and other classical composers as well as hymns and gospel spirituals. Before she was in her teens, she was playing these professionally at church functions and social gatherings. By the time she entered high school, however, she was devoting much of her time to jazz. Under the influence of her brother Ernie, she was drawn particularly to bebop, a fast-paced, harmonically intricate style that began to dominate jazz in the late 1940s.

Long a center of the jazz world, Detroit enthusiastically embraced the new style. Local clubs, notably the famous Blue Bird Inn, and radio programs encouraged young musicians throughout the city to follow in the footsteps of bebop's leading practitioners, including the saxophonist Charlie Parker, the trumpeter Dizzy Gillespie, and the pianist Bud Powell. It was in this exciting atmosphere that Alice began appearing at jazz clubs, often accompanied by her brother on bass. Following graduation from high school, she was offered a scholarship to the Detroit Institute of Technology, but turned it down to travel to Paris, where she studied with Powell and married vocalist Kenny (Pancho) Hagood, with whom she had a daughter. The union would end in divorce in 1965.

Met John Coltrane

After a brief return to Detroit, where she resumed playing gigs with her brother, Alice moved to New York City in 1962. While playing with vibraphonist Terry Gibbs at Birdland, another famous club, shortly after her arrival, she met John Coltrane for the first time. The two were soon living together, though they would not marry until the finalization of Alice's divorce from Hagood in 1965. By all accounts, the relationship was a close one, with children born in 1964 (John Jr., who died in a car accident in 1982), 1965 (Ravi), and 1967 (Oran). Eleven years her senior, John introduced Alice to several Eastern religious traditions, notably the ancient Hindu scriptures known as the Vedas, which would exert a profound influence on much of her later life. In addition to caring for her young children, Alice joined John's band in 1965, replacing McCoy Tyner as pianist. The change coincided with the saxophonist's desire to move further into experimental or avant-garde jazz, with the ultimate goal of expressing through music the spiritual wisdom he had found in the ancient texts. Alice strongly supported this change and embraced her husband's related suggestion to take up the harp, a common instrument in Eastern religion but then almost unknown in the context of jazz. Among the albums she recorded with her husband are *Live in Japan* (recorded

in 1966 and released in 1973); *Expression* (1967), his last studio album; and *The Olatunji Concert* (recorded in 1967 and released in 2001), his last live recording.

John Coltrane's death from liver cancer in 1967 left his widow with four young children and the responsibility, as the executor of his estate, for all of his financial and artistic assets, most of which were organized under a holding company he had established, Jowcol Music. Alice Coltrane's astute handling of these complex business arrangements was widely admired, and she would run Jowcol Music profitably until her death forty years later. Despite these demands on her time, she continued to record music, releasing a series of albums under her own name between 1968 and 1978. Such highly regarded recordings as *A Monastic Trio* (1968), *Ptah the El Daoud* (1970), and *Universal Consciousness* (1971) were an innovative, often trancelike mixture of African and Asian rhythms and instrumentation.

Evident in all was Coltrane's increasing dedication to spiritual matters. Sacred chants from the Hindu tradition, for example, were prominently featured. Coltrane, who took a vow of celibacy for religious reasons after her husband's death, made the first of several trips to India in the early 1970s, where she studied with several well-known gurus, or mystical teachers, including Swami Satchidananda and Sathya Sai Baba. After gaining the rank of teacher herself, she adopted the name of Turiyasangitananda, sometimes shortened to Turiya.

Founded Religious Institute

Following the release of *Transfiguration,* a live album, in 1978, Coltrane ceased recording commercially for more than twenty-five years. Though she continued to record music throughout that period, the results were intended only for use in the religious observances that occupied an increasing proportion of her time. In 1975 she founded a religious institute in San Francisco, the Vedanta Center, devoted to the mystical traditions of Hinduism. Eight years later she moved the center to a large property in Agoura Hills, California, outside Los Angeles, and expanded it into the Sai Anantam Ashram, with residential facilities for several dozen full-time students. In addition to overseeing every aspect of the transfer and expansion, Coltrane continued to manage her late husband's estate and the John Coltrane Foundation, a charitable organization she founded that began providing scholarships to music students in 2004.

That year also saw the triumphant resumption of her commercial recording career with the release of *Translinear Light.* Featuring Coltrane on piano, organ, and synthesizer, *Translinear Light* included the work of several highly regarded musicians, including her son Ravi, an accomplished saxophonist and the album's producer; the drummer Jack DeJohnette; and the bassist Charlie Haden. Her other surviving son, Oran, also played saxophone on several tracks. Critics responded enthusiastically to the album's mixture of traditional jazz rhythms, gospel melodies, and sacred Hindu chants, with Thom Jurek of *allmusicguide.com* calling it a "defining, aesthetically brilliant statement from a master composer, improviser, and player."

Although Coltrane made only a handful of public appearances in the 1980s and 1990s, these increased somewhat as she worked on *Translinear Light* and its successor, the posthumously released *Sacred Language of Ascension* (2007), which added ancient Hebrew chants to what the blogger Jim Harrington, reviewing a 2006 concert, called Coltrane's "musical nutrition for the soul." On January 12, 2007, shortly before *Sacred Language of Ascension* was due for release, Coltrane died of respiratory failure in West Hills, California, a suburb of Los Angeles. At a memorial concert held several months later in New York, Ravi Coltrane expressed the views of many who had experienced his mother's music and spiritual guidance. "She truly was," he was quoted as saying by the *New York Times,* "the mother of many."

Selected discography

With the John Coltrane Quintet

Live in Japan, Impulse!, 1966 (released 1973).
Expression, Impulse!, 1967.
Live at the Village Vanguard Again!, Impulse!, 1967.
The Olatunji Concert (live), Impulse!, 1967 (released 2001).

Solo/bandleader

A Monastic Trio, Impulse!, 1968.
Huntington Ashram Monastery, Impulse!, 1969.
Ptah the El Daoud, Impulse!, 1970.

Journey in Satchidananda (live), Impulse!, 1970.
Universal Consciousness, Impulse!, 1971.
World Galaxy, Impulse!, 1971.
Lord of Lords, Impulse!, 1973.
Eternity, Warner Brothers, 1975.
Radha-Krsna Nama Sankirtana, Warner Brothers, 1976.
Transcendence, Sepia Tone, 1977.
Transfiguration (live), Sepia Tone, 1978.
Translinear Light, Impulse!, 2004.
Sacred Language of Ascension (posthumous), Kindred Rhythm, 2007.

Sources

Periodicals

New York Times, January 15, 2007, p. A13; May 19, 2007, p. B7.
Washington Post, October 21, 2006; January 15, 2007, p. B06.

Online

"Alice Coltrane," *All about Jazz,* http://www.all-aboutjazz.com/php/musician.php?id=5848 (accessed July 5, 2008).
"Biography," Alice Coltrane Turiyasangitananda, http://www.alicecoltrane.org/biography.html (accessed July 5, 2008).
Harrington, Jim, "Alice Coltrane Shows 'A Love Supreme,'" Alice Coltrane Turiyasangitananda, November 5, 2006, http://www.alicecoltrane.org/newsReview3SF.html (accessed July 5, 2008).
Jurek, Thom, review of *Translinear Light,* allmusic, http://www.allmusicguide.com/cg/amg.dll?p=amg&sql=10:39fuxqlsldje (accessed July 8, 2008).

—R. Anthony Kugler

Edward E. Cornwell III

1956—

Trauma surgeon, educator

As one of the top trauma surgeons in the United States, Edward E. Cornwell saves the lives of hundreds of patients each year who come into the emergency room with gunshot wounds and other devastating injuries. His bloody hands, he has voiced, are a testament to the scourge of violence in U.S. cities—which is why he has become a leading advocate for violence prevention in American communities. In his work at some of the best trauma centers in the country over two decades, not only has Cornwell led the way in the surgical treatment of gunshot wounds and the administration of critical care, he also has become a powerful voice for cultural change. Cornwell's goal is nothing short of ambitious: to fundamentally change the way Americans think about and portray violence.

Edward Eugene Cornwell III was born on November 30, 1956, in Washington, DC, the son of Edward Cornwell II, a surgeon, and Shirley Cornwell. After graduating from Sidwell Friends School, he studied biology at Brown University, receiving a bachelor's degree in 1978. He went on to attend Howard University College of Medicine, completing his MD degree with honors in 1982. Though he had not intended to follow in his father's footsteps, his own experience on the operating table redirected his career path: "My father was a surgeon. When I was a little boy, I wanted to be a football player and a mathematician in the off-season. But when I had my own operation, a cornea transplant ... that really cemented my desire to become a physician and probably a surgeon," Cornwell told talk show host Oprah Winfrey in 2000.

Cornwell trained as a surgeon in two of the toughest urban areas in the country, first completing his internship and residency in trauma surgery at the Los Angeles County/University of Southern California (USC) Medical Center (from 1982 to 1987), and then a fellowship at the Maryland Institute for Emergency Medical Services in Baltimore (from 1987 to 1989), where he studied trauma and critical care and the administration of emergency management. In both cities he experienced firsthand the gory realities of violence-plagued neighborhoods, treating the victims of gunshot wounds and other violent injuries—many of them young African-American men—on a daily basis. In a 2006 interview published in *Johns Hopkins Magazine,* he stated, "Before each day I was on call during my residency, I would stop and pray that I would be able to handle whatever was about to come into that trauma center."

Cornwell began his professional career in 1989 at Howard University Hospital in Washington, DC—his birth place. In 1993 he returned to the Los Angeles County/USC Medical Center, an elite trauma center that was treating a staggering twelve hundred gunshot wounds every year. Five years later he was recruited for the position of chief of adult trauma at Baltimore's Johns Hopkins Hospital, which was then in the process of upgrading its trauma facilities to Level I, the highest level of care.

At Johns Hopkins Cornwell operated on nearly three hundred gunshot-wound victims each year. Many of his patients, he found, were repeat customers, and nearly

At a Glance . . .

Born Edward Eugene Cornwell III on November 30, 1956, in Washington, DC; son of Edward E. Cornwell II and Shirley Cornwell; married Maggie Burdette Covington, June 24, 1989; children: Michael. *Education:* Brown University, BA, biology, 1978; Howard University College of Medicine, MD, 1982.

Career: Howard University College of Medicine, assistant professor of surgery, 1989–93, surgeon-in-chief of Howard University Hospital and chair of Department of Surgery, 2008–; University of Southern California, assistant professor of surgery, 1993–97; Johns Hopkins Hospital, chief of adult trauma, and professor of surgery for Johns Hopkins Medical School, 1998–2008.

Memberships: American Association for the Surgery of Trauma; American College of Surgeons; National Medical Association, past president of Surgical Section; Society of Black Academic Surgeons, past president; Society of Critical Care Medicine; Society of University Surgeons; TraumaNet Maryland, past chair.

Awards: "What's Right with Southern California" Community Service Award, KCBS-TV, 1998; Martin Luther King Jr. Community Service Award, Baltimore, 1999; Maryland Governor's Volunteer Service Award, 2000; named one of America's Leading Black Doctors, *Black Enterprise* magazine, 2001; Champion of Courage Award, FOX-45 TV, 2003; Whitney M. Young Jr. Award, Greater Baltimore Urban League, 2005; Speaker's Medallion, Speaker of the House of Delegates of Maryland, 2006.

Addresses: *Office*—Howard University Hospital, Department of Surgery, Suite 4B-02, 2041 Georgia Ave. NW, Washington, DC 20060-0002.

a third were young men under the age of nineteen. In his interview published in *Johns Hopkins Magazine,* Cornwell recalled performing a series of operations to save the life of a fifteen-year-old gunshot victim who had been brought to the emergency room by a cab driver. "That boy's mother called me last July to tell me he'd been shot in the head while sitting in a car," he said.

Cornwell's experiences in the emergency room prompted him to turn his sights to the streets outside the hospital and to become a vocal advocate for violence prevention. According to Cornwell, the problem lies in Americans' cultural attitudes toward violence: "Long before Virginia Tech, long before Columbine, we've been a country that glamorizes violence. We live in a culture of violence. Kids from all ages and all backgrounds are inundated with images of violence that glorify it," he said in a question-and-answer session at Stanford University in 2007. Cornwell aims to combat those images by giving young people a dose of reality, exposing the true effects of violence.

In 2000 Cornwell was featured in the ABC television series *Hopkins 24/7,* a six-part documentary that followed him in his work in the emergency room and in the East Baltimore community. In one episode Cornwell brought a group of young people to the hospital to visit a gunshot victim whom he had operated on. The series brought considerable attention to his antiviolence message: Soon he was hearing from lawmakers, appearing in *People* magazine, and talking with Oprah Winfrey.

In 2003 executives at MTV approached Cornwell to get his input on an antiviolence video they had produced starring 50 Cent, a rapper whose lyrics were filled with just the sort of violent imagery Cornwell was trying to counter. He was appalled by the video, which seemed to have the opposite effect, glamorizing violence. According to Cornwell' interview in *Johns Hopkins Magazine,* "I told them I was offended by this as a black male, as a father, and as a trauma surgeon." Instead, he proposed that the network splice scenes from *Hopkins 24/7* with images from their video to point out the difference between the fantasy of rap videos and real life.

MTV never took him up on his offer, but in 2005 Cornwell lent his support to a state-sponsored antiviolence program—"Hype vs. Reality"—initiated by Maryland governor Robert Ehrlich Jr. The program, given star backing by basketball superstar Carmelo Anthony, who lived in Baltimore from the age of eight, aimed to stem the tide of urban violence by exposing the false images and messages that the media conveys about violence.

In 2008 Cornwell left Johns Hopkins to return, once again, to Howard University, becoming chair of the Department of Surgery in the College of Medicine and surgeon-in-chief of Howard University Hospital. At Howard, Cornwell's goal focused on developing centers of excellence in trauma and critical care, transplant surgery, and cardiovascular surgery, and establishing the university as a top training site for surgeons. Still, his most important work, as he saw it, was to continue to push his antiviolence message outside the hospital.

Cornwell has garnered many accolades for his medical and community service work. In 1996 he was nominated for the USC Good Neighbor Volunteer Award and was chosen as the commencement speaker at the USC School of Medicine by the graduating class. He received the "What's Right with Southern California" Community Service Award in 1998, the Martin Luther King Jr. Community Service Award in 1999, and the Maryland Governor's Volunteer Service Award in 2000. *Black Enterprise* magazine named Cornwell one of America's Leading Black Doctors in 2001. He was honored with the Champion of Courage Award from FOX-45 television in 2003 and the Greater Baltimore Urban League's Whitney M. Young Jr. Award in 2005. Finally, in 2006, Cornwell was presented with the Speaker's Medallion from the Speaker of the House of Delegates of Maryland, in recognition, according to the *Journal of the National Medical Association,* of his "contributions ... to the cause of a better life for all Marylanders."

Selected writings

(With others) "National Medical Association Surgical Section Position Paper on Violence Prevention: A Resolution of Trauma Surgeons Caring for Victims of Violence," *Journal of the American Medical Association,* June 14, 1995, p. 1788.

(With others) "Health Care Crisis from a Trauma Center Perspective: The LA Story," *Journal of the American Medical Association,* September 25, 1996, p. 940.

"Enhanced Trauma Program Commitment at a Level I Trauma Center: Effect on the Process and Outcome of Care," *Journal of the American Medical Association,* November 26, 2003, p. 2644.

"African-Americans' Participation in Clinical Research: Importance, Barriers, and Solutions" (editorial), *American Journal of Surgery,* January 2007, p. 40.

Sources

Periodicals

Johns Hopkins Magazine, April 2006.
Journal of the National Medical Association, April 2008, pp. 357–358.
New Scientist, May 22, 2004, p. 4.

Online

"5 Questions: Edward Cornwell on Youth Violence," *Stanford Report,* May 16, 2007, http://news-service.stanford.edu/news/2007/may16/med-cornwell-051607.html (accessed July 18, 2008).

"Inside Look: Real Life ER," *Oprah Winfrey Show,* http://www.oprah.com/tows/pastshows/tows_2000/tows_past_20001101_d.jhtml (accessed July 18, 2008).

—Deborah A. Ring

Chaka Fattah

1956—

Politician

Fattah, Chaka, photograph. AP Images.

After serving twelve years in the Pennsylvania state legislature, Chaka Fattah earned a seat in 1995 in the U.S. House of Representatives, where, in 2006, he was elected to his seventh term. During his tenure in the House Fattah has distinguished himself as a champion of educational and housing reform. In July of 2008 he oversaw the bipartisan reauthorization of the Higher Education Opportunity Act, which included funding for Gaining Early Awareness and Readiness for Undergraduate Programs (GEAR UP), a national college preparatory program for underprivileged high school students that Fattah created in 1998. Also in 2008 Fattah was appointed chairman of the Congressional Urban Caucus by House Speaker Nancy Pelosi. Fattah also serves on the House Appropriations Committee and on the subcommittees on Homeland Security; Commerce, Justice, Science, and Related Agencies; and Energy, Water, and Development.

Even prior to his election to Congress, Fattah demonstrated his commitment to urban issues by organizing national conferences on cities and making proposals to the George H. W. Bush and Bill Clinton presidential administrations. Aware that he was asking for more federal and state aid to urban areas, at a time when government belt-tightening had become fashionable, Fattah offered passionate arguments for his position. "The majority of Americans live in metropolitan areas, and therefore, are impacted to the degree that as the core decays— crime, poverty, drug abuse—it moves out, it spreads to the suburbs surrounding that core," he commented in the *Philadelphia Inquirer Magazine*. "So, the suburbs are inextricably tied to the cities, and this beating up on cities is a false political argument..... The country would be much more productive if we had everyone in the game, if we focused our resources on lifting those boats stuck at the bottom."

Followed Path of Activist Parents

Fattah was born Arthur Davenport, the fourth of six sons of a U.S. Army sergeant named Russell Davenport and a journalist and activist named Frances "Frankee" Brown. His mother worked for the *Philadelphia Tribune* and as an occasional publicist for musicians such as Sam Cooke and Otis Redding. The Davenport marriage failed while Arthur was still young, and his

advantage," Fattah noted in the *Philadelphia Inquirer Magazine.* "It makes people pay attention. All ethnic groups in this country have ethnic names.... Had it not been for slavery, my name would have been more African anyway."

As a young teen, Fattah moved with his family to the 1400 block of Frazier Street in West Philadelphia. There his mother began a study of Philadelphia's gang wars for her magazine. When she discovered that another of her sons was a member of a gang, she took an unusual step to keep him off the streets: She invited his whole gang to live in the Frazier Street row house. Fattah's home was suddenly a makeshift hostel for as many as twenty-five youths at a time. "I thought it was great," the congressman remembered in the *Philadelphia Inquirer Magazine.* "All my older brothers and their friends, they were my idols.... Having more than a dozen people with all kinds of perspectives and experiences—good and bad—was helpful in getting a more dynamic view of life."

Falaka Fattah's personal war on gangs became the House of Umoja, an urban "Boy's Town" that developed into a nationally known youth program. Chaka Fattah himself played a part in the project's success. As the need for space quickly outpaced his mother and stepfather's modest home, he began to eye the twenty-odd abandoned houses on his block that were simply rotting away. It seemed to him that the House of Umoja might expand into some of these empty dwellings if they could be donated to the project. After consulting with his parents—who admired his initiative, but doubted that anyone would listen to him—Chaka produced a slide presentation and written report on his idea and asked to see the president of the First Pennsylvania Bank, which held the mortgages to some of the houses. Fattah was fourteen years old at the time, but Jim Bodine, the bank president, agreed to see him. Bodine was impressed by the earnest young man and his proposal. A few months later the bank turned over several of the properties to Falaka Fattah.

Gained Interest in Politics

Fattah became interested in politics while he was a student at Shoemaker Junior High School in Philadelphia. He signed on as a campaign volunteer for mayoral candidate Hardy Williams and learned grassroots politicking by handing out leaflets, tacking up posters, and cheering at rallies. After his parents founded the House of Umoja, Fattah met influential congressman Bill Gray, who helped them to secure a federal grant to fix up the abandoned houses they had received from the bank. Fattah supported Gray through some of his early campaigns, and the two remained friends. As a student at Overbrook High School, Fattah helped to organize the Youth Movement to Clean Up Politics, a junior wing of the black political movement aimed at ousting the old-style, white-run Democratic machine in Philadelphia. Fattah and his friend, Curtis

mother became deeply involved in the civil rights movement. At a 1968 national conference on black power, she met a fellow activist named David and married him two months later. Together they founded the magazine *Umoja,* a Swahili word for unity. They also decided to take new names that would emphasize their African roots. Frankee Brown became Falaka Fattah; Arthur became Chaka Fattah, named after the Zulu warrior Chaka.

For Fattah, the African-inspired name became not only a source of racial pride but also a means by which to establish his individuality. "I think my name is an

Jones, participated in voter registration drives and helped black constituents to get to the polls on Election Day in an effort to give citizens in their community more power over the political process.

Fattah decided to run for elected office himself. In 1978 he persuaded Jones to join him as a candidate for city commissioners. The commissioners' race was a city-wide contest in which the top two vote-getters from each party face off for three open slots. Tens of thousands of votes would be required for either Fattah or Jones to win a position. Undaunted, the two young men found a benefactor who bought each of them a business suit and dress shoes. A local printing company, called the Resistance Press, printed their campaign flyers at cost. With the Youth Movement behind them, the pair raised about $7,000 and posed together for a poster in which they appeared pushing brooms—as if to imply they would sweep the established candidates out of office. So persistent were the two young men that they won endorsements from the *Philadelphia Inquirer* and its rival, the *Philadelphia Bulletin*. On election day Fattah placed fourth in a field of twenty-four Democrats. Only after the election did anyone bother to find out his age—at twenty-two, he was three years too young even to qualify for the commissioner's job.

Reflecting on those days, Fattah observed in the *Philadelphia Inquirer Magazine*: "We had a lot of fun, we got to see the city and meet a lot of people. It was the foundation for the beginning of a political organization that has a great deal of credibility in Philadelphia today." Fattah learned from his experience in the commissioners' campaign. For his next try at public office, he assembled an effective grassroots team from block captains to wards and district leaders. These volunteers helped him spread his message in door-to-door fashion and provided him with enthusiastic teams of helpers at special events in the city. According to Vanessa Williams in the *Philadelphia Inquirer Magazine,* Fattah went on to establish "one of the city's most effective independent political operations." Williams added that Fattah had the services of "an almost unlimited supply of talent, time, and tenacity" among his many volunteers. Indeed, high-ranking workers in any Fattah campaign were asked to sign "mission statements" in which they pledge to work diligently and display "intelligence," "initiative," and "caring."

In 1982 Fattah—who was then working for Philadelphia's Housing and Community Development office—announced his plans to run for the Pennsylvania General Assembly. It was the first of many occasions when the maverick Fattah would challenge the veteran politicians in the Democratic Party. Fattah won a seat in the state House of Representatives by fifty-eight votes over Nicholas Pucciarelli, an established politician with a widespread power base. At age twenty-five, Fattah became the youngest person ever elected to the Pennsylvania General Assembly. As he learned the process

of shaping state government, Fattah also completed his education, earning a master's degree in government administration from the Fels School for State and Local Government at the University of Pennsylvania.

Fattah served as a state representative until 1988, when he won an election for state senator in the Seventh District, comprising parts of West and North Philadelphia, East Falls, Germantown, and Manayunk. By the time he assumed his senate seat, Fattah was a seasoned lawmaker with the education and experience to handle politics in Harrisburg. In an arena where hundreds of pieces of legislation are proposed in any given term, Fattah saw seven bills he had sponsored become law, including a job-training bill, an act that toughened regulation of for-profit trade schools, and an act intended to protect the rights of people without credit cards.

With Fattah's new responsibilities also came increased publicity for his ideas—and he had plenty of them. It was Fattah who in 1990 persuaded more than twenty corporations, colleges, and foundations to make advance payments on their city wage taxes in order to help Philadelphia meet its payroll when funds ran short. Fattah crusaded against high-rise public housing projects, launching a campaign to relocate families from the grim public apartment complexes in the city to rehabilitated single-family neighborhood homes. The audacious state senator also proposed a Big City Initiative, challenging the federal government to invest $100 billion per year for ten years to rebuild one hundred of the nation's largest cities. The proposal won Fattah an invitation to the White House to discuss the issue with an aide to then-president George H. W. Bush. Fattah also organized a 1992 national conference during which urban officials from all over the country described their ideas about fixing America's crumbling cities.

Won Seat in Congress and Ran for Mayor

State Senator Fattah's interests were obviously leaping beyond the bounds of his Philadelphia senatorial district. In 1991 no one was particularly surprised when he announced himself as a candidate to fill the congressional seat vacated suddenly by his old mentor, Bill Gray. Fattah was one of three candidates in a special congressional election held that year. In the race he finished a distant second to Lucien Blackwell, a "long-time party warhorse," according to Williams. Blackwell finished the rest of Gray's term and won a subsequent term as well. In 1994 Fattah challenged him again. Williams described the primary election, held on May 10, 1994: "Fattah and his machine emerged like a stealth bomber. He annihilated Blackwell, beating him by 16 percentage points. And in November, when a [Republican] GOP [Grand Old Party] juggernaut crushed Democrats from coast to coast, Chaka Fattah defied the trend: He won his seat with 85 percent of the vote, the largest margin of victory for any incoming freshman in [the 1995] Congress."

Just a few years after winning his seat, Fattah gained national prominence when he developed GEAR UP, his college readiness program for low-income students in seventh through twelfth grades. The legislation was signed into law in 1998 and went on to become a hallmark grant and scholarship program of the U.S. Department of Education. According to Fattah's congressional Web site, GEAR UP has served millions of students in impoverished urban areas, contributing, as of 2008, at least $2 billion in grant and scholarship money. In keeping with his interest in developing educational opportunities for inner-city youths, Fattah created two subsequent educational aid programs: the CORE (College Opportunity Resources for Education) Philly Scholarship and the College Retention Program. The former offers scholarships to low-income Philadelphia students attending Pennsylvania state colleges and universities, while the latter is a financial assistance program that offers resources such as work-study opportunities and low-interest loans to help students continue their educations.

In 2006 Fattah announced his intention to run for mayor of Philadelphia the following year, despite his popularity as a representative and the fact that he had just been reelected to serve another term. Fattah ran on a platform promising to lower both crime—at the time Philadelphia was experiencing an average of one murder per day—and poverty and to clean up corruption in the mayoral office after the convictions of twelve members of the administration of Philadelphia's Mayor John Street. Initially Fattah was the frontrunner in the race, but his public statement regarding his belief that Mumia Abu-Jamal, who had served twenty-five years on death row for the murder of a police officer in 1981, should be granted a new trial due to widespread controversy over the fairness of the original trial drew the ire of many, including Philadelphia's Fraternal Order of Police. Despite receiving support from former president Bill Clinton and the endorsement of Senator Barack Obama, Fattah's campaign was plagued by charges of corruption similar to that of the administration he sought to replace. In the end, Fattah finished a disappointing third and returned to his seat in the House.

Sources

Periodicals

Associated Press, May 7, 2007.
Philadelphia Inquirer, October 25, 1991, p. 1B; October 29, 1991, p.8A; January 16, 1993, p.1B; May 12, 1994, p. 1B; January 5, 1995, pp. 9A, 15A.
Philadelphia Inquirer Magazine, January 15, 1995, pp. 23–28.
Philadelphia Magazine, February 1992, pp. 49–53.
Washington Post, May 16, 2007.

Online

Congressman Chaka Fattah, 2nd District of Pennsylvania, http://www.house.gov/fattah/index.htm (a ccessed August 11, 2008).
"Gaining Early Awareness and Readiness for Undergraduate Programs (GEAR UP)," U.S. Department of Education, http://www.ed.gov/programs/gearup/index.html (accessed August 11, 2008).

—Anne Janette Johnson and Nancy Dziedzic

Laurence Fishburne

1961—

Actor

After working steadily in films, television, and plays for more than twenty-five years, Laurence Fishburne played what would arguably become his best-known role, as Morpheus, in the 1999 science fiction movie *The Matrix*; he reprised the role in two subsequent films, *The Matrix Reloaded* and *The Matrix Revolutions* (both 2003). After winning further acclaim on the stage in productions of August Wilson's *Fences* and in the one-man Broadway play *Thurgood,* based on the life of U.S. Supreme Court Justice Thurgood Marshall, Fishburne announced in 2008 that he would be joining the cast of the hit television series *CSI: Crime Scene Investigation* the following year.

Fishburne, Laurence, photograph. AP Images.

Fishburne was born in Augusta, Georgia, in 1961. His father, a corrections officer, frequently took him to the movies, but it was his mother, a schoolteacher, who introduced him to the stage. The family moved to a middle-class neighborhood in Brooklyn, New York, when Laurence was young, and soon he was auditioning for parts in local plays. "I've always been an actor," he remarked to James Ryan in *Premiere*; he informed *New York* magazine that his first role was in the second

grade: "I was Peter Pan, the boy who never grows up. I still am—I play make-believe for a living." At age ten he appeared in the play *In My Many Names and Days* at the New Federal Theater. "I played a little 10-year-old baseball freak from Brooklyn who used to dig going to Ebbitts Field and watching Jackie Robinson," Fishburne recalled to David Mills in the *Washington Post*.

Fishburne next landed a role in the 1972 television film *If You Give a Dance, You Got to Pay the Band,* which led to a part on the soap opera *One Life to Live* when he was eleven years old that lasted three years. One year after joining the daytime series, he appeared in the dramatic film *Cornbread, Earl and Me*. Fishburne told Patrick Pacheco in the *Los Angeles Times* that after *Cornbread*'s release, "My father took all the guys at this juvenile correction facility in the Bronx to see it. Afterward, we got together and they told me that I was doing good, that I had something really fine going on for myself and that if I ever [messed] up, they'd be waiting. That kept me in line." The actor earned a part in a Negro Ensemble Theater production and was accepted into the prestigious High School of Performing Arts in New York City. Then, at age fifteen, Fishburne embarked on the acting experience that would utterly transform him: a role as a member of the boat crew in Francis Ford Coppola's Vietnam epic *Apocalypse Now.*

Grew Up on Apocalypse Set

Pacheco quoted Fishburne as saying that shooting *Apocalypse* was "the most formative event" of his life. He had a chance to observe several luminaries of American film acting—Marlon Brando, Robert Duvall, Martin Sheen, and others—and to consult them for advice. Coppola taught Fishburne that acting "could be taken seriously, as art, with potential for educating, entertaining, and touching people." And in the drenching rain and chaos of filming in the Philippines, Fishburne lived a sporadically unsupervised fantasy of adolescence: "I was smoking reefer like everybody else," he told Pacheco. "My mother was there with me, but she couldn't control me so she called in the big guns, my father. Everybody in the company referred to him as 'the jailer,' but all he had to do was say, 'OK, that's enough of that,' and I'd come around."

Recalling his return to the United States, Fishburne recounted to Ryan, "I figured I was one of the baddest motherf—ers on the planet. And I came to L.A. and nobody gave a s—. I was really pissed off about that. I couldn't get work. I think a lot of people thought I was crazy, and I probably was." Fishburne made the second of what would be a series of appearances in Coppola films, portraying Midget in *Rumble Fish,* before playing a heavy in *Death Wish II.* "I was only getting work playing bad guys, and I wanted to be an actor and didn't want to wait tables," he said to Tom Perew in *Black Elegance.* "But I would have [done so, if necessary]." In what Mills called Fishburne's "least dignified professional moment," the actor's *Death Wish* character "shielded his head with a boom box while fleeing vigilante Charles Bronson."

Fishburne was concerned with balancing the roles he portrayed and combating Hollywood stereotypes. He succeeded by appearing in two more Coppola films, *Gardens of Stone* and *The Cotton Club,* as well as in Steven Spielberg's *The Color Purple.* He also participated in the PBS drama *For Us, the Living,* based on the story of Medgar Evers, a crucial figure in the civil rights movement of the late 1950s and early 1960s. Fishburne explained in the *Los Angeles Times* that "this is a gig where I had to put myself up and pay my own transportation, but to be involved with Roscoe Lee Browne, Howard Rollins, Dick Anthony Williams, Irene Cara. Well, that was my ancestors saying to me, 'OK, here's some work we can do.'" He further confided that "I work with somebody on what is called 'ancestral memory,' and I find it a source of spiritual strength," because the struggles of the past "are not something to be embarrassed by, but a resource to be valued and respected."

Took Diverse Film Roles

In the meantime, an ambitious young director had been keeping an eye on Fishburne. One day in the mid-

1980s, reported Mills, Fishburne was watching a street performance when someone tapped him on the shoulder. "I don't know who this guy is. He says, 'You're Larry Fishburne.... You're a good actor.' So he introduced himself and said he was from Brooklyn and he was making movies." The Brooklyn filmmaker was Spike Lee, who wanted Fishburne to appear in a film called *Messenger.* The movie was never made, but Lee used Fishburne in *School Daze;* the actor played the campus activist Dap in that collegiate musical comedy.

Fishburne later passed up the role of Radio Raheem in Lee's 1988 smash *Do the Right Thing,* criticizing the film's plot for straying from reality. "I'm from Brooklyn too," he told Mills. "And I didn't grow up in that kind of Brooklyn." Though Fishburne experienced some friction with Lee, the actor's refusal of roles in subsequent Lee films has evidently had more to do with Fishburne's desire for a starring part than any lingering hard feelings.

While working on *School Daze,* Fishburne met Hajna Moss, a casting agent and producer. The two eventually married and had two children, settling in the Bedford-Stuyvesant section of Brooklyn. Fishburne accepted the role of an orderly in the horror film *A Nightmare on Elm Street III* in order to make the down payment on a house. "My wife likes horror movies, we wanted to buy a house, and they offered me a gig," he explained to Ryan. "[The film's supernatural villain Freddy Krueger] and I never met." He and Moss divorced in the 1990s. Fishburne also played a cop in the thriller *Red Heat,* and, starting in the late 1980s, had the recurring role of the lovable Cowboy Curtis on the Saturday morning television series *Pee-Wee's Playhouse.* Among his other television projects were the film *A Rumor of War* and guest appearances on episodes of *Hill Street Blues* and *Miami Vice.*

Took on More Prominent Roles

In 1990 Fishburne landed an important role playing "New Jack Gangster" Jimmy Jump in Abel Ferrara's *King of New York,* costarring Christopher Walken and Wesley Snipes. Though the part was originally written for an Italian-American, Fishburne lobbied for it. His extravagant and overblown performance portraying what he called a "lovable badman" was lauded by critics. Fishburne also began working with playwright August Wilson in 1990 to develop the character of Sterling in the play *Two Trains Running.*

True to his commitment to balance the cinematic "nuts" with responsible characters, Fishburne played an attorney working for activist lawyer Gene Hackman in Michael Apted's 1991 film *Class Action. Sight and Sound* praised "a perfectly formed performance from Larry Fishburne, a great black actor spoiling for a part in something really big." Fishburne also appeared in Martin Sheen's *Cadence,* a military drama costarring Sheen and his son Charlie.

Fishburne's next big project was *Boyz n the Hood,* a film directed by then-twenty-three-year-old John Singleton, who had been a production assistant on *Pee-Wee's Playhouse.* As Furious Styles, the entrepreneur-activist father who guides his son out of trouble, Fishburne earned rave reviews. *Sight and Sound* declared, "Larry Fishburne continues to be a matchless screen presence in the central role of Furious," while Stanley Kauffmann in the *New Republic* wrote that the actor "brings an even-tempered, unforced authority to the role."

Even critics who disliked the film's tone admired Fishburne's work. Ralph Novak in *People* noted that Fishburne "acts his way through most of Singleton's verbiage, conveying the determination of a father trying to give his son a chance." Edmond Grant in *Films in Review* lamented that "the finest actor in the film ... gets the corniest role." Christine Dolen of the *Detroit Free Press* observed that with *Boyz* Fishburne "seemed to leap, like a major movie star at the height of his power, from the screen into our startled and appreciative consciousness." Fishburne is quoted in the same piece as saying that "*Boyz n The Hood* did take my career to a different level. But I did what I've been doing for the last 20 years. I think it was the power of the whole film. I give the credit to the writing and the execution of that film."

Won Awards for Stage Role

For his next role, in Wilson's stage play *Two Trains Running,* which opened on Broadway in 1992, Fishburne won a Tony Award for best featured actor in a play and also picked up Outer Critic's Circle, Drama Desk, and Theater World awards. As Sterling, an ex-convict espousing the black empowerment philosophy of civil rights activist Malcolm X, Fishburne once again stunned the critics. Frank Rich in the *New York Times* wrote that the actor "greets each of Sterling's defeats with pride and heroic optimism" and called Fishburne and his costar Roscoe Lee Browne "the jewels of the production."

Perew claimed that Fishburne's work in *Two Trains Running* "should convince any doubters that Larry Fishburne will forever play lead roles" and added: "Watching the play, you get black history the way Sterling has seen it. Fishburne is quirky, insightful, often humorous and, finally, a profound Sterling." Of the role, the actor himself stated in his interview with Pacheco that "Sterling's a man with an idea, and that's what makes him dangerous," and that the character has "just got out of jail, he's got no money and he's got no job. When a brother's got to get himself a hustle, that makes him dangerous." He told Dolen that working with Browne, Wilson, and director Lloyd Richards was a bigger thrill than winning a Tony: "This is the longest time I've worked in the theater. It's the most exciting; it requires real discipline and develops your concentration to a level that I know when I come off this, no matter what the part is in what movie, I'll be able to do it. Because I feel like a bona fide actor now."

Returning to film in 1992, Fishburne portrayed a genuinely challenging character in *Deep Cover*: Russell Stevens Jr., an undercover cop who gets drawn into the world of drug dealing and begins to lose his moral bearings. Director Bill Duke found Fishburne's subtlety and range perfect for the part: "Larry can show a side of himself that will do whatever is necessary to get what he wants. He becomes as ferocious a bad guy as [he does] a cop. Looking in Larry's eyes, you don't see a lie, and that's what you want in an actor," Duke observed to Ryan, adding that he found Fishburne "confident but not egotistical." Commenting on Duke's improvisational, actor-centered approach, Fishburne observed in an *Entertainment Weekly* profile, "It's collaborative here. Everyone throws in his two cents." Duke contended in the same article that Fishburne was at first uneasy with the director's approach: "Larry hated working with me in the beginning. He's used to rehearsing a scene the way it's going to be shot. I said, 'Larry, that's not how I work.' It always made him nervous, but he started to trust me and we had a good collaboration."

Fishburne himself found playing Stevens a rich opportunity. "What makes Stevens special for me," he told Ryan, "is he's a cop and he's a criminal at the same time. He has to do bad in order to do good. White actors get to play this type of stuff a lot, and we don't. It's an opportunity to show up and be a man on the screen—not a black man, not a white man, not a superman, just a man." Owen Gleiberman of *Entertainment Weekly* pointed to Fishburne's performance as one of the strengths of a film he judged inconsistent: "Fishburne, with his hair-trigger line readings and deadly reptilian gaze, conveys the controlled desperation of someone watching his faith unravel."

Performed More Multilayered Roles

In 1993 Fishburne again played a character with a dark side when he starred opposite Angela Bassett in the movie version of singer Tina Turner's autobiography, *What's Love Got to Do with It.* Although he initially turned down the role of Turner's abusive husband, Ike Turner, because he thought it was too one-sidedly evil to be realistic, the opportunity to work with Bassett again (they acted opposite each other in *Boyz n the Hood*) proved to be too much of a draw. But rather than accept the flat character, Fishburne reworked his portrayal of Ike to demonstrate the humanizing charm that made Ike so attractive prior to his descent into drug abuse and violence. Rita Kempley in the *Washington Post* said, "Fishburne's performance is astounding for the humanity he brings to the thinly-drawn Ike." That same year he stepped down from star billing in order to play a street-smart chess player in *Searching for*

Bobby Fischer. Fishburne's character mentors a young chess prodigy who resists outside pressure to play chess competitively.

The year 1995 was a full one for the actor as six of his projects came to life. In a career move not unlike his decision to act in *For Us, the Living,* Fishburne took a pay cut in order to lend the weight of his celebrity to the HBO movie *The Tuskegee Airmen.* He played Hannibal Lee, a pilot who endures racial prejudice in the course of his flying career with the all-black 99th Squadron of the 332d Fighter Group of the U.S. Air Force during World War II. Fishburne earned an Emmy nomination for his performance in this dramatization of the real-life elite fighting unit.

For the movie *Higher Learning* Fishburne once again teamed up with director John Singleton, this time to play a West Indian professor at an American university that is a racial and ideological war zone. Although the role of Professor Phipps is a smaller one in the film, critic Roger Ebert remarked that Fishburne's portrayal is "all the more effective because it is so subtle." While some critics found Singleton's characterizations rigidly stereotypical and the plot overblown, Fishburne was singled out in reviews time and again as outstanding.

Earned Accolades Playing Othello

In 1995 Fishburne became the first African American to play Shakespeare's Othello on the silver screen. Following in the footsteps of such legendary actors as Sir Laurence Olivier and Orson Welles, Fishburne brought the Moor Othello to life in the 1995 production, which also starred Kenneth Branagh as Iago and Irene Jacob as Desdemona. While critics debated the merits of this version, which cut the play by a third, Fishburne received good reviews for a role he admitted scared him initially. "It's definitely scary before you start. And harder to shake off afterwards. After all, Othello has been around for almost 400 years," he remarked in an interview with *Insight on the News.* Even though some critics faulted his inexperience with Elizabethan English for the diminished impact of his lines, the sheer charisma of Fishburne's screen presence won over audiences. Janet Matlin in the *New York Times* wrote, "With no previous Shakespearean experience, he at first displays an improbable loftiness, sounding very much the rarified thespian beside Mr. Branagh's deceptively regular Joe. But Mr. Fishburne's performance has a dangerous edge that ultimately works to its advantage, and he smolders movingly through the most anguished parts of the role."

In 1997 Fishburne became involved with another HBO movie based on historical facts when he starred with Alfre Woodard in *Miss Evers' Boys.* The story is based on an actual medical experiment conducted by the United States government between 1932 and 1972, in which African-American men suffering from syphilis were left untreated so that the effects of the disease could be studied. Woodard played a nurse, Miss Evers, who acts as friend and confidante to the men while, at the same time, she is aware of the deception her participation in the experiment necessitates. Fishburne played one of the victims of the experiment who becomes Miss Evers' romantic interest. Fishburne was also a producer of the movie, which won numerous awards and honors, including an Emmy.

In 1998 Fishburne played a compassionate ex-convict in the HBO movie *Always Outnumbered.* Based on stories by acclaimed African-American author Walter Mosely, the story follows Socrates Fortlow—Fishburne's character—as he attempts to help his community after serving nearly thirty years in jail. The positive portrayal of African-American men is particularly important to Fishburne, who acknowledged in a *Jet* article the scarcity of such images in movies. "Socrates is a character who reminds people that not all [African-American men] are ignorant, not all of us beat up women, not all of us are what you would think we are. Most of us are decent human beings."

Faced Unreality in The Matrix

Fishburne closed out the century in the reality-bending science-fiction thriller *The Matrix.* Also starring Keanu Reeves, the cerebral action movie concerns a group of rebels who are trying to expose the matrix, a virtual reality that has been imposed on humanity by a machine to fool them into believing that they are free. Fishburne played Morpheus, the leader of this collection of renegades, who recruits Reeves's character to spearhead the rebellion. The movie raised many philosophical issues, including those related to Eastern religions, Gnostic Christianity, cyberpunk, and the mind-body connection, and visually it paid homage to Japanese anime and the martial arts film genre. A critical and box office triumph, winning four Academy Awards and earning nearly half a billion dollars worldwide, *The Matrix* also became a pop-culture tour-de-force, inspiring video games, fan sites and blogs, and academic probing into its meaning. Peter Travers summed up the *Matrix* effect in *Rolling Stone:* "Not since *2001: A Space Odyssey* and the first *Star Wars* trilogy has the youth audience latched onto a cinematic vision of a future generation and mined it so vigorously for truth about its own."

In May of 2003 the second film in the *Matrix* trilogy was released. *The Matrix Reloaded* picked up the story of the last human city of Zion, with Fishburne reprising his role as Morpheus, captain of the hovercraft *Nebuchadnezzar.* Although *Reloaded* was one of the most anticipated sequels in film history, critics were less than enthusiastic, and fans, in many cases, left the theatre more confused than satisfied. Kenneth Turan in the *Los Angeles Times* noted, "Good intentions and great effects notwithstanding, in dramatic terms this is basically an expensive place holder, a rest stop where

the narrative can catch its breath before moving on." In November of 2003 the *Matrix* story did move on, to its conclusion, with the release of *The Matrix Revolutions.* While *Matrix* diehards—and they number in the millions—continued to find meaning and relevance in the final film, critics failed to see the draw. Travers in *Rolling Stone* wrote succinctly, "At the risk of overstatement, *The Matrix Revolutions* sucks." Nevertheless, fascination with *The Matrix* continued, and Fishburne lent his vocal talents to two *Matrix* video games, in 2003 and 2005.

Fishburne's next two projects teamed him again with *What's Love Got to Do with It* costar Bassett. In *Akeelah and the Bee* Fishburne played an English professor who supports a young girl's dream of winning a national spelling bee, with Bassett playing the girl's mother. In their reviews critics simultaneously lambasted the film for its stereotypical characters and formulaic plot and cheered its good intentions and fine performances, particularly that of Fishburne, who, as some reviewers noted, brought much-needed gravity to an otherwise light movie. Similarly, Fishburne was praised for his role as a former Negro League baseball player in a 2006 Pasadena Playhouse production of Wilson's *Fences,* in which he starred with Bassett. Critics noted that the two actors revived the sexual tension and relationship nuances they had created so successfully as Ike and Tina Turner.

Played Animated Characters and Supreme Court Judge

In late 2006 Fishburne was part of a large ensemble cast in Emilio Estevez's directorial debut, *Bobby,* which explored seemingly unrelated events surrounding the assassination of Democratic presidential candidate Robert F. Kennedy in 1968. For his next two films, Fishburne chose much lighter material, and in fact never actually appeared on screen. In 2007 he narrated a computer-generated animation version of *Teenage Mutant Ninja Turtles* and provided the voice of the Silver Surfer in *Fantastic Four: Rise of the Silver Surfer.* In 2008 Fishburne switched gears once more, playing a casino enforcer in the card-counting movie *21.* None of these films did well at the box office or with critics.

In mid-2008, however, Fishburne returned to the stage in a Broadway production of *Thurgood,* a one-man show based on the life and career of Thurgood Marshall, the first African-American Supreme Court justice. Presented as a lecture given by Marshall to a class of students at Howard University, Marshall's alma mater, the play features Fishburne gradually becoming younger as he recounts the events that led to his rise from civil rights activist and NAACP attorney to Supreme Court justice. Written by first-time playwright George Stevens Jr., *Thurgood* received mixed reviews for what some critics considered an overly long, plodding storyline. Fishburne's performance, however, was widely admired. Reviewer Brian Scott Lipton wrote on the TheaterMania Web site that Fishburne "instantly commands the stage with consummate ease, wringing enormous humor, pathos, and, above all, inspiration from his subject's life and Stevens' words…. In fact, he is now a serious contender to earn his second Tony Award."

Selected works

Films, as actor

Cornbread, Earl and Me (as Laurence Fishburne III), 1975.
Fast Break (as Laurence Fishburne III), 1979.
Apocalypse Now (as Larry Fishburne), 1979.
Willie and Phil (as Laurence Fishburne III), 1980.
Death Wish II (as Laurence Fishburne III), 1982.
Rumble Fish (as Larry Fishburne), 1983.
The Cotton Club (as Larry Fishburne), 1984.
The Color Purple (as Larry Fishburne), 1985.
Quicksilver (as Larry Fishburne), 1986.
Band of the Hand, 1986.
A Nightmare on Elm Street III: Dream Warriors (as Larry Fishburne), 1987.
Gardens of Stone (as Larry Fishburne), 1987.
Cherry 2000 (as Larry Fishburne), 1987.
School Daze, 1988.
Red Heat (as Larry Fishburne), 1988.
King of New York (as Larry Fishburne), 1990.
Cadence (as Larry Fishburne), 1990.
Class Action (as Larry Fishburne), 1991.
Boyz n the Hood (as Larry Fishburne), 1991.
Deep Cover (as Larry Fishburne), 1992.
What's Love Got to Do with It, 1993.
Searching for Bobby Fischer, 1993.
Higher Learning, 1995.
Bad Company, 1995.
Just Cause, 1995.
Othello, 1995.
Fled, 1996.
Event Horizon, 1997.
(And executive producer) *Hoodlum*, 1997.
The Matrix, 1999.
(And producer and screenwriter) *Once in the Life*, 2000.
Osmosis Jones, 2001.
Biker Boyz, 2003.
The Matrix Reloaded, 2003.
Mystic River, 2003.
The Matrix Revolutions, 2003.
Assault on Precinct 13, 2005.
Kiss Kiss Bang Bang (uncredited), 2005.
(And producer) *Akeelah and the Bee*, 2006.
Mission: Impossible III, 2006.
(And producer) *Five Fingers*, 2006.
Bobby, 2006.
Teenage Mutant Ninja Turtles, 2007.
Fantastic Four: Rise of the Silver Surfer, 2007.
The Death and Life of Bobby Z, 2007.
Tortured, 2008.

21, 2008.

Television, as actor

If You Give a Dance, You Gotta Pay the Band (movie), 1972.
One Life to Live (series), 1973–76.
The Six O'Clock Follies (series), 1980.
A Rumor of War (movie), 1980.
Trapper John, MD (series), 1981.
MASH (series), 1982.
Strike Force (series), 1982.
I Take These Men (movie), 1983.
For Us, the Living: The Medgar Evers Story (movie), 1983.
Hill Street Blues (series), 1986.
Miami Vice (series; as Larry Fishburne), 1986.
Pee-Wee's Playhouse (series; as Larry Fishburne), 1986–87.
Spenser: For Hire (series), 1987.
The Equalizer (series), 1989.
Decoration Day (movie), 1990.
The American Experience (series), 1991.
Tribeca (series), 1993.
The Tuskegee Airmen (movie), 1995.
(And executive producer) *Miss Evers' Boys* (movie), 1997.
(And executive producer) *Always Outnumbered* (movie), 1998.
Decoded: The Making of "The Matrix Reloaded" (documentary), 2003.
CSI: Crime Scene Investigation (series), beginning 2009.

Plays, as actor

In My Many Names and Days, New Federal Theater, New York City, 1971(?).
Eden, St. Mark's Playhouse, New York City, 1976.
Short Eyes, McGinn-Cazale Theatre, New York City, 1985.
Loose Ends, McGinn-Cazale Theatre, New York City, 1988.
Two Trains Running, Walter Kerr Theatre, New York City, 1992.
The Lion in Winter, Criterion Center Stage Right, New York City, 1999.
Fences, Pasadena Playhouse, Pasadena, CA, 2006.
Thurgood, Broadway production, 2008.

Video Games

Enter the Matrix, 2003.
The Matrix Online, 2005.
True Crime: New York City, 2005.

Sources

Periodicals

Back Stage, March 26, 1999.
Black Elegance, June/July 1992.

Chicago Sun-Times, January 11, 1995; December 29, 1995.

Detroit Free Press, June 2, 1992.

Entertainment Weekly, April 24, 1992.

Film Comment, July/August 1990.

Films in Review, February 1992.

Insight on the News, January 15, 1996.

Jet, July 15, 1991; February 24, 1997; March 23, 1998.

Los Angeles Times, January 12, 1992; May 14, 2003.

New Republic, September 2, 1991.

New York, July 22, 1991.

New York Times, April 14, 1992.

Newsweek, July 15, 1991.

Parade, June 28, 1992.

People, March 25, 1991; April 1, 1991; July 22, 1991.

Premiere, May 1992.

Rolling Stone, May 14, 2003; November 3, 2003.

San Francisco Chronicle, August 4, 1995; August 27, 1997.

Sight and Sound, July 1991; August 1991; November 1991.

Time, May 11, 1992.

Variety, August 18, 1997.

Video Review, March 1992.

Washington Post, July 7, 1991; June 11, 1993; January 20, 1995; December 29, 1995.

Online

Laurence Fishburne Official Web Site, http://www.laurence-fishburne.com.

Lipton, Brian Scott, "*Thurgood,*" TheaterMania, May 1, 2008, http://www.theatermania.com/content/news.cfm/story/13713 (accessed September 30, 2008).

Other

Additional information for this profile was obtained from a press biography on Fishburne.

—Simon Glickman, Rebecca Parks, and Nancy Dziedzic

Harold E. Ford Jr.

1970—

Financial executive, politician, political analyst

The election of Harold E. Ford Jr. to the U.S. House of Representatives in November of 1996 was a noteworthy event for a number of reasons. At age twenty-six, Ford became the second youngest member of Congress in U.S. history. He was also the first African American to succeed a parent in office; Ford's father, Harold E. Ford Sr., represented Tennessee's ninth district for eleven terms before retiring in 1996. Even though Ford no longer serves in Congress, having narrowly lost his 2006 bid for a seat in the U.S. Senate, he remains a political force as chair of the Democratic Leadership Council and as a highly visible political commentator on television and in the print media. He has also made his mark in the business world as an executive with the major financial firm Merrill Lynch & Co.

Harold Eugene Ford Jr. was born in Memphis, Tennessee, in 1970. Ford began his political involvement at age four, when he spoke in a radio advertisement that was part of his father's first campaign for Congress. According the *Congressional Quarterly Weekly Report,* when his father was sworn in as a member of Congress in January of 1975, Ford turned to his mother, Dorothy, and said, "This is what I want to do

Ford, Harold E., Jr., photograph. Alex Wong/Getty Images for Meet the Press.

when I grow up." As a boy, Ford accompanied his father to Congressional Black Caucus meetings, and he fondly recalls bouncing on the knee of Representative Charles B. Rangel of New York. He also remembers spending several happy hours at the Washington home of the Reverend Jesse Jackson, whose son, Jesse Jr., entered Congress in 1997 as a representative from Illinois.

Arrived in House with Connections

The oldest of three brothers, Ford spent his first nine years in Memphis, where he attended a public elementary school. In 1979, with Ford Sr. securely entrenched in Congress, the Ford family moved to the Washington, D.C., area. There, Ford attended St. Alban's School, an exclusive Episcopal boys' school that has educated many sons of the Washington power elite. Ford viewed his familiarity with the ways of Washington as an asset. As a Ford campaign spokesman told the *New York Times* in 1996, "Whoever wins is going to be a freshman and our candidate not only knows where the restrooms are, but where the committee rooms are." Indeed, Ford's early political ties reach the highest

position, he wrote policy papers promoting economic recovery in the Los Angeles area after the 1992 riots. Encouraging economic development in urban areas was among Ford's major goals as a member of Congress.

Ran Father's Reelection Campaign

Ford attended the University of Michigan Law School, taking time out from his legal studies to coordinate his father's 1994 campaign. Ford eventually earned his law degree in 1996. That spring, Ford Sr. announced that he would not seek a twelfth term in Congress and was supporting his son as his successor. "I want to go out on top. I think that public opinion polls show that I'm stronger than ever in my career. I want to come back home to Memphis and be apart of this city. I went with a new vision in 1974 and I think it's time for a new vision and a new generation to come," Ford Sr. announced at a Memphis press conference, as quoted in *Jet.*

The Ford family is deeply entrenched in the Memphis business and political scenes. Ford's grandfather, Newton Jackson Ford, was a prominent funeral home director. Ford's uncle, John Newton Ford, served in the Tennessee state senate until his political career was abruptly ended by a bribery scandal in 2005. Another uncle, James W. Ford, was a member of the Memphis city council and a Shelby County commissioner. With this family history, name recognition made Ford the front runner in the ninth district Democratic primary during his first campaign for Congress. Campaign buttons and T-shirts simply said "Jr." Ford's opponents in the primary were Rufus Jones, a state representative, and Steve Cohen, a state senator. Because all three candidates espoused liberal views, the campaign hinged on family and racial matters. According to the *Congressional Quarterly Weekly Report,* the Memphis mayor W.W. Herenton, a political rival of the Ford family and an African American, "openly shopped around for a heavy-hitting politician to back for a run against Ford, but could not recruit his top-choice candidates." Herenton had to settle for Jones, his former brother-in-law. Cohen, the only white candidate in the race, hoped that Ford and Jones would split the black vote (the ninth district is 60 percent African American and encompasses most of Memphis and some of its suburbs). Jones proved to be a weak candidate, and Cohen failed to draw much support from the district's white voters, most of whom tend to vote Republican.

Ford was accused of racism when he labeled Cohen "the great Republican hope." Cohen claimed that the remark was meant to point out his race rather than his political views because the Republican Party in Memphis is overwhelmingly white. Ford denied that his remarks were racially motivated, arguing that local

ranks of government. Ford Sr. served alongside the former vice president Al Gore Jr. in the Tennessee congressional delegation, and Ethnic NewsWatch described Ford as "practically a godson" to Gore.

After graduating from St. Alban's in 1988, Ford enrolled at the University of Pennsylvania, an Ivy League college in Philadelphia. While studying for a degree in American history, Ford was an active campus leader and journalist. Believing that the opinions of minority students were not being given sufficient hearing, Ford co-founded *The Vision,* an African-American student newspaper. After receiving his bachelor's degree in 1992, Ford returned to Tennessee to coordinate his father's congressional campaign. He then joined the Justice/Civil Rights Cluster of the 1992 Clinton Transition Team as a special assistant.

In 1993 Ford worked under the U.S. secretary of commerce Ron H. Brown, a longtime friend of the Ford family, as a special assistant to the Economic Development Administration. While serving in this

Republicans had tried for more than two decades to unseat Ford Sr. and would be pleased to see Cohen defeat Ford Jr. Ford won the August of 1996 Democratic primary with 62 percent of the vote. According to the *New York Times*, Ford said at a victory rally that his triumph was "a victory for young people who are seeking guidance and hope and opportunity." In the November general election, Ford easily defeated Republican Rod DeBerry, an African American who had run against Ford's father in 1994 to represent the heavily Democratic ninth district. Soon after being sworn in as a member of the House, Ford was elected Second Vice President of the 105th Congress's freshman class.

Reelected with Little Resistance

Ford happily exploited his "Washington insider" status, but during his tenure in Congress he was careful to point out that family connections alone cannot get anybody elected. Ford explained in the *Chattanooga Free Press*, "If I went out and said, I'm Harold Ford, Jr., and couldn't construct a sentence, nobody would vote for me. You can't inherit it. You've got to go out and earn it."

As a U.S. representative, Ford championed the interests of the people in his district. "You don't send people to Washington who can't deliver. You send someone who knows the system and the process, who can deliver for the district," Ford told *Black Enterprise*. He sought to transform Memphis into more of an international business center. Ford explained to Ethnic NewsWatch, "I think we should communicate more with the Department of Commerce in developing the city as a foreign trade zone.... Memphis has an opportunity to really grow from a global perspective and become a major player."

Ford visited nearly one hundred schools during his first campaign, and once in office he urged the U.S. Department of Education to ensure that all classrooms have Internet access. Ford was also a strong supporter of Head Start, a preschool education program that was created during President Lyndon B. Johnson's war on poverty. Those were tough positions to take during a period that saw the popularity of government-based solutions to social problems plummet. Ford told Ethnic NewsWatch, "I certainly don't want to be portrayed (or misunderstood) as one who feels the federal government ought to come in and dictate how, when, where and what kids should be taught, but I do say that the federal government has the responsibility to ensure that young people are exposed to the highest level of education that his country can afford."

Lost Senate Bid

A self-described workaholic who took the stairs rather than wait for the slow elevators in the U.S. Capitol building, Ford dove into his job with gusto, treating his one-bedroom apartment in Arlington, Virginia, across the Potomac from Washington, as little more than a place to sleep. In true bipartisan spirit, two of his best friends in Congress during his first years in the House were young Republicans: John Ensign of Nevada and Jon L. Christiansen of Nebraska. For Ford, working long hours did not necessarily represent a sacrifice. He said of his job to the *Memphis Commercial Appeal,* "I am serious about this but you have to understand: This is fun for me. I enjoy this. I got hooked on politics early. I'm here to do a job and I take it very seriously, but I'm having the time of my life."

Ford won his 1998 reelection contest by a huge margin, and in 2000 the Republicans did not bother to field a candidate for the seat. That year, Ford was the keynote speaker at the Democratic National Convention, where the fellow Tennessean Al Gore was nominated as the Democratic presidential candidate. Ford was easily reelected again in 2002 and 2004. In 2005 he announced that he was planning to run in 2006 for the U.S. Senate seat being vacated by Senate Majority Leader William Frist, who had earlier indicated that he would not seek reelection. In November of 2006 Ford lost a hotly contested race to Republican Bob Corker. After that disappointment, Ford wasted little time licking his wounds. In January of 2007 he was elected chair of the Democratic Leadership Council, an organization that promotes centrist policy priorities within the Democratic Party. A month later, Ford accepted a position as vice chairman and senior policy adviser at the investment bank Merrill Lynch & Co. Apparently these two jobs were not enough; Ford also filled his postcongressional days with a visiting professorship at Vanderbilt University and as a political analyst with NBC News. However, while he is managing to keep busy outside of the halls of government, do not count on this lifelong insider to remain outside too long; the *New York Observer* reported in July 2007 that when asked "What's next?" by the NBC executive Vic Garvey, Ford replied: "I'm gonna be Governor."

Sources

Periodicals

American Prospect, September 2007, p. 23.
Atlanta Constitution, July 22, 1997, p. A8.
Black Enterprise, November 1996, p. 20.
Chattanooga Free Press, October 9, 1996, p. A7.
Congressional Quarterly Weekly Report, January 4, 1997, pp. 84–85.
Houston Chronicle, January 5, 1997, p. A4.
Jet, May 6, 1996, p.6; January 17, 1997, pp. 4–6.
Memphis Commercial Appeal, November 7, 1996, p. B1; January 2, 1997, p. B1; January 15, 1997, p. B1; January 29, 1997, p. A11; March 17, 1997, p. B1; March 26, 1997, p. B2; June 17, 1997, p. B2; August 10, 1997, p. E1; August 28, 1997, p. A8.
Nashville Tennessean, April 20, 1997, p. B7.

Newsweek, October 30, 2006, p. 26.

New York Observer, July 3, 2007.

New York Times, June 9, 1996, p. A26; July 30, 1996, p. B7; August 2, 1996, p. A20; November 5, 2006, p. A1.

People, November 18, 1996, pp. 50–55.

Time, August 13, 2007.

Tri-State Defender, November 13, 1996, p. A1.

Washington Post, November 7, 1996, p. A39; November 12, 1996, p. D3; March 11, 1997, p. E2; April 29, 1997, p. B2; June 14, 1997, p. A7.

Information for this profile was also obtained from Ethnic NewsWatch.

Online

"Harold E. Ford, Jr.," Merrill Lynch & Co., http://www.ml.com/?id=7695_8134_8302_76005 (accessed September 9, 2008).

Other

"Former Congressman Harold E. Ford, Jr. Joins Merrill Lynch as Vice Chairman," Merrill Lynch & Co. press release, February 14, 2007, http://www.ml.com/index.asp?id=7695_7696_8149_74412_75268_75567 (accessed September 9, 2008).

—Mary C. Kalfatovic and Bob Jacobson

Johnny Ford

1942—

Politician

In 1972 Johnny Ford became the first African American elected mayor of Tuskegee, Alabama. His historic victory was heralded as a sign that a new generation of young, well-educated black politicians was stepping into leadership in the years following the civil rights movement. When he took office, he was quoted by the *New York Times* as saying that "the South is the new frontier for black accomplishment." Ford served as mayor until 1996, when he was elected to the state legislature. He was reelected mayor of Tuskegee in 2004.

Ford, Johnny, photograph. AP Images.

Born on August 23, 1942, in Midway, Alabama, Ford was adopted at age four by his uncle, Charlie Benjamin Ford. They moved to Tuskegee, home of the Tuskegee Institute, which was founded in 1881 to educate the children of freed slaves. During Ford's youth the famed Tuskegee Airmen—the first all-black corps of military pilots, who had compiled a noteworthy record during World War II—were a source of both local and national pride for African Americans. Yet Tuskegee, like the rest of the South, was a deeply segregated place, and Ford attended the city's all-black public schools.

Worked for Kennedy Campaign

Ford won a scholarship to Knoxville College, a historically black school in Tennessee, where he studied history and sociology. He had hoped to become a lawyer, but after earning his bachelor's degree in 1964, he realized he was unable to afford the tuition at most law schools. He moved to New York City, where he worked for the Greater New York Council of the Boy Scouts of America, first as a recruiter in the rough Bedford-Stuyvesant area of Brooklyn and later as director of all Boy Scout activities in the South Bronx. Through this job he met Robert F. Kennedy, the senator from New York, who was running for president. Ford was hired as a strategist for the campaign. "Mind you, I didn't know anything about politics," he told Ray Jenkins in the *New York Times*.

In June of 1968 Kennedy was shot and killed, only minutes after winning the California primary. His death came just two months after the assassination of Martin Luther King Jr. in Memphis, Tennessee. Ford told Jenkins that, later that night, in private, "I fell down on

At a Glance . . .

Born on August 23, 1942, in Midway, AL; son of a hospital employee; adopted by his uncle, Charlie Benjamin Ford, at age four; married Frances Rainer (a social worker), 1970 (divorced); married and divorced two more times; married Joyce London Alexander (a judge), 2006; children: Johnny, Christopher, Tiffany. *Politics:* Republican. *Religion:* Baptist. *Education:* Knoxville College, BA, 1964; Auburn University, MPA, 1977.

Career: Boy Scouts of America, Greater New York Council, recruiter and supervisor, 1964–68; campaign strategist for presidential candidate Robert F. Kennedy, 1968; Model Cities Program, executive coordinator in Tuskegee, AL, 1969–70; campaign manager for Alabama House of Representatives candidate Fred Gray, 1970; Multi Racial Corporation, assistant director, 1970–72; U.S. Department of Justice, Montgomery, AL, office, 1971–72; mayor of Tuskegee, AL, 1972–1996 and 2004—; member of Alabama House of Representatives, 1997–2004; Johnny Ford and Associates Inc., president.

Memberships: National Conference of Black Mayors, founding member and president-emeritus; World Conference of Mayors, founder and director general; National Association for the Advancement of Colored People (NAACP); Tuskegee Optimist Club, founding president.

Addresses: *Office*—Tuskegee City Hall, 101 Fonville St., PO Box 830687, Tuskegee, AL 36083.

my knees and started praying. I wondered where America was heading."

Ford returned to New York City. But when he visited his family in Tuskegee at Christmas, he learned that his hometown had been selected for the Model Cities Program, a new federal initiative. He was hired as its executive coordinator in Tuskegee. Ford then managed Fred Gray's campaign for the Alabama House of Representatives. Gray, who had served as counsel to both Rosa Parks and King, became the first African American elected to the state house since Reconstruction.

Elected Mayor

For a time Ford worked in the Montgomery office of the U.S. Department of Justice, ensuring compliance with the Civil Rights Act of 1964 and the Voting Rights Act of 1965. In 1972 he made his own run for office, becoming mayor of Tuskegee. Tuskegee occupied an unusual place in both African-American history and the South: It was essentially a college town, home to the prestigious Tuskegee Institute (later Tuskegee University). At the time, the city had a population of eleven thousand, about 80 percent of whom were African American. The Tuskegee Institute's faculty and student body numbered around thirty-six hundred, which at the time was believed to be the largest group of professional and middle-class blacks in the South. Several African Americans had already been elected to local office in Tuskegee and Macon County.

Ford's win at the polls in October of 1972 prompted a visit from *New York Times* reporter Jon Nordheimer, who was intrigued by the fact that both Ford and another young African American had just been elected mayor of Alabama cities. A. J. Cooper, who had run for the office in a working-class suburb of Mobile, held a law degree from New York University. He had also worked for the Kennedy campaign. "The ceremonies," wrote Nordheimer, "symbolized the return of educated young blacks to their roots in the South's Black Belt—a dream of decades [that] saw the brightest and most talented members of each generation leave home for better economic and social opportunities in the North and never return."

A few weeks later the *New York Times* ran another story, "The Tuskegee Mayor and His Wife: A Very Visible Interracial Marriage," which noted that mixed-race marriages were still technically illegal in the state. Ford and his wife, Frances Rainer, a social worker from a well-connected white family in another town, had started dating during Ford's tenure with the Model Cities program. They often met in the larger city of Montgomery, about forty minutes away by car. Theirs was the first interracial marriage in Macon County. Even though antimiscegenation laws had been declared invalid by the U.S. Supreme Court three years earlier, Alabama's law was still on the books, so the newlyweds, the minister who married them, and the clerk at the county office who had issued the marriage license were subject to criminal penalties. "A lot of people marry for money," Ford told Ray Jenkins, the *New York Times* reporter. "A lot of people marry for class. Maybe some people marry for political reasons. But we married for love."

Served Twenty-four Years

Ford's first term in office was so tumultuous that he had a security detail for personal protection. He also angered some local black leaders when he admitted to voting for the Republican incumbent, Richard M. Nixon, in the 1972 presidential race. "Other places may be losing Federal funds because of cuts, but not Tuskegee. I've prevented that," he told B. Drummond Ayres in the *New York Times*. "I'm a practical man and that makes for good politics."

Ford was reelected mayor five more times, serving until 1996. A year later he won a seat in the Alabama House of Representatives, representing Macon County, and served for six years. In 2003 he switched party affiliation from Democratic to Republican, which made him the first black Republican to serve in the Alabama state house since Reconstruction. "I see this as an opportunity to work from within the Republican Party to bring about change and accomplish goals," a report in *Jet* quoted him as saying. A year later, he ran again for mayor of Tuskegee and won.

Ford's marriage to Rainer ended in divorce, as did his second and third marriages. In December of 2006 he wed Joyce London Alexander, who in 1979 had become the first African-American woman to be appointed a magistrate judge in the United States. In 1996 she was named chief magistrate judge in Massachusetts. Because of their career commitments, their union became a long-distance one.

During his seventh term as Tuskegee mayor, Ford focused on making Tuskegee an important stop on African-American heritage tours. The airfield where the Tuskegee Airmen had trained had been named a National Historic Site, and Ford wanted a similar designation for the Tuskegee Veterans Hospital. "The Tuskegee Veterans Hospital was to medicine what the Tuskegee Airmen were to aviation as far as African Americans getting involved and making history," he told Rick Harmon in the *Montgomery Advertiser*. "Because the hospital here is where black doctors, black social workers, black nurses and others helped make history for their professions."

Sources

Periodicals

Jet, February 3, 2003, p. 6.
Montgomery Advertiser (Montgomery, AL), March 6, 2008.
New York Times, October 5, 1972, p. 97; November 9, 1972, p. 54; June 27, 1973, p. 41.

—Carol Brennan

Bernardin Gantin

1922–2008

Church official

Gantin, Bernardin, photograph. Francois Lochon/Time Life Pictures/Getty Images.

Bernardin Gantin, a cardinal of the Roman Catholic Church, was the highest-ranking black African in the modern era of his church before his death in 2008. For nearly two decades he served as dean of the College of Cardinals, the body that meets upon the death of a pope to choose his successor. He was a close friend and colleague of Pope John Paul II, the Polish pontiff who led the world's Roman Catholics from 1978 to 2005, and Gantin's rise owed much to the pope's vision for the church in the twenty-first century. "Along with the Nigerian Cardinal Francis Arinze, who headed Vatican work on interreligious dialogue," noted Peter Stanford in the Guardian, Gantin "was a potent symbol of John Paul II's determination to break the European stranglehold on the College of Cardinals."

The son of a railway worker, Gantin was born in 1922 in Benin, the West African nation known as Dahomey prior to 1975. At the time of his birth, his homeland was a colony of France, and Benin's European masters left a distinct religious and cultural imprint, including a staunch Roman Catholicism, that remained long after it was granted independence in 1960. Gantin entered a seminary at the age of fourteen, and was ordained a priest on January 14, 1951, a few months before his twenty-ninth birthday. His earliest years as a priest included assignments as a teacher of languages and a village pastor. In 1953 he departed Africa for Rome to study theology and canon law at two Catholic institutions—Pontifical Urban University and Pontifical Lateran University, both located in the Vatican, the seat of the Roman Catholic Church. He earned an advanced degree in theology and canon law.

Gantin was consecrated as titular bishop of Tipasa of Mauritania, a North African country, and auxiliary bishop of Cotonou in Benin in 1957, making him one of the youngest bishops in the church at the time. In January of 1960 Pope John XXIII made him the newest archbishop of Cotonou, the newly independent Benin's largest city, and over the next several years Gantin emerged as a leader among Africa's Catholic clergy. According to Stanford writing in the Guardian, Gantin's efforts "in building schools, encouraging local vocations and enabling indigenous nuns to set up healthcare projects won him a national reputation, but also brought him into conflict with turbulent politicians in his homeland."

At a Glance . . .

Born on May 8, 1922, in Toffo, Benin; died on May 13, 2008, in Paris, France; son of a railway worker. *Religion:* Roman Catholic. *Education:* Studied at the Pontifical Urban University and Pontifical Lateran University; earned licentiate in theology and canon law, 1956(?).

Career: Ordained Roman Catholic priest, 1951; consecrated bishop of Tipasa of Mauritania and Auxiliary of Cotonou, 1957; Archbishop of Cotonou, 1960–71; Congregation for the Evangelization of Peoples, adjunct secretary, 1971–73, secretary, 1973–77; appointed cardinal, 1977; Pontifical Council for Justice and Peace, president after 1977; Pontifical Council Cor Unum, president after 1978; prefect of the Congregation for Bishops, 1984–98; named Cardinal Bishop of the suburbicarian diocese of Palestrina, 1986; College of Cardinals, dean, 1993–2002.

In 1969 Pope Paul VI made a historic papal visit to Africa and met Gantin for the first time. The political turmoil in Benin continued, and with his bishop's safety in mind the pope summoned him to Rome in 1971. Gantin was appointed the adjunct secretary of the Congregation for the Evangelization of Peoples, the division of the Church that oversees all missionary work. Two years later, in 1973, he was made secretary of the department. In June of 1977 Paul VI made Gantin a cardinal, the second-highest rank in the Church. With that appointment came a new role as head of the Pontifical Council on Justice and Peace, a job whose duties included representing the Vatican at United Nations meetings. Gantin was the first black African in the modern era to hold a position of such authority in the Church.

Paul VI died in 1978, and journalists who gathered in Rome for the funeral and the subsequent election of a new pope reported on rumors that Gantin was among the "papabili," the handful of likely contenders to succeed the pope. Interviewed by a correspondent for the *Times*,, Gantin noted that Paul VI had made great strides in bringing Africans and others from the developing world into the Church, but declined to speculate any further. "We shall let ourselves be guided by the Holy Spirit," the *Times* quoted him as saying. "What counts is not the contribution of a single continent or of a culture, but the universal spirit which must animate the church."

Gantin participated in two papal elections: The first conclave, in August of 1978, chose an Italian cardinal,

Albino Luciani, who was named John Paul I—and who died just thirty-three days later. During his brief tenure, however, John Paul I named Gantin the president of the Vatican charity Cor Unum. The College of Cardinals met again in October and chose the archbishop of Krakow, Poland, Karol Wojtyla, to succeed the unlucky John Paul I. Taking the name Pope John Paul II, Wojtyla was an active, globe-trotting pontiff who determined to make the church more relevant to its faithful around the world, not just among its historic core of support in Western Europe. In 1982 John Paul II made his own visit to several African nations, accompanied by Gantin, who was greeted by enthusiastic crowds in Benin. Two years later John Paul named Gantin prefect of the Congregation for Bishops, the administrative department of the Church that chooses new bishops and disciplines those who stray from church doctrine.

Gantin and John Paul II met weekly for two hours each Saturday evening to discuss various bishop-related matters, and on a few occasions Gantin signed the excommunication decree against persistently rebellious ones. These included Archbishop Marcel Lefebvre of France, whom Gantin had known from the French cleric's many years of service in Africa. "John Paul and Gantin deliberately appointed conservative bishops in what they saw as unacceptably liberal dioceses," noted Gantin's obituary in the *Independent*. "Conflicts ensued in the Netherlands, Austria and particularly Switzerland. Gantin played a leading role from 1990 in defending the controversial conservative Bishop Wolfgang Haas of the Swiss diocese of Chur, whose sweeping dismissals of priests and the blocking of the appointment of a new seminary rector had provoked widespread demonstrations." In another controversy, Mexican bishop Samuel Ruiz García was disciplined for what the Vatican viewed as his Marxist interpretation of the Church's teachings, but formal removal of Ruiz was thwarted by widespread protests in Chiapas, the Mexican state where Ruiz had become a popular figure.

In 1993 Gantin became the first black African bishop to serve as dean of the College of Cardinals. Gantin would have chaired the conclave upon the death of John Paul II, but the cardinal retired in 2002, before the Polish pontiff's death. Gantin returned to Benin, which had been restored to democracy by then and had seen a significant rise in the number of Catholics since the 1970s. He died in Paris in May of 2008, five days after his eighty-sixth birthday.

Sources

Periodicals

Guardian (London), May 15, 2008, p. 38.
Independent (London), May 20, 2008, p. 32.
National Catholic Reporter, May 28, 1999, p. 8.
New York Times, February 27, 1973, p. 2.
Time, April 23, 1984, p. 65.

Times (London), August 10, 1978, p. 3; June 8, 1993, p. 13.

Online

"Gantin Card. Bernardin," Holy See Press Office, http://www.vatican.va/news_services/press/docu mentazione/documents/cardinali_biografie/cardi nali_bio_gantin_b_en.html (accessed August 25, 2008).

—Carol Brennan

Kevin Garnett

1976—

Professional basketball player

Garnett, Kevin, photograph. Stephen Shugerman/Getty Images.

When most basketball fans first heard of Kevin Garnett, he was known as the high school basketball player who was going directly into the National Basketball Association (NBA) because he couldn't qualify academically to play in college. Many NBA observers assumed he was a disaster waiting to happen and too immature to succeed. But by his second season in the league, Garnett had surprised many by becoming one of the NBA's young crop of budding stars. At 6-foot-11 he has the power and size of a center, but he also has the speed and ball-handling skills of a guard. In his early days in the league, Garnett quickly silenced his critics by developing a reputation as one of the league's classy young players. After starring for more than a decade for the often-hapless Minnesota Timberwolves, Garnett was traded before the 2007–08 season to the Boston Celtics. There, along with longtime Celtic star Paul Pierce and fellow newcomer Ray Allen, he led a revitalized Celtic squad to an NBA title. In the process, he shed his reputation as a player who, despite incredible talent, could not bring home a championship.

Garnett was born on May 19, 1976, in Mauldin, South Carolina. His mother, Shirley Irby, raised three chil-

dren: Kevin, an older sister, Sonya, and a younger sister, Ashley. The family lived in Mauldin, a quiet, middle-class bedroom community, for the first eighteen years of Garnett's life. Garnett showed promise as a basketball prospect early on and attracted considerable attention from college scouts. At the end of his junior year at Mauldin High School, he was named Mr. Basketball for the state of South Carolina.

Transferred to Chicago High School

A major change in Garnett's life came following his junior year in high school. He was involved in an incident in which he and several of his friends were accused of assaulting a white student, a touchy accusation in the racially tense town. His record was cleared after he participated in a pretrial program for first-time offenders, but staying in the area was problematic after that. Garnett met the coach from Chicago's Farragut Academy High School at a basketball camp before his senior year, and he and his mother moved to that city so he could transfer to Farragut. The move was a dramatic one in most every way, particularly going

At a Glance . . .

Born Kevin Garnett on May 19, 1976, in Mauldin, SC; son of Shirley Irby; married Brandi Padilla, 2004; children: one daughter.

Career: Member of Minnesota Timberwolves, 1995–2007; U.S. Olympic men's basketball team, member, 2000; member of Boston Celtics, 2007—.

Awards: Mr. Basketball for state of South Carolina, 1994; Mr. Basketball for state of Illinois, 1995; named National High School Player of the Year by *USA Today*, 1995; named to *Parade* All-America First Team, 1995; McDonald's All-America Game, Most Outstanding Player, 1995; named to the National Basketball Association (NBA) All-Star Team, eleven seasons; voted NBA All-Rookie Second Team, 1996; Olympic gold medal as member of the U.S. basketball team, 2000; Most Valuable Player, NBA All-Star Game, 2003; NBA Most Valuable Player, 2004; NBA Defensive Player of the Year, 2008.

Addresses: *Office*—Boston Celtics, 226 Causeway St., Fourth Floor, Boston, MA 02114.

from a quiet southern community to a gang-infested urban environment. Garnett said he had to learn to survive in Chicago, telling *Newsweek* the city was "total hell—gangs, guns, crime. I had to deal with a gang leader named Seven-Gun Marcello. No fun."

The move was a successful one from a basketball standpoint, however, as Garnett averaged 25.2 points per game, 17.9 rebounds, 6.7 assists, and 6.5 blocks during his one year at Farragut. In 1995 he was named Mr. Basketball in his adopted state, selected as *USA Today*'s National High School Player of the Year, and placed on *Parade*'s All-America First Team. Following the season, he played in the McDonald's All-America Game, where he grabbed eleven rebounds, scored eighteen points, and was named the game's Most Outstanding Player. Scouts were unanimous in their opinion that Garnett was a top-notch basketball prospect.

However, there was one problem with the logical and traditional next step in the career of a top-notch basketball talent: Garnett was not a top-notch student. While several college programs wrestled with the question of whether to accept this marginal student with remarkable basketball skills, Garnett wrestled repeatedly with the ACT entrance exam. The question be-

came moot when he failed for the fourth time to gain a score that would allow him to play basketball as a freshman. With college out of the picture, Garnett declared himself eligible for the NBA draft.

Jumped Straight to the NBA

Garnett's move from South Carolina to Chicago had generated a bit of controversy in the basketball world, but nothing compared to his decision to jump from high school to the pros. Everyone seemed to have an opinion as to whether Garnett was ready, physically and emotionally, to make the big step. Of the three players who had previously done so, Moses Malone had unqualified success, Darryl Dawkins had some success, and Bill Willoughby had limited success. The most recent of those players had entered the league twenty years before Garnett; another player, Shawn Kemp, skipped college basketball but did attend college for a year. On the one hand, many basketball people questioned whether any nineteen-year-old was mature enough to avoid the pitfalls of the NBA's spotlight. On the other hand, they also thought that if he could handle the attention and forego the temptations, his physical assets could make him a superstar for years to come.

The Minnesota Timberwolves, a young franchise eager to improve its future, took a gamble and chose Garnett with the fifth pick overall in the 1995 NBA entry draft. The team signed him to a contract for $5.6 million over three years. While it was thought Garnett had the potential to play nearly any position, the Timberwolves decided his rail-thin 6-foot-11, 220-pound frame was best suited to small forward until he filled out with a few more pounds. He rented an apartment in Minnetonka, a suburb of Minneapolis, and shared it with a roommate, Bug Peters, an old friend from South Carolina. Garnett allayed fears of his getting into trouble, telling *Newsweek* that he was basically a homebody. "I don't drink or smoke or go out much at all," he declared. "I've done all that, and it got me in trouble. I have an image to uphold. People are watching; kids are watching. I prefer staying home with Bug, playing CDs and Sega." Garnett was also largely confined to his hotel room on road trips. As teammate Sam Mitchell attested in *Newsweek,* "The kid's not old enough to get in anyplace where he can get into trouble."

Another place Garnett avoided trouble was on the basketball court. Not surprisingly, he didn't immediately set the world on fire with his statistics, but when his rookie season was over there was enough evidence to suggest that the Timberwolves' gamble would probably pay off. He played in the Rookie Game at the All-Star break, finishing with eight points, four rebounds, and six assists. Midway through the season he cracked the Wolves' starting lineup, and he ended up leading the squad with a 49.1 percent field goal percentage. He also broke a team record for blocked shots in a season with 131. In addition, he led the team in rebounds in half the games after he became a starter and had double digits in points and rebounds in twelve games.

As the season rolled on, Garnett attracted rave reviews from seasoned observers of the game. Atlanta Hawks general manager Pete Babcock told *Sports Illustrated* late in the season, "He's a special player. Earlier in the year you saw flashes of it. But he has so much more confidence now. He extends so high on his turnaround jumper and shoots so soundly, he's become very difficult to stop." Timberwolves vice president Kevin McHale told *Sports Illustrated,* "What this kid has accomplished is amazing. If you put him in a college situation right now, where it's not as physical and there's zone coverage, he'd be doing things that would have people in awe."

Grew into Pro Stardom

Garnett's strong play continued into his second professional season, and so did the growth in his reputation. One national magazine included Garnett in an article about the young players in the league with strong character and respect for the game. When he was named to the NBA Western Conference All-Star Team as an injury replacement in February, he became the youngest player ever selected in the history of the league. It was less than two years after he had graduated from high school, and Kevin Garnett was already a star in the NBA. People could only wonder how good he might be after his twenty-first birthday.

In 1997 Garnett signed a new contract with the Timberwolves that made him the highest-paid player in the NBA, and in any other sport. In August of that year, he turned down a six-year, $102-million offer from the Timberwolves. He held out and later signed for $126 million. He played the 1997–98 season under his original contract, with the new deal starting the following season. Garnett's contract was credited with sparking the labor dispute that delayed the start of the 1998–99 season until February of 1999, as basketball team owners insisted on a new player agreement with a salary cap to limit superstar salaries.

For years, Garnett was the undisputed star of the Timberwolves, making the NBA All-Star Team several times. However, for seven straight seasons, the Timberwolves did not make it past the first round of the playoffs. Commentators began to question Garnett's leadership abilities and his aggressiveness. Frustrated, Garnett, who was about to become a free agent, pressed the Timberwolves to upgrade the team by adding some veteran players. Management responded by acquiring established vets Latrell Sprewell and Sam Cassell. Garnett signed a five-year contract for $100 million. Given the huge contracts of NBA superstars, it was less than he could have demanded, but it left the Timberwolves money under the NBA salary cap to sign other talented players.

Surrounded by an improved collection of talent, Garnett performed better than ever in the 2003–04 season, with career highs of 24.2 points per game and 13.9 rebounds per game, the latter of which led the league. The Timberwolves earned the Western Conference's best record, 58-24, and they advanced to the third round of the playoffs before losing to the Los Angeles Lakers. Garnett won the league's Most Valuable Player award for the season, and *Sports Illustrated* named him its NBA Player of the Year.

Brought Title to Boston

However, Sprewell and Cassell left the Timberwolves in 2005, and the team missed the playoffs for three years straight. Again, critics began wondering if Garnett would ever lead a team to the NBA's highest levels. Garnett himself began to realize that if he was to ever be part of a championship team, perhaps it would have to be somewhere other than Minnesota. In July of 2007 the Timberwolves traded Garnett to the Boston Celtics, which were trying to become an elite team again after twenty-one years without a championship and posting the second-worst record in the league the previous season. Garnett had vetoed a trade to the Celtics earlier that summer. This time, however, the Celtics were a more appealing option, having already acquired star Ray Allen. The new Celtics, led by the trio of Garnett, Allen, and longtime member Paul Pierce, quickly became favorites to win the Eastern Conference in the 2007–08 season.

The new-look Celtics did not disappoint their fans. They quickly established themselves as the team to beat in the Eastern Conference. In January of 2008 Garnett received the most votes in the league in balloting for the NBA All-Star Game. The following month, Garnett was named a starter for the Eastern Conference All-Star Team, and two months later he was voted Defensive Player of the Year in the NBA. Along the way, he played some offense too. In March he became the thirty-second player in NBA history to score twenty thousand points in a career, making him one of only four active players to reach that landmark. After recording the best record in the league during the regular season, the Celtics trounced the Los Angeles Lakers in the NBA Finals to claim the championship. For Garnett, the victory put to rest any lingering notions that he was destined to remain a "perennial loser" and solidified his position as one of the very best players of his generation, and perhaps of all time.

Sources

Periodicals

Boston Globe, April 22, 2008.
Chicago Tribune, December 9, 2007.
Evening Standard (London), October 8, 2007, p. 15.
Jet, May 29, 1995, p. 50.

Minnesota Timberwolves 1996–97 Media Guide, p. 8.

Newsweek, December 4, 1995, p. 72.

Sporting News, December 9, 2005, p. 54.

Sports Illustrated, June 26, 1995, p. 65; March 11, 1996, p. 61; May 3, 1999, p. 38; December 29, 2003, p. 92; July 5, 2004, p. 94; August 13, 2007, p. 66.

USA Today, December 5, 2006, p. 7C; March 11, 2008, p. 8C.

Online

"Boston's Kevin Garnett Top Vote-Getter among All-Stars," NBA.com, http://www.nba.com/allstar 2008/allstar_starters_080124.html (accessed September 10, 2008).

"Kevin Garnett Reaches 20,000-Point Plateau," NBA. com, http://www.nba.com/news/garnett20k_080 307.html (accessed September 10, 2008).

—Mike Eggert and Bob Jacobson

Haile Gebrselassie

1973—

Athlete

Ethiopia's Haile Gebrselassie is one of the world's fastest runners and has held several world records in long-distance events. A two-time Olympic gold medalist in the men's 10,000-meter race, Gebrselassie is also a top marathon runner and set a new world record time of 2:04:26 with his win in the 2007 Berlin Marathon. Like many of the world's best runners, he hails from a part of the African continent known for both its high altitude and dire poverty, and he has invested his earnings in several business ventures back in his homeland as a mission to create jobs, end famine, and improve the lives of ordinary Ethiopians.

Born in 1973, Gebrselassie grew up near the town of Asela, in the Arsi zone in central Ethiopia. His earliest years were a time of political upheaval: In 1974 the country's longtime monarchy was ousted by a Communist military dictatorship, which then engaged in a brutal campaign, known as the Red Terror, to root out dissent. Thousands, including the emperor, were killed. A period of famine followed in the early 1980s. Although the Arsi area was not one of the hardest hit, Gebrselassie recalled his early years as a time of abject poverty. His father owned some livestock and could grow a few crops when the weather cooperated, but Gebrselassie, his five brothers, and four sisters were all expected to pitch in, especially after their mother died from cancer in 1979, the year Gebrselassie turned six. "My family worked so hard day and night," he told Jim Denison, who interviewed him for *Runner's World* in 2005. "Yet we were still poor. Our conditions never seemed to change. For months at a time it was the same thing for breakfast, lunch, and dinner—corn,

corn, corn…. I used to dream of how I could make my life better, or how I could become someone famous or important. I thought about becoming a pilot, or maybe an artist."

One of his family's few luxuries was a radio, and in the summer of 1980 the seven-year-old was entranced by broadcasts from the 1980 Moscow Olympics. That year an Ethiopian runner, Miruts Yifter, won the men's 10,000-meter race. As Gebrselassie witnessed Ethiopia's jubilation, he made winning an Olympic gold medal his goal. He did not formally enter the sport until he was in his teens but, like many in his family and region, usually ran to and from school, a trip of a little more than six miles each way. Because the Arsi area was so far above sea level, which meant its air had less oxygen, his heart and lungs had to work harder—but that also conditioned them to work at maximum-performance levels. There were other challenges on the daily trek, he recalled in an interview with Jim White for the *Guardian*. "In the rainy season, sometimes to get to the first lesson we had to run really quick, because we had to cross the river to school and we'd have to go up and down the bank to find a place to cross because there is no bridge."

Disobeyed His Father

When Gebrselassie competed for the first time in a formal event—at age fourteen in a race at his school—he won the 1,500-meter contest, even though he was the youngest in the group. His father discour-

At a Glance . . .

Born on April 18, 1973, in Asela, Arsi, Ethiopia; son of Bekele Gebrselassie (a farmer) and Ayelech Degtu (a farmer); married Alem Te Lhun; children: Eden, Melat, Bete.

Career: Ethiopian national junior track-and-field team, 1991–92; Ethiopian national men's track-and-field team, 1993—; Ethiopian Olympic team, 1992, 1996, 2000, 2004, and 2008.

Awards: Gold medal, 10,000-meter race, International Association of Athletics Federation World Championships, 1993, 1995, 1997, 1999; gold medal, 10,000-meter race, 1996 Atlanta Olympics and 2000 Sydney Olympics; winner, 2005 Amsterdam, 2006 Berlin, 2006 Fukuoka (Japan), 2007 Berlin, and 2008 Dubai marathons.

Addresses: *Office*—c/o Ethiopian Athletics Federation, PO Box 3241, Addis Ababa, Ethiopia.

aged his further participation, however, asserting that spare time should be devoted either to studying or to helping with farm chores. At age fifteen he defied his father and traveled to Addis Ababa, Ethiopia's capital, to compete in a 10-kilometer race. When he arrived, he learned that the race had been canceled. But a marathon—a 26.2-mile race—was still set to start. Having gone that far—about one hundred fifty miles—he decided to run anyway. Although he did poorly, the race gave him his first taste of serious long-distance running. When he returned home, he recounted later, his father was angry at him for having traveled so far just to run in a race. For several months he abided by his father's order to quit running.

About a year later he moved to Addis Ababa to live with two of his brothers. The plan was that he would join the army, but his brother Assefa, who had earned a college degree and could support him, urged him to keep running instead. For the next year he trained daily at Jan Meda, a track used for national track-and-field events (it was originally built for the emperor's racehorses). In 1991, after winning a spot on the Ethiopian junior national team, he boarded a plane for the first time and flew to Antwerp, Belgium, where he competed in the World Cross Country Championships, the top event for amateur runners, which is sponsored by the International Association of Athletics Federa-

tions (IAAF). Running in both the junior 5,000-meter and 10,000-meter events, he did not do very well. However, a year later, at the IAAF World Junior Championships in Seoul, South Korea, he took first place in both races. At the 1993 IAAF World Championships in Stuttgart, Germany, he moved up from the junior team to compete in the men's division. He won the 10,000-meter race and came in second in the 5,000-meter race.

The following year Gebrselassie set a new world record time of 12:56.96 in the 5,000-meter race. In 1995 he broke the world record in the 10,000 meters by a stunning nine seconds, finishing the annual Adriaan Paulen Memorial Race in Hengelo, The Netherlands, in 26:43.53. At the 1996 Atlanta Olympics he won a gold medal in the men's 10,000-meter and returned to Ethiopia a national hero. The airport in Addis Ababa was also host to his engagement party for his upcoming wedding to Alem Te Lhun, who had worked at her family's snack kiosk near the Jan Meda track. *Endurance,* a docudrama about Gebrselassie's quest for Olympic gold, was released a few years later.

Broke His Own World Record

At the 1997 track-and-field championships in Zurich, Switzerland, Gebrselassie broke his own 5,000-meter record. The following year he set new indoor records in the 2,000-meter and 3,000-meter races. At the 2000 Summer Olympics in Sydney, Australia, he beat Kenya's Paul Tergat by 0.09 seconds to win his second Olympic gold medal in the men's 10,000-meter race. Tergat and another Kenyan, Daniel Komen, were Gebrselassie's top rivals at IAAF meets during this period of his career. He was also being challenged by a younger Ethiopian runner, Kenenisa Bekele, whom Gebrselassie had mentored. Both competed in the 10,000 at the 2004 Athens Olympics; Bekele won the gold medal while Gebrselassie, who had injured his Achilles tendon, came in fifth.

Gebrselassie won his first marathon in Amsterdam in 2005. A year later he won both the Berlin and Fukuoka (Japan) marathons. He set a new world record for a marathon, 2:04:26, in Berlin in 2007. Four months later he won the 2008 Dubai Marathon with a time of 2:04:53. In 2008 he opted out of the marathon event at the Beijing Olympics, citing the city's polluted air, but did run in the 10,000-meter race, finishing sixth. "The marathon is more exciting than 10,000 meters," Gebrselassie told Denison in *Runner's World.* "The lead vehicle up front, the police motorbikes and their sirens, and the photographers, television cameras, and journalists. My favorite part, though, is the millions of people along the street shouting my name. Can you imagine hearing people cheer for you for over two hours? Oh, it's just fantastic."

In addition to prize money, Gebrselassie reportedly earned a fee of $1 million just for showing up at some of the world's top marathons. In Addis Ababa, where he lives with his wife and three daughters, he invested in real estate and construction ventures, employing his siblings and more than two hundred others. His construction company built schools in underserved rural areas. He also worked with several charitable initiatives, including HIV/AIDS prevention and efforts to improve sanitation. "The most important thing is to create jobs for these people," he told Paul Kimmage in the *Sunday Times*. "I am trying to contribute my share. All the money I have, I spend in this country…. This is where I was born. This is where I will die. I am proud of this country. I am proud of these people."

Sources

Periodicals

Guardian (London), April 8, 2002, p. 20.
New York Times, March 11, 2008, p. D1.
Runner's World, May 2005, p. 93.
Sports Illustrated, July 20, 1998, p. 34.
Sunday Times (London), June 2, 1996, p. 11; February 23, 2003, p. 18.

Online

"Q & A with Haile Gebrselassie," CNN.com, November 9, 2007, http://edition.cnn.com/2007/TECH/09/26/revealed.HaileG.qanda/.

—Carol Brennan

Sylvia Harris

1967(?)—

Professional jockey

Harris, Sylvia, photograph. AP Images.

Sylvia Harris is a woman who knows what it is like to be down on her luck. She has been there again and again in her life. She also knows what it is like to achieve her dreams. In late 2007 Harris, who had harbored a lifelong goal of becoming a professional jockey, won her first thoroughbred race. At the age of forty she made horse-racing history as one of the oldest rookie jockeys in the sport and only the second African-American woman to win a thoroughbred race. In doing so, she overcame twenty years of adversity that included bouts with manic depression, difficult personal relationships, and a period of homelessness. "Human triumph," Harris said of her win, in a 2008 interview with the *New York Times.* "That's what it comes down to." Indeed, Harris's story is nothing short of amazing.

Harris was born in Frankfurt, Germany, to Edward Harris Sr. and Evaliene Harris, both of whom served in the U.S. Army. Raised in Santa Rosa, California, Sylvia Harris was a star athlete in track and field and gymnastics, setting many records in her hometown. From a young age she was "animal crazy," developing a fondness for horses while visiting Golden Gate Fields and Bay Meadows with her father, according to an inter-

view with the Web site Female on the Horse. "I remember leaning over the fence and watching them run," Harris told reporter Jason Schandler in Bloodhorse.com in 2008. "I was enthralled."

Harris aspired to become a jockey, but her parents discouraged a career in horse racing as an impractical goal for an African-American woman. Instead she enrolled in Santa Rosa Junior College, considering veterinary medicine as an occupation. Within two years, however, Harris became pregnant with her first child and needed to support her new family as a single mother.

When Harris was nineteen year old, her parents divorced. The event triggered the first of many episodes of manic depression, which would progressively grow worse. Staying up for days on end writing poetry, she began to experience delusions and eventually was hospitalized. Over the following years, she went through alternating periods of mania and stability, culminating in a major breakdown in 1995 while she was living in Virginia with her father. She spent three months at Western State Hospital, a psychiatric institution in Staunton, and lost custody of her children.

At a Glance . . .

Born in 1967(?) in Frankfurt, Germany; daughter of Edward Harris Sr. and Evaliene Harris; children: Atlanta, Rory, Toshi. *Religion:* Buddhist. *Education:* Santa Rosa Junior College.

Career: Worked at stables and training facilities in California, Florida, Virginia, and Illinois, grooming and galloping horses and cleaning stalls; became professional jockey in 2007.

By 1999, with her illness under control with medication, Harris was living in Florida. Hoping to make a fresh start, she enrolled at Full Sail Academy, a music, design, film, and entertainment school located in Winter Park. But it seemed that the deck was stacked against her. One day Harris's car was stolen. With no transportation to get to work, she lost her job. With no income to pay the rent, she was soon evicted from her apartment. She ended up homeless, sleeping in abandoned cars or on the streets of Orlando and eating in soup kitchens. She had hit rock bottom. As Harris told the *New York Times,* "I had no idea how I was going to get my life back together."

Harris saw a glimmer of hope when she met a minister at a Florida homeless shelter. When he asked her what she wanted to do with her life, Harris recalled her childhood dream and told him that she would like to work with horses. By the end of the day, the minister had arranged for Harris to go to Ocala, Florida, the center of the state's thoroughbred breeding industry. She soon found work at a local training center, grooming and galloping horses and cleaning stalls. In a 2008 interview with Associated Press sportswriter Andrew Seligman, which appeared in *USA Today,* she recalled that the work "reawakened all of the childhood memories and wants and dreams, and loving animals and wanting to be around horses."

Still, Harris continued to harbor dreams of becoming a jockey, even though she was now well into her thirties. While working at Ocala Breeders' Sales Company, she met a jockey who told her he had not started riding until age thirty-seven, and he had won his first race at age forty-two. Harris decided that her goal was not out of reach yet.

In 2005 she spotted a classified ad for a small racetrack in Saskatchewan, Canada, that was looking for jockeys. She answered the ad and drove to Marquis Downs in Saskatoon to find work. Once she arrived, however, she discovered that the papers she needed in order to work in Canada had not been completed by her sponsor, and she would have to drive to the U.S.

consulate in Detroit, Michigan, in order to do so. Not only that, she would need some $3,000 in order to get matters straightened out—money she did not have and could not get.

With less than a hundred dollars in her pocket, Harris began driving south, first through Minneapolis and then on to Chicago, where some of the most competitive horse-racing tracks in the United States are located. Once again, Harris started over, finding employment galloping horses in local stables while working toward getting her jockey's license.

Harris had difficulty finding mounts, as few trainers seemed willing to take a chance on an inexperienced female jockey who was pushing forty. In August of 2007 she finally landed her first thoroughbred race at Arlington Park outside of Chicago, finishing third. Then, a few months later, Harris met trainer Charlie Bettis at Hawthorne Race Course, earning occasional mounts from him.

Harris's big break would come on November 7, when Bettis offered to put her on Wildwood Pegasus, a four-year-old gelding who suffered from arthritic knees. No other jockey would ride the horse, fearing injury. But Harris seized the opportunity, and she and the horse finished third that day. Encouraged, Bettis kept her in the saddle, and Wildwood Pegasus won his next start on December 1 by seven-and-a-half lengths. The victory made Harris the second African-American woman ever to win a thoroughbred race—the first was Cheryl White in the 1970s—and the first to do so in Chicago. Harris went on to take two more firsts that season, and steady work has followed.

After her historic win, Harris told Bloodhorse.com, "It was a dream come true, a dream that took 30 years to fulfill. I'm 40 now and my prayers were finally answered." Harris's inspirational story has brought her much media attention. In early 2008 she was profiled in the *New York Times,* and she later appeared on *Good Morning America,* the *Today Show,* and *Inside Edition.* Having achieved her own dream, she also became involved with the Make-a-Wish Foundation, so that she could help make the dreams of others come true, too.

Sources

Periodicals

New York Times, January 9, 2008.
USA Today, January 17, 2008.

Online

Schandler, Jason, "Harris' Long Climb to the Top," January 7, 2008, http://racing.bloodhorse.com/article/43022.htm (accessed July 21, 2008).

"Sylvia Harris," interview, Female on the Horse, http://www.femalejockeys.com/Sylvia.html (accessed July 21, 2008).

—Deborah A. Ring

Shannon Holmes

1973(?)—

Writer

Shannon Holmes wrote his first novel, *B-More Careful,* while serving time in prison on drug charges. Published independently in 2002, *B-More Careful* went on to spend ten months on *Essence* magazine's best-seller list. Since then Holmes has turned out several more works in the genre sometimes dubbed urban lit or hip-hop literature. "It's street, it's grimy, it's graphic," Holmes said of his fiction in an interview with Melody K. Hoffman for *Jet.* "This isn't a lifestyle; this is my life. What's ironic about the situation now is that some of the same things I did that got me locked up is the same things I write about."

Born in New York City in the early 1970s, Holmes came of age in the Bronx, which during the height of the crack cocaine epidemic in the 1980s had one of the highest per-capita crime rates in the nation. Like many of his peers, he was pulled into illegal activities in his neighborhood, and in a nearly inevitable outcome entered the penal system. In 1995 he was sentenced to serve five years on drug charges. "There was this dude in jail that spent a lot of time in the library like me, I was really influenced by the writing he was doing," Holmes told the Web site BallerStatus.com about his first efforts at writing fiction. "I start putting my thoughts down and called my dad, I told him 'I think I'm on to something in here.' He sent me the money and it was probably the best hundred dollars he's spent in his life."

While still incarcerated Holmes inked a deal with Teri Woods Publishing, an independent house, to issue *B-More Careful,* which was published under Woods's company name, Meow Meow Productions, in January of 2002. The story of a savvy Baltimore teenager, Holmes's debut novel follows Netta's life from an abusive home in the projects to her leadership of a ruthless gang of young women with connections to some of the most powerful drug lords in the city. *B-More Careful* earned comparisons to earlier novels by two other African-American writers, Donald Goines and Iceberg Slim, who also chronicled street life in frank prose. Their books had sold millions back in the 1960s and 1970s, and Holmes had read them as a teenager.

For a time Holmes was affiliated with Triple Crown Publications, considered the leading independent publisher of the genre. Triple Crown Publications was founded by Vickie Stringer, an ex-felon who self-published her semiautobiographical *Let That Be a Reason,* written while serving time for drug trafficking. She had sold that first book out of the back seat of her car, going on to a lucrative career as a publisher and literary agent for other storytellers of urban life. "At a time when the National Endowment for the Arts warns that book readership is declining, 'hip-hop lit' is finding a larger audience," journalist Dinitia Smith wrote in the *New York Times* about the phenomenon of writers like Stringer and Holmes. "There are no hard sales figures on the books because most are self-published and marketed the same way as hip-hop music was a generation ago: out of cars, in the streets, through flyers, in beauty salons and car washes in African-American neighborhoods. But now, as it did with hip-hop, the mainstream is beginning to notice."

At a Glance . . .

Born in 1973(?) in New York, NY.

Career: Author of novels.

Addresses: *Home*—New York, NY. *Office*—c/o Author Mail, St. Martin's Press, 175 Fifth Ave., New York, NY 10010.

Based on high sales figures for *B-More Careful,* Holmes signed in 2003 with Atria Books, an imprint of Simon & Schuster, for a reported six-figure deal. His second novel, *Bad Girlz,* became an *Essence* number one best-seller in the spring of 2004. Like his debut, it featured a female protagonist, Tonya, who is a teenager being raised by her unhappy single mother, Veronica. One day Veronica's boyfriend offers Tonya a joint laced with PCP and then rapes her; the act causes Tonya's life to spiral quickly out of control. One day, Holmes writes, "Tonya came home from school and thought her home had been burglarized. The apartment was empty. It wasn't until she saw that everything was gone except her clothes that it occurred to her that her mother had moved out. There was no note, no forwarding address left for Tonya. She was on her own.... She bounced around from family member to family member for months, looking for a stable home. She found no takers. Her mother had dragged her name through the mud, ruining the girl's reputation with their family. She told the story of how her household was broken and made Tonya the villain."

Holmes's third book *Never Go Home Again,* appeared in 2004. Its focus is sixteen-year-old Corey, who is awaiting sentencing as the story opens. The title refers to the future that Corey knows awaits some young men like himself who enter the penal system at an early age, are charged as adults, and then cannot break free of a criminal life once they are finally released. Holmes returned to Tonya's story in a 2008 sequel, *Bad Girlz 4 Life.* After leaving behind her first job as an exotic dancer, Tonya finds initial success as a hairdresser. But when her business fails she returns to her former life—this time with an even more sordid twist as the organizer of underground sex parties.

Holmes is also the author of *Dirty Game,* his first for a new publisher, St. Martin's Griffin. This 2007 novel portrays a man's battle to save his daughter from falling prey to the forces at work in their rough-and-tumble world, and to her own coming-of-age recklessness. Holmes still lives in New York City, where in the summer of 2008 production began on *Hardwhite,* a Bronx-set feature film whose script he wrote from his own experiences. "I can't write about corporate America, because I haven't been in corporate America," he joked with Bernadette Adams Davis in an interview for *Black Issues Book Review.* In the Baller-Status.com profile, he admitted that his writing had brought him great financial success, but was also a consistent reminder of his roots. "Every time I travel I go straight to the hood to see what their lives are like," he said. "Each time I discover that I'm not that far removed from a life on the streets. I'm not just another writer writing about things I've heard about; seven years of successful writing can't take you away from a lifetime."

Selected works

B-More Careful, Meow Meow Productions, 2002.
Bad Girlz, Atria Books/Simon and Schuster, 2003.
Never Go Home Again, Atria Books/Simon and Schuster, 2004.
Dirty Game, St. Martin's Griffin, 2007.
Bad Girlz 4 Life, St. Martin's Griffin, 2008.

Sources

Books

Holmes, Shannon, *Bad Girlz,* Atria, 2003.

Periodicals

Black Issues Book Review, January–February 2004, p. 40; March–April 2005, p. 46.
Jet, April 7, 2008, p. 48.
New York Times, September 8, 2004, p. E6.

Online

Willow, "Turn Off Your Hellavision: Interview with Author Shannon Holmes," BallerStatus.com, July 31, 2007, http://www.ballerstatus.com/article/editorialscolumns/2007/07/3494/ (accessed August 25, 2008).

—Carol Brennan

Tom Jackson

1951—

Sports broadcaster, professional athlete

Jackson, Tom, photograph. Al Messerschmidt/Getty Images.

Tom Jackson is a television sports analyst who spent fourteen years as a professional football player in the National Football League (NFL). During his football career Jackson played on the formidable "Orange Crush" defensive line for the Denver Broncos. He joined the broadcasting team of the cable sports channel ESPN in 1987. Discussing his perspective as a television commentator in 2000, Jackson said in the Louisville, Kentucky, *Courier-Journal,* "I feel that my opinion—from playing in this league for fourteen years and from covering it for another fourteen—is a very viable opinion. ... I've been in enough locker rooms, seen enough football, talked to enough players and coaches, to understand what I'm seeing in front of me."

Jackson was born in 1951 in Cleveland, Ohio, where his first sports allegiance was to the hometown Cleveland Browns of the NFL. From 1957 to 1965 the star player on the team was running back Jim Brown, one of football's pioneering African-American talents. Jackson dreamed of a career as a running back like the record-setting Brown, but the coach at John Adams High School decided he would be better utilized as a linebacker. Others discouraged Jackson from pursuing a football career at all, telling him he was too small for the sport. However, he was courted by Lee Corso at the University of Louisville and received an athletic scholarship to play football there.

As a Louisville Cardinal, Jackson helped lead the team to its first appearance in a bowl game in a dozen years. He was named the Missouri Valley Conference Player of the Year twice and served as team captain. Dave Boling, a columnist for the *News Tribune* of Tacoma, Washington, was Jackson's teammate at Louisville. He recalled that Jackson "stayed busy offering surprises. Waiting for our keys in a hotel lobby on a road trip, we heard somebody doing a nice job on Chicago's 'Colour My World' on the lobby piano. We walked over to take a look. Tom Jackson at the keyboard. As far as I could gather, nobody had a clue he could play. Game after game, this guy came up with stunning plays that helped us to a 9–1 record and a ranking in the Top 20 as seniors."

Jackson was drafted by the Denver Broncos of the NFL in 1973. The Broncos had been perennial losers since their debut in 1960; the year Jackson was drafted was the first in which they finished with a winning season.

At a Glance . . .

Born on April 4, 1951, in Cleveland, OH; married Diana Maria Hill (divorced); married Jennifer Jackson; children: Andrea (first marriage; deceased 1997), Taylor, Morgan (second marriage). *Education:* University of Louisville, 1969–73.

Career: Denver Broncos, linebacker, 1973–87; ESPN, football analyst, 1987—.

Addresses: *Office*—ESPN, Inc., ESPN Plaza, 935 Middle St., Bristol, CT 06010-7454.

Under coaches John Ralston and Red Miller, the team's fortunes began to improve, largely because of a solidly crafted line of defense—Jackson and fellow linebackers Randy Gradishar and Bob Swenson—that was soon dubbed the Orange Crush because of the team's uniform colors. The Broncos finished the 1977 season as the American Football Conference champions. They went on to their first Super Bowl, in New Orleans in January of 1978, where they were trounced by the Dallas Cowboys, 27–10.

Jackson was a three-time Pro Bowl athlete in the late 1970s. Twice he was voted Most Valuable Player by his teammates. The Broncos even created a Most Inspirational Player award just for him in 1979; he won it six times. "Jackson is one of the smallest linebackers in the league at 5 feet 11 and 220 pounds," wrote William N. Wallace in the *New York Times* a decade later. "But he remains a productive player because of his speed and his anticipation. The speed is eroding now, but he is still a valuable commodity and his teammates know it." When Jackson announced his retirement, he was the longest-serving player in the history of the franchise. He left on a high note: The Broncos made their second appearance at the Super Bowl, in Pasadena in January of 1987, which they lost to the New York Giants, 39–20.

The Broncos offered Jackson a slot on the team's coaching staff, but he opted for a career in broadcasting instead. He joined ESPN as an analyst for two of the sports channel's Sunday staples: the pregame show *NFL Countdown* (later renamed *NFL Sunday Countdown*) and *NFL Prime Time,* an early-evening recap of all the day's highlights. Jackson, anchor Chris Berman, and their staff spent more than twelve hours collectively watching every minute of every matchup played every Sunday.

Jackson and his colleagues at *NFL Sunday Countdown* found themselves mired in controversy in September of 2003 not long after conservative radio talk-show host Rush Limbaugh joined the program as a commentator. Discussing Philadelphia Eagles quarterback Donovan McNabb, Limbaugh said, "What we have here is a little social concern in the NFL," according to a *New York Times* report by Richard Sandomir. "The media has been very desirous that a black quarterback can do well—black coaches and black quarterbacks doing well. There is a little hope invested in McNabb, and he got a lot of credit for the performance of this team that he didn't deserve." Jackson and Steve Young were on the air with Limbaugh at the time, and they continued discussing the Eagles and McNabb without acknowledging Limbaugh's comment about race and media favoritism.

Many in the viewing audience, however, erupted in furor. U.S. Army General Wesley K. Clark, a presidential hopeful, and Representative Harold Ford Jr. (D-Tennessee) both called on ESPN to fire Limbaugh. Limbaugh resigned three days later. Limbaugh's remarks "made us very uncomfortable at the time, although the depth and the insensitive nature of which weren't fully felt until it seemed too late to reply," Jackson said afterward, according to *Sports Illustrated.*

Jackson's marriage to Diana Hill ended in divorce. His ex-wife and their nine-year-old daughter, Andrea, who was known as "Dre," were killed in an automobile accident in Colorado in the summer of 1997. Jackson flew to Denver to see Andrea, before giving doctors permission to remove her from life support, which had been started to allow for organ donation. As quoted by Marilyn Robinson in the *Denver Post,* Jackson said, "I choose to believe that she is at peace and that she is happy and contented.... I see it as Dre's life going on, as Dre's life continuing."

Sources

Periodicals

Courier-Journal (Louisville, KY), October 28, 2000.
Denver Post, August 8, 1997, p. B1; September 22, 2005, p. F9.
News Tribune (Tacoma, WA), November 6, 2006.
New York Times, January 8, 1987, p. D23; October 2, 2003, p. D1.
Sports Illustrated, October 13, 2003, p. 22.

—Carol Brennan

Benjamin Jealous

1973—

Civil rights leader

Jealous, Benjamin, photograph. AP Images.

When Benjamin Jealous accepted the job of president of the National Association for the Advancement of Colored People (NAACP) in May of 2008, he knew that he would have a tough road ahead of him. Even before he took office in September, some members of the NAACP, the nation's oldest civil rights organization, were critical of him, arguing that he was too young—just thirty-five years old at the time of his selection, the youngest president in NAACP history—and too inexperienced. Others, however, heralded Jealous as a bright leader who could breathe new life into the organization, which has struggled to redefine its mission and to keep pace with financial pressures in the face of declining membership. Jealous, for his part, has emphasized his commitment to the NAACP's core civil rights and social justice concerns, but all the while signaling his intention to move the organization into the twenty-first century to connect with the younger generation.

Benjamin Todd Jealous was born on January 18, 1973, in Pacific Grove, California. His parents, Fred Jealous, a counselor, and Ann Todd Jealous, a marriage and family therapist, both became involved in the civil rights movement during the 1950s, and they imparted their values and activism to their son. At age seven Benjamin Jealous declared that he planned to become a civil rights lawyer, and at age fourteen he participated in his first voter registration drive.

Jealous attended the York School in Monterey, California. During that time he spent a semester in Washington, DC, as a page for Democratic congressman Leon Panetta, and later served as an intern to Representative Sam Farr. After graduating from high school, Jealous took a job with the NAACP Legal Defense Fund as a community organizer in Harlem in New York City, where he led the neighborhood's residents and local churches in a campaign against the elimination of obstetrical services at St. Luke's Women's Hospital.

At age twenty-one Jealous went to Mississippi, where he worked as a field organizer on a campaign to halt the state's plan to close two of its three historically back universities. Soon he began writing for the *Jackson Advocate,* Mississippi's oldest black newspaper. His investigative reporting there uncovered corruption among high-ranking officials at the state penitentiary in

At a Glance . . .

Born Benjamin Todd Jealous on January 18, 1973, in Pacific Grove, CA; son of Fred and Ann Todd Jealous; married Lia Beth Epperson (a constitutional law professor and former civil rights attorney), July 27, 2002; children: Morgan. *Education:* Columbia University, BA, political science, 1996; Oxford University (Rhodes scholar), MS, comparative social research, 1998.

Career: *Jackson Advocate,* managing editor, 1993–95; National Newspaper Publishers Association, executive director, 1999–2002; Amnesty International, director of U.S. Human Rights Program, 2002–05; Rosenberg Foundation, president, 2005–08; National Association for the Advancement of Colored People, president, 2008—.

Memberships: Asia Society; Association of Black Foundation Executives; California Council for the Humanities; Northern California Grantmakers; PowerPAC.

Awards: Rhodes Scholarship, 1997; Special Achievement Award, National Coalition to Abolish the Death Penalty; Exceptional Communicator Award, New California Media; Charles Tisdale Award, *Jackson Advocate;* Emerging Leader Award, National Coalition on Black Civic Participation; "30 Leaders of the Future," *Ebony* magazine, 2001.

Addresses: *Office*—c/o National Association for the Advancement of Colored People, 4805 Mount Hope Dr., Baltimore, MD 21215-3206.

Parchman, and he provided evidence to acquit a black farmer who had been wrongfully charged with arson. In 1993 Jealous became managing editor of the *Advocate.*

Jealous completed his undergraduate degree in political science at Columbia University in 1996. The following year he was named a Rhodes scholar and traveled to Oxford University, where he earned a master's degree in comparative social research. Upon his return to the United States, he took a position as executive director of the National Newspaper Publishers Association, a trade association representing more than two hundred black community newspapers. During his tenure he launched an initiative that doubled the number of

newspapers publishing online and helped reorganize the news service.

From 2002 to 2005 Jealous served as director of the U.S. Human Rights Program at Amnesty International, an organization dedicated to social justice worldwide. He led the organization's campaigns to pass federal legislation against prison rape, focus attention on racial profiling, and expose the sentencing of children to life in prison. Subsequently, Jealous became president of the Rosenberg Foundation, a private institution based in San Francisco that advocates on behalf of California's immigrant population and working families.

Jealous was one of three candidates under consideration for the presidency of the NAACP in early 2008. The short list also included the Reverend Frederick D. Haynes III, senior pastor of Friendship-West Baptist Church in Dallas, and Alvin Brown, a former White House official then working on Hillary Clinton's presidential campaign. Jealous, the youngest of the three, lacked the traditional credentials for the job—all but one of the organization's sixteen previous leaders had been politicians or ministers. Jealous's résumé included media skills, technological savvy, and a history of grassroots activism.

By the time the NAACP's annual convention began on May 17, the search committee had narrowed the choices down to one. Jealous was the sole candidate presented to the organization's sixty-four-member board of directors, which approved his appointment by a vote of thirty-four to twenty-one. As the NAACP's seventeenth leader, he was the youngest in the organization's nearly hundred-year history.

The selection process, however, proved contentious, revealing a generational divide within the organization and philosophical differences over the NAACP's mission and direction. Some longtime members opposed the choice of Jealous, whom they viewed as inexperienced and uninspiring in leadership ability. Other members interpreted his appointment as a signal that the NAACP was poised to go in a new direction, to make itself relevant to a generation facing different forms of racial injustice than their parents did.

"It was time for the NAACP to take this step," Mary Frances Berry, who sat on the fifteen-member search committee, told the *Chronicle of Philanthropy.* "There was no need to have another traditional civil-rights leader just to have another traditional civil-rights leader. What Jealous brought was youth, energy, creativity, and vision. He can connect across the generational divide, and he understands the technological changes that have taken place."

In an interview with the Associated Press, quoted in the *Washington Post,* Jealous expressed his excitement about the board's choice: "I think that it's a real affirmation that this organization is willing to invest in the future, to invest in the ideas and the leadership of the generation that is currently raising black children in this country."

Jealous took the reins of the NAACP at a challenging time. He succeeded Bruce S. Gordon, who had resigned in March of 2007 after only nineteen months on the job, citing irreconcilable differences with the board of directors. A few months later the organization disclosed a budget shortfall of $1 million, necessitating a 40 percent reduction in its workforce and the closing of seven regional offices. Adding to its woes, the organization faced declining membership and philanthropic contributions.

As the NAACP approached its centennial, Jealous began to forge his agenda for the organization. For him, the most pressing issues that the NAACP needed to address, in addition to its management challenges, included employment discrimination, inner-city violence, and segregation in schools. He also cited the nation's record-high incarceration rate, especially among African Americans, as cause for concern.

For his accomplishments, Jealous has received numerous awards. In 2001 he was named to *Ebony* magazine's list of "30 Leaders of the Future." He has also received the Special Achievement Award of the National Coalition to Abolish the Death Penalty, and the Emerging Leader Award of the National Coalition on Black Civic Participation.

Sources

Periodicals

Baltimore Sun, July 18, 2008.
Chronicle of Philanthropy, May 29, 2008.
San Francisco Chronicle, May 27, 2008.
Washington Post, May 18, 2008, p. A06.

Online

"Benjamin Todd Jealous," NAACP, http://www. naacp.org/about/leadership/executive/jealous/in dex.htm (accessed July 23, 2008).

—Deborah A. Ring

Michaëlle Jean

1957—

Governor general

Jean, Michaëlle, photograph. AP Images.

Michaëlle Jean represents England's Queen Elizabeth II as Canada's governor general, a position that remains the final legacy of Canada's colonial past as a possession of Britain. The post carries with it some extensive political rights, but these are rarely exercised, and Canada's government is permitted to function independently without interference from either the British monarch or his or her representative in Ottawa. Jean is the first black woman to serve as the vice-regal, and is an enormously popular public figure. Sometimes dubbed her country's version of Oprah Winfrey, she was born in Haiti and emigrated from there with her family as a child. In her historic installation speech in 2005, a transcript of which appeared on her official Web site, Jean noted that Canadians "are encouraged to believe that everything is possible in this country and my own adventure represents for me and for others a spark of hope that I want kept alive for the greatest number."

Jean was born in 1957 in Port-au-Prince, Haiti's capital. Her father, Roger, was a professor of philosophy and literature, and the family lived in Bois Verna, an affluent district of the city. In the same year she was born, François "Papa Doc" Duvalier won the presidency in a questionable election and began a dictatorial regime that endured until his son, Jean-Claude "Baby Doc" Duvalier, was finally ousted during a period of civil unrest in 1986. The long Duvalier era included widespread human rights abuses and blatant corruption, with the family was later accused of bankrupting the nation while maintaining an opulent lifestyle that mimicked a royal court.

When Jean reached school age, her parents home-schooled her because at the time all schoolchildren in Haiti had to swear an oath of allegiance to the senior Duvalier. Her father was targeted as one of the intellectuals who posed a threat to the regime, and when the young Jean was ten years old her father was detained and tortured. Upon his release, the family fled, as many middle-class Haitians had already done. Her parents' marriage did not survive the transition to Quebec, and Jean lost touch with her father for many years.

The Jeans first settled in Thetford Mines, Quebec, a mining town that was likely a bleak and drastic departure from a Caribbean villa home, but they later moved to Montreal. Her mother, Luce, returned to work as a nurse to support Jean and her sister, Nadege. As a teenager, Jean earned top grades at École Marguerite-de Lajemmerais, a Montreal high school for the musically gifted. She went on to study Italian and Hispanic languages and literature at the University of Montreal, earning an undergraduate degree and then a graduate degree in comparative literature. Study-abroad stints in Italy further polished her fluency, and she taught Italian studies at the University of Montreal for a time. For nearly a decade she also worked at a domestic-violence shelter in the city.

Jean began considering a career move into journalism, and made a fortuitously timed visit to Haiti with a graduate student and budding filmmaker in February of 1986, just as Baby Doc Duvalier's regime was drawing to its violent close. In 1988 Jean was hired by Radio-Canada, the French-language national broadcasting service, as a reporter. She went on to a long career with that and other networks, appearing on or anchoring *Montréal ce soir* ("Montréal Tonight"), *Le Point, Le Monde ce soir* ("The World Tonight"), and *Horizons francophones.* After 1999 she served as host of the documentary-film showcases *The Passionate Eye* and *Rough Cuts* on the Canadian Broadcasting Corporation (CBC), the English-broadcasting network. In 2004 she launched *Michaëlle,* her own in-depth news and interview program on Radio-Canada.

By then Jean was married to Jean-Daniel Lafond, a documentary filmmaker who had emigrated from France in the early 1970s. They lived in the Montreal quarter known as Little Burgundy, a predominantly black area, and worked together on a number of documentaries, including *Haiti in All Our Dreams,* in which Jean interviewed her well-known uncle, French-Haitian writer René Depestre.

One of her husband's projects became a topic of debate not long after Canadian prime minister Paul Martin put forth Jean's name to serve as the next governor general of Canada in August of 2005. The separation of the French-speaking province of Quebec from the rest of Canada has long been a contentious issue in Canada, and in her husband's 1991 documentary *The Black Way,* Jean makes a toast to independence—though it is unclear whether she is speaking about Quebec or the Caribbean island of Martinique. Her French citizenship—which she applied for and received after her marriage to the French Lafond—was also held up for criticism, and Francophone and Anglophone news outlets in Canada debated whether Jean possessed sufficient loyalty to the federal system.

Through public statements Jean reiterated her allegiance to an intact Canada, and she renounced her French citizenship shortly before she was sworn in as governor general on September 27, 2005. She became the first black Canadian to hold the post, and the twenty-seventh to serve in the post's history, which dates back to 1760. Jean's home and office is Rideau Hall, a small palace in Ottawa. She and her husband are parents to daughter Marie-Éden, who was adopted from Haiti.

In the Canadian system the head of the political party with the majority in parliament is the head of government, while the British monarch serves as head of state. Jean was the vice-regal for Queen Elizabeth II, and her formal title was an impressive one: Her Excellency the Right Honourable Michaëlle Jean, Chancellor and Principal Companion of the Order of Canada, Chancellor and Commander of the Order of

Military Merit, Chancellor and Commander of the Order of Merit of the Police Forces, Governor General and Commander-in-Chief in and over Canada. The governor general's duties are largely ceremonial, though her actual powers include the ability to appoint Supreme Court justices and call an assembly of the lower house of the Canadian parliament. These are rarely exercised, but as chief executive, the British monarch does hold reserve powers known as the Royal Prerogative and, theoretically at least, may direct the governor general to intervene in government affairs.

The bulk of Jean's duties, however, involved public appearances and representing Canada on goodwill visits abroad. She also delivered the annual Speech from the Throne, which marked the opening of the new parliamentary session. Her 2007 Speech from the Throne typically reiterated several fundamental goals of domestic and foreign policy, and concluded by noting that "Canadians can be proud of their country and its achievements. Working together we have built a nation that is prosperous and safe.... Like the North Star, Canada has been a guide to other nations; through difficult times, Canada has shone as an example of what a people joined in common purpose can achieve."

Sources

Periodicals

Globe & Mail (Toronto), August 5, 2005, p. A1; August 18, 2005, p. A1; March 23, 2007, p. A23.
Maclean's (Toronto), January 14, 2008, p. 20.

Online

"Installation Speech," Governor General of Canada, September 27, 2005, http://www.gg.ca/media/doc.asp?lang=e&DocID=4574 (accessed August 25, 2008).
"Speech from the Throne: Strong Leadership. A Better Canada," Government of Canada, October 16, 2007, http://www.sft-ddt.gc.ca/eng/media.asp?id=1364 (accessed August 25, 2008).

—Carol Brennan

Kevin Johnson

1966—

Mayor of Sacramento, former professional basketball player

Johnson, Kevin, photograph. Barry Gossage/NBAE via Getty Images.

Kevin Johnson first rose to prominence as a professional basketball player. After twelve seasons as a point guard for the Phoenix Suns, he retired from basketball to pursue a career in business and philanthropy. His charitable activities are focused on St. HOPE, an organization he founded in 1989 to provide after-school activities to children in his hometown of Sacramento, California. From those modest beginnings, St. HOPE has grown into a multifaceted program with an ambitious mission, according to its Web site: "to revitalize inner-city communities through public education, civic leadership, economic development and the arts." As part of that mission, Johnson won city approval in 2003 to take over ailing Sacramento High School and transform it into the flagship of a faith-based charter-school program. Five years later Johnson gave up day-to-day control of St. HOPE in order to run for mayor of Sacramento.

Kevin Maurice Johnson was born on March 4, 1966, in Sacramento. His mother, Georgia Johnson, is the daughter of a black father and a white mother (also named Georgia); the latter later married George Johnson, a white sheet-metal worker. Kevin's father died shortly after his birth, and he was raised by his maternal grandparents in the city's troubled Oak Park section. Like many of their neighbors, the family often struggled financially. George Johnson has nevertheless described the period as a happy one, while Kevin has repeatedly credited his grandfather with instilling in him the values of hard work, self-confidence, generosity, and personal ethics. A standout star in both baseball and basketball for Sacramento High School (the school he would later take over), Johnson also did well enough academically to secure a scholarship to the University of California at Berkeley, where he majored in political science and again excelled at both baseball and basketball. In 1986, after being signed as a prospect by the Oakland Athletics, a professional baseball team, he spent several summers playing in the minor leagues. It was in basketball, however, that Johnson attracted the most notice, particularly in his junior and senior years, when he was named to the Pac-10 athletic conference's First Team, an annual honor given to only five of the league's players. In the spring of 1987, when Johnson was only a few credits shy of his bachelor's degree (he would

At a Glance . . .

Born Kevin Maurice Johnson on March 4, 1966, in Sacramento, CA; son of Georgia Johnson; raised by maternal grandparents George and Georgia Johnson. *Religion:* Christian. *Education:* University of California–Berkeley, BA, political science, 1997; completed Summer Leadership Institute for leaders of faith-based nonprofits, Harvard Divinity School, 2000.

Career: Cleveland Cavaliers, point guard, 1987–88; Phoenix Suns, point guard, 1988–98, 1999–2000; NBC Television, basketball commentator, 2000–01; St. HOPE, founder and chairman, 1989–2008; mayor of Sacramento, 2008—.

Awards: First Team, Pac-10 athletic conference, 1985–86 and 1986–87; All-Star Team, National Basketball League, 1989–90, 1990–91, and 1993–94; J. Walter Kennedy Citizenship Award, National Basketball Association, 1990–91; National Caring Award, Caring Institute, 1992; named 411th Point of Light by President George H. W. Bush, 1991; John R. Wooden Lifetime Achievement Award, Paralysis Project of America, 2008.

Addresses: *Office*—City Hall, 915 I Street, Sacramento, CA 95814-2604.

complete the degree ten years later), the Cleveland Cavaliers of the National Basketball Association (NBA) selected him in the first round of that year's draft; he was the seventh choice overall.

Johnson's first months in the NBA were something of a disappointment, as he lost the role of starting point guard to Mark Price, a more experienced veteran. In February of 1988, however, Cleveland traded him, along with teammates Tyrone Corbin and Mark West, to the Phoenix Suns in exchange for Larry Nance, Mike Sanders, and a future draft pick. Johnson thrived in Phoenix, winning a host of awards including Rookie of the Month (April of 1988) and Most Improved Player (1988–89). He was also named to the league's All-Star team three times (1990, 1991, and 1994) and played on the U.S. team that won the gold medal at the 1994 International Basketball Federation championship in Toronto, Canada. In Phoenix, Johnson was known for his competitiveness on the court, as well as for his generosity and religious faith. A devout Christian, he often led prayer groups with teammates and opponents before games. He also made a habit of buying ten

tickets to every home game and distributing them free to friends, acquaintances, and strangers. His personal life was not without problems, however, the most serious of which involved allegations that he molested a sixteen-year-old girl in 1995. Though the Maricopa County (Arizona) District Attorney's office declined to file charges on the grounds that a conviction was not likely, the incident has continued to affect Johnson's career, particularly following his decision to enter politics in 2008.

Focused on Charitable Work

Johnson retired from basketball at the end of the 1998 season, though he returned for six games in the 1999–2000 season when Jason Kidd, his replacement at point guard, was injured. Retirement allowed him to pursue a variety of personal and professional projects. In addition to spending a year from 2000 to 2001 as a basketball commentator for the television program *The NBA on NBC*, he managed his investments and promoted several real estate developments. Above all, however, he worked to expand St. HOPE, a faith-based charitable organization he founded in 1989 to provide after-school activities to poor, mostly African-American students in Oak Park, his old Sacramento neighborhood.

Johnson's return to Sacramento after retirement coincided with the beginning of a period of explosive growth for the St. HOPE organization, as it moved under his direction from an after-school program to a comprehensive community-development organization focused on economic growth, redevelopment, and charter schools. In May of 2003, for example, St. HOPE's property development division opened the 40 Acres Art and Cultural Center, an award-winning mixed-use facility in the center of Oak Park. Other divisions within St. HOPE include the Hood Corps, which offers neighborhood youth a variety of public-service opportunities, and St. HOPE Public Schools (SHPS), which oversees the group's charter schools.

SHPS is by far the largest component of the St. HOPE organization. Key to its expansion was the 2003 decision by the Sacramento School Board to cede control of Sacramento High School, a struggling inner-city institution, to St. HOPE, which reorganized and reopened it as the flagship of its charter school system. The change was a controversial one, with many city residents expressing unease at the idea of a faith-based organization running a public school; such an arrangement, they felt, violated the principle of the separation of church and state. According to local media accounts, intensive lobbying efforts by the charismatic Johnson were an important factor in the school board's decision. The controversy dissipated soon thereafter, even as St. HOPE continued to expand the program. As of the spring of 2008, the organization was running a total of seven charter schools, with a combined enrollment of more than fifteen hundred students from prekindergarten through grade twelve. According to its Web site, St. HOPE planned to expand across the United States, with its first school outside Sacramento, the St. HOPE Leadership Academy, scheduled to open in the Harlem district of New York City in August of 2008.

In January of 2008 Johnson resigned his chairmanship of St. HOPE in order to focus on his political career. Less than two months later, on March 5, 2008, he officially announced his campaign to become mayor of Sacramento. On June 3, 2008, he faced his major opponent, incumbent Heather Fargo, and a number of other candidates in a nonpartisan primary election. According to California law, a runoff election can be avoided if a candidate in a nonpartisan primary wins a majority of votes cast. Though Johnson won with a 7 percent margin over Fargo, he failed to win a majority, and a runoff election was therefore scheduled for November of 2008. Johnson has campaigned on a modest, uncontroversial platform, promising better schools, reduced crime, and economic development. Fargo, for her part, has emphasized her experience, contrasting her years on the city council and as mayor with Johnson's status as a political newcomer. The merits of the candidates, however, have been repeatedly overshadowed in a bitter campaign of mudslinging, much of it aimed at Johnson. The 1995 incident of alleged sexual misconduct, for example, received renewed scrutiny when a minor candidate, Leonard Padilla, drew attention to similar allegations made against Johnson in 2007 by a female student at Sacramento High School. Though the Sacramento Police Department found the charges to be without merit, the episode received significant media attention. Equally troubling for Johnson's campaign were news reports in April of 2008 that AmeriCorps, a public-service program of the federal government, was conducting an investigation of St. HOPE, a major recipient of AmeriCorps funds. Though the alleged incident at Sacramento High School was the major focus of the AmeriCorps investigation, there were also allegations of financial impropriety. However, these charges did not seem to have a lasting impact on Johnson's political career since Johnson won the Sacramento mayoral election in November of 2008.

Sources

Periodicals

New York Times, March 7, 2008, p. D5; June 9, 2008, p. A14.

Online

"About Kevin," Kevin Johnson for Mayor, http://www.kevinjohnsonformayor.com/about/bio (accessed July 8, 2008).

"History & Timeline," St. HOPE, http://sthope.org/history-1.html (accessed July 8, 2008).

"Kevin Johnson," NBA Encyclopedia: Playoff Edition, http://www.nba.com/history/players/kevjohnson_stats.html (accessed July 8, 2008).

—R. Anthony Kugler

Van Jones

1968—

Activist, attorney

Jones, Van, photograph. Vince Bucci/Getty Images.

Van Jones is a social activist whose work to combine job creation with "green" initiatives in the San Francisco Bay area has served as a model for urban renewal programs throughout the country. An active proponent of police reform and human rights issues, Jones is also credited with bringing the environmental movement—a cause usually associated with white, middle-class advocates—to urban centers, where chronic unemployment and crime are often considered more pressing concerns than pollution. "Too often we have said: 'We are overwhelmed with violence, bad housing, failing schools, excessive incarceration, poor healthcare and joblessness. We can't afford to worry about spotted owls, redwood trees and polar bears,'" he wrote in *ColorLines* in 2007. "But Hurricane Katrina and its aftermath taught us that the coming ecological disasters will hit the poor first and worst."

Jones, the son of two teachers, was born in 1968 and grew up in Jackson, Tennessee. He studied journalism and political science at the University of Tennessee in Martin and, after graduating with a degree in communications in 1990, went on to Yale University Law School. Already active in raising awareness about campus racial and administration issues, Jones was spurred to activism in the spring of 1992, when riots erupted in Los Angeles following the acquittal of white police officers charged with brutally beating black motorist Rodney King. Jones was working as an intern for a civil-rights attorney in San Francisco at the time; he returned to the Bay Area permanently after earning his law degree in 1993.

Police brutality was the focus of his earliest efforts. In 1995 he founded Bay Area Police-Watch. Every day his office fielded as many as twenty complaints from area residents who believed they had been victims of unlawful behavior by police officers in San Francisco, Oakland, and other nearby communities. In 1997 the organization was instrumental in the firing of San Francisco police officer Marc Andaya. Jones had already compiled a long list of complaints against Andaya when a suspect named Aaron Williams died after being arrested by Andaya and other officers in 1995. Witnesses testified that Andaya kicked Williams in the head after he had subdued him with pepper spray; the coroner ruled, however, that Williams's death was attributable to the cocaine in his system. When the charges against Andaya were dismissed, community protests ensued,

At a Glance . . .

Born Anthony Jones in 1968 in Jackson, TN; married Jana; children: two sons. *Education:* University of Tennessee at Martin, BA, communications, 1990; Yale Law School, JD, 1993.

Career: Bay Area PoliceWatch, founder, 1995; Ella Baker Center for Human Rights, cofounder, 1996; Green For All, founder, 2007, and president, 2007—.

Memberships: Center for American Progress (senior fellow), National Apollo Alliance, Rainforest Action Network, Social Ventures Network.

Awards: Next Generation Leadership Fellowship, Rockefeller Foundation, 1997; Reebok Human Rights Award, Reebok Foundation, 1998, Hunt Prime Mover Award, 2008; Paul Wellstone Award, Campaign for America's Future, 2008; George Lucas Foundation's "Daring Dozen," 2008.

Addresses: *Office*—Green For All, 414 13th St., Ste. 600, Oakland, CA 94612.

and Jones's group helped publicize other incidents, such as the time Andaya choked a suspect who was already in handcuffs. In the end, the San Francisco Police Commission fired Andaya. As a result of his advocacy work, Jones was granted a Next Generation Leadership Fellowship from the Rockefeller Foundation and won a Reebok Human Rights Award.

In 1996 he cofounded the Ella Baker Center for Human Rights, which was named after the longtime civil rights activist who pressured the national Democratic Party leadership to take a firmer stand against racial discrimination both in the South and within the party. The Baker Center's first effort was the creation of a Green Job Corps in Oakland. The state of California, which had been a leader in progressive environmental laws since the 1970s, had passed legislation requiring that both new construction and existing structures adhere to strict energy-efficiency standards. Under the law, older buildings had to be weatherproofed, retrofitted with solar panels, or renovated in other ways. Jones worked with both the Oakland city government, which provided $250,000 in start-up funding, and the local electricians' union to train unemployed residents to do these jobs. There was potential for steady work because the jobs could not be outsourced. "You can't take a building you want to

weatherize, put it on a ship to China and then have them do it and send it back," Jones told Thomas L. Friedman in the *New York Times.* "Those green-collar jobs can provide a pathway out of poverty for someone who has not gone to college."

In 2007 Jones founded Green For All, an organization that works on a national level to train unemployed urban residents for jobs in the renewable-energy and retrofitting sector. As its founding president, Jones joined forces with Democratic Representative Nancy Pelosi, who later became Speaker of the House, to get $1 billion in federal funding to create 250,000 new jobs by 2012. Jones explained the practicality of such expenditures in a *Forbes* article in 2006. Federal and state governments were already spending nearly $35 billion annually for prisons and jails, he noted, and many of those dollars went to private companies that received government contracts to build or manage incarceration facilities. For those companies to earn profits, Jones pointed out, they had to keep the jails full—in other words, the companies had little financial incentive to rehabilitate prisoners. Noting that 57 percent of parolees in California end up back in prison, Jones asserted that "the system is so broken that the very people we entrust to rehabilitate prisoners actually profit from prolonged prisoner stays and quick prisoner returns."

Jones's adopted hometown of Oakland has been the starting point for several significant social-justice movements that later spurred change at the national level, including early labor union organizing and minority political participation based on the work of the Black Panthers, a militant group active in the city during the 1960s. Jones has been hailed as a pioneer for merging environmental issues with efforts to solve such urban problems as neighborhood decay, job loss, and poverty. For many years the green movement was viewed as a concern primarily of the affluent and college-educated. However, as Jones explained to writer Alwin Jones in *Black Enterprise,* "green values are very consistent with African and indigenous values in the first place. Western society is coming back around to values that were and are a part of our core, our heritage, our history. We shouldn't think about it as jumping on a white bandwagon because it's our bandwagon in the first place."

Sources

Periodicals

Black Enterprise, May 2008, p. 51.
ColorLines, September–October 2007, p. 9.
Forbes, April 24, 2006.
New York Times, October 17, 2007, p. A27; March 26, 2008; April 20, 2008.

—Carol Brennan

Eddie Levert

1942—

R&b singer, songwriter

Levert, Eddie, photograph. Larry Marano/Getty Images.

As the lead singer of the legendary O'Jays, the vocal group best remembered for their "Philly soul" sound, Eddie Levert lent his voice to such chart-topping tunes as "Back Stabbers," "Love Train," and "For the Love of Money." Throughout the 1970s Levert and the O'Jays racked up more than thirty hit singles, becoming a crossover success in both pop and R&B. Inducted into the Rock and Roll Hall of Fame in 2005, the O'Jays have stood the test of time, continuing to record and perform live. For Levert, musical collaboration has been a family affair as well—with son Gerald Levert he recorded two popular albums and wrote a book before Gerald's untimely death in 2006.

Edward Levert was born on June 16, 1942, in Bessemer, Alabama. When he was eight years old, his family relocated to Canton, Ohio, where he spent his youth. He began singing at an early age, first teaming up with an elementary school friend, Walter Williams, to perform as a gospel duo on local radio. At McKinley High School in Canton, Levert and Williams, together with pals William Powell, Bill Isles, and Bobby Massey, were inspired to form their own vocal group after attending a show by Frankie Lyman and the Teenagers.

Launched in 1958, the quintet initially called themselves the Triumphs. The group began performing locally, attracting enthusiastic crowds. Before long, Cincinnati, Ohio, producer Syd Nathan had signed them to his King label; now calling themselves the Mascots, the group released their first single, "Miracles," in 1961. The song enjoyed moderate success in the Cleveland, Ohio, area.

Levert and his group had an early fan—and mentor—in Eddie O'Jay, a popular Cleveland disc jockey who featured them at sock hops that he hosted. O'Jay offered them career advice, notably suggesting a name change, and considered becoming their manager for a time. As an homage to the DJ, the group renamed themselves the O'Jays. They soon signed with Imperial Records, working with producer H. B. Barnum. Their first chart-making song, "Lonely Drifter," was released in 1963. More would follow, including the 1967 hit "I'll Be Sweeter Tomorrow (Than I Was Today)," which landed Levert and the O'Jays their first top-ten single on the R&B charts.

The group's big break would come in 1968. Performing at the Apollo Theater in New York City, they met

Philadelphia-based producers Kenny Gamble and Leon Huff, who were then representing the Neptune label, distributed by Chess Records in Chicago. The O'Jays' first single for the producers, "One Night Affair," rose to number fifteen on the R&B charts in the summer of 1969. A few years later, when Gamble and Huff established their own label, Philadelphia International, the O'Jays became their flagship act. The group, now pared down to a trio—Levert, Williams, and Powell—was considered a pioneer of Philly soul (also called the Philadelphia Sound or Sweet Philly), a style of soul music marked by funk influences, strong strings and horns, and gospel harmonies.

The O'Jays' inaugural album with Philadelphia International, *Back Stabbers* (1972), epitomized Philly soul. The record's title track, featuring Levert's soulful lead vocals, became the band's first crossover hit, breaking the top five on the pop music chart and propelling them to stardom. The follow-up single, "Love Train," topped both the pop and R&B charts. The O'Jays enjoyed tremendous success over the course of the 1970s, releasing the hit albums *Ship Ahoy* (1973), *Survival* (1974), *Family Reunion* (1975), *Message in the Music* (1976), and *So Full of Love* (1978). During the decade they had hit after hit, including "Time to Get Down," "Put Your Hands Together," "For the Love of Money," "I Love Music," and "Livin' for the Weekend."

Founding member Powell left the group in 1975 and died of cancer two years later. Levert and Williams continued to record, replacing Powell with Sammy Strain, previously of Little Anthony and the Imperials, but the group produced fewer hits. As the times changed, so did Americans' taste in music. The 1979 album *Identify Yourself* marked the beginning of the O'Jays' decline in popularity as disco and funk music were replaced by the New Wave electronica of the 1980s. The group left Philadelphia International in 1987. They recorded *Let Me Touch You*, featuring the song "Lovin' You," for EMI Records that year, attempting to update their classic soul sound with a more contemporary R&B flair.

During the 1980s two of Levert's sons, Gerald and Sean, continued their father's musical tradition by forming the urban trio LeVert (with Marc Gordon) and issuing solo albums. Eddie Levert collaborated with son Gerald on the 1995 recording *Father and Son*, featuring the song "Wind beneath My Wings." In 2007 the pair's second album, *Something to Talk About*, came out alongside their book, *I Got Your Back: A Father and Son Keep It Real about Love, Fatherhood, Family, and Friendship*. Sadly, however, just before the release of both of these works, in November of 2006 Gerald died at age forty of an accidental combination of prescription and over-the-counter medications, just as work on the album and book was being completed. Levert lost a second son in March of 2008, when Sean died while in a Cleveland jail after pleading guilty to being behind in child support payments.

The book *I Got Your Back* takes its title from a song that Gerald wrote for the record *Father and Son*. In it, Eddie and Gerald reflect on their father-son relationship and the importance of family relationships. In a 2007 interview with *Jet* magazine, Eddie Levert recalled that his fondest memories of his son were of the music they made together: "The proudest moments in my career were onstage with that kid. The O'Jays is what I do, that's my job. But some of my greatest and proudest moments were when I was with him onstage…. With me and him, we'd look at each other and we knew what to do, that's how close we were."

Levert and the O'Jays have continued to record and perform for enthusiastic audiences, releasing *For the Love* in 2001 and *Imagination* in 2004. The group received the Pioneer Award from the Rhythm & Blues Foundation in 1998, and they were inducted into the Vocal Group Hall of Fame in 2004 and the Rock and Roll Hall of Fame in 2005. Levert made a big-screen appearance in the film *The Fighting Temptations* (starring Cuba Gooding Jr.) in 2003, and in 2006 the O'Jays performed live at the ESPY Awards, hosted by Lance Armstrong. PBS television recorded a live performance by the O'Jays on June 8, 2008, at Atlantic City's Borgota Hotel to commemorate the group's fiftieth anniversary in the music industry.

Selected works

Albums with O'Jays

Back Stabbers, Philadelphia International, 1972.
Ship Ahoy, Philadelphia International, 1973.
Survival, Philadelphia International, 1974.
Family Reunion, Philadelphia International, 1975.

Message in the Music, Philadelphia International, 1976.
So Full of Love, Philadelphia International, 1978.
Identify Yourself, Philadelphia International, 1979.
My Favorite Person, Philadelphia International, 1982.
Love Fever, Philadelphia International, 1984.
Let Me Touch You, EMI, 1987.
Serious, EMI, 1989.
Emotionally Yours, EMI, 1991.
Heartbreaker, EMI, 1993.
Love You to Tears, Volcano, 1997.
For the Love, MCA, 2001.
Imagination, Sanctuary, 2004.

Albums with Gerald Levert

Father and Son, EastWest America, 1995.
Something to Talk About, Atlantic, 2007.

Books

(With Gerald Levert and Lyah Beth Leflore) *I Got Your Back: A Father and Son Keep It Real about Love,* *Fatherhood, Family, and Friendship,* Broadway Books, 2007.

Sources

Books

Jackson, John A., *A House on Fire: The Rise and Fall of Philadelphia Soul,* Oxford University Press, 2004.

Periodicals

Jet, July 24, 2006, p. 54; June 18, 2007.

Online

"The O'Jays," Rock and Roll Hall of Fame and Museum, http://www.rockhall.com/inductee/the-ojays (accessed July 11, 2008).
The O'Jays Home Page, http://theojayshomepage.com/index_1.html (accessed July 11, 2008).

—Deborah A. Ring

Ramsey Lewis

1935—

Jazz musician, radio host

Lewis, Ramsey, photograph. Bryan Bedder/Getty Images.

The divide between popular taste and elite critical opinion in jazz is amply illustrated by the career of pianist Ramsey Lewis. Lewis has consistently drawn large audiences and numerous record buyers over more than forty-five years of musical activity, but since the appearance of his hit 1965 album *The In Crowd,* he has been criticized by many jazz writers for what they have considered excessive commercialism. Scott Yanow on the allmusic Web site was perhaps typical when he refused to classify much of Lewis's music as jazz at all, contending that "Lewis has mostly stuck to easy listening pop music during the past 30 years." Yet Lewis, who became well known to Chicago radio audiences in the late 1990s as an on-air jazz-show host, set the tone for much of the successful jazz-pop fusion that followed his own 1960s breakthrough. Ignoring critical orthodoxy, he became an unusually influential musician. He has also been one of jazz's best public ambassadors, through his series of radio and television shows and recordings distributed under the "Legends of Jazz" umbrella.

Ramsey Emmanuel Lewis Jr. was born in Chicago on May 27, 1935. He grew up in the Cabrini Homes housing project that also spawned soul vocalists Curtis Mayfield and Jerry Butler. When he was barely more than a toddler, his sister, Lucille, began taking piano lessons. Lewis raised a fuss until his parents gave in and agreed to pay 50 cents per week for lessons for him as well, with a local church organist who would hit his fingers with a ruler if he made a mistake. At age eleven Lewis switched to another teacher, Dorothy Mendelson, who, Lewis told *Down Beat,* told him, "'You must make the piano sing.' I found that fascinating. 'Listen with the inner ear.' Her lessons were a means to an end, about making music, not about technique." Inspired, Lewis began practicing until late in the evening, and his parents began to worry that he was neglecting his other studies.

Joined Seven-Piece Band

Lewis's first appearances as a pianist came at church, where his father served as choir director. When he was age sixteen he joined the Clefs, a locally popular seven-piece band that found work performing at parties and college dances. Several members of the group were drafted into the military during the Korean War during the 1950s, but Lewis and two other band members, bassist Eldee Young and drummer Redd Holt, were not called. Chicago radio DJ Daddy-O Daylie, mindful of the rising popularity of straight-ahead jazz, advised the three remaining Clefs to join together as the Ramsey Lewis Trio.

Daylie arranged an audition for Lewis's trio with Phil Chess, one of two brothers who created the Chess label and put Chicago on the rhythm-and-blues recording map. Chess was impressed, and Lewis's debut album, *Ramsey Lewis and His Gentlemen of Swing,* was released some months later when Daylie promised to give the music air play. It was the beginning of a string

of several dozen releases for Lewis on Chess and related labels, stretching into the early 1970s, when Lewis moved to the Columbia label.

Though jazz purists value his music of the late 1950s and early 1960s over his later work, Lewis was alert to pop trends even at this early stage. In 1962, at the height of the country/rhythm-and-blues crossover trend stimulated by Ray Charles and vocalist Solomon Burke, Lewis's trio released *Country Meets the Blues.* That same year they released a bossa nova album to capitalize on that growing craze.

Appeared at Birdland

Lewis had honed his piano skills with studies at the Chicago Music College and DePaul University, and the trio won mainstream jazz fans with a 1959 appearance at New York's prestigious Birdland club and subsequent gigs at the Village Vanguard and the Newport Jazz Festival. They seemed on their way to an artistically rewarding but financially dicey future in modern jazz when, in 1964, a coffee shop waitress enamored of the Dobie Gray pop hit "The In Crowd" suggested that they cover the song. Introducing their instrumental version to a hardcore jazz audience at Washington, DC's Bohemian Cavern, Lewis was nervous. But the audience was won over, and the resulting album, 1965's *The In Crowd,* brought the trio a platinum-selling album and a Grammy Award for best small-group recording.

The other titles on *The In Crowd* were indicative of the range of Lewis's musical interests; they include a movie-score number (the "Love Theme" from *Spartacus*), a bossa nova song (Antonio Carlos Jobim's *Felicidade*), a country-pop standard ("Tennessee Waltz"), a jazz classic (Duke Ellington's "Come Sunday"), and yet more styles. "This album is one of the places where Afro and funk-jazz started," noted Matthew Greenwald on allmusic, and in general even Lewis's critics have had to concede the rhythmic infectiousness of his playing. Lewis followed up his initial success with other covers that cracked pop charts—"A Hard Day's Night" and "Hang On Sloopy." In the 1970s the original Lewis trio broke up under the pressures of stardom, but Lewis forged ahead with a new group that included drummer Maurice White, who later founded the popular R&B group Earth, Wind & Fire.

Now heading a septet, Lewis toured with Earth, Wind & Fire twice in the 1970s, and recorded *Sun Goddess,* one of his most successful albums, with a band that included members of that group. Lewis experimented with synthesizer keyboards and horn sections, but much of his work after the early 1980s was in the more intimate trio and quartet formats with which he was most familiar. Lewis also emerged on occasion as a formidable solo pianist. The *Los Angeles Times,* reviewing a duet concert he played with pianist Billy Taylor, noted that "his solo during 'Body and Soul' was stunning, an imaginative impromptu that was a virtual definition of chamber jazz at its best."

Recorded with Classical Musicians

Lewis continued to branch out into new musical areas, recording with classical musicians on the 1988 release *A Classic Encounter* (with the Philharmonic Orchestra), and the following year employing contemporary dance rhythms on his *Urban Renewal* release under the tutelage of his producer son, Kevyn. A pair of albums with chanteuse Nancy Wilson, 1984's *The Two of Us* and 2002's *Meant to Be,* were particularly successful. A year rarely passed without the release of one or more Lewis albums, and most, despite the critics' disapproval, reached the top levels of jazz album sales charts.

Lewis remained philosophical about the split between critics and audiences. "This is a very sensitive area that we're entering into," he told *Down Beat.* "Jazz as entertainment and jazz as art.... Count Basie and Duke Ellington's playing was for dancers, but something happened where jazz entertainment came to be looked down upon by musicians ... Well, that's OK, but the music became so complex you couldn't dance to it, and the guy who worked all day in an office, drove a truck, whatever, at the end of the week, he didn't feel that he could spend his 88 or his 810 going to school, so he stopped going [to jazz clubs]."

Indeed, as modernism loosened its stranglehold on jazz aesthetics, critics began to recognize Lewis's contributions and to treat his new releases more kindly. By the turn of the century, Lewis was a jazz leader and tastemaker in his own right, serving as artistic director of the jazz series at Ravinia, the summer concert venue of the Chicago Symphony Orchestra, and hosting a syndicated radio show based at Chicago's WNUA. His album *Appassionata,* released on the Narada label in late 1999, revealed that Lewis's taste for crossing musical boundaries remained undiminished. The album included arrangements of classical pieces by Fauré, Chopin, and others, an Art Tatum tribute, a gospel medley, and a piece by Lewis's youthful Chess Records compatriot Charles Stepney. The release appeared to signal that Lewis had come closer to the jazz ideal of creative freedom than his critics had initially understood.

In 2003 Lewis released another well-received album with vocalist Wilson, *Simple Pleasures.* That year, Lewis, along with partners Larry Rosen—founder and former president of GRP Records—and Lee Rosenberg formed LRSmedia, a production company devoted to making jazz products in a variety of media. The company's highest profile project was *Legends of Jazz,* a thirteen-part television series that aired in 2006, featuring profiles of many of the greatest jazz artists of all time. In 2005 Lewis formed the Ramsey Lewis Foundation, whose mission was to give disadvantaged youth the opportunity to play musical instruments, especially jazz. As he wrote in a May 10, 2008, column in *Billboard,* "We must find ways to reach into our local communities to expose youth to this music. If not, jazz will continue to be America's classic music, but not popular." In 2007 Lewis was officially designated a Jazz Master by the National Endowment for the Arts, and around that time he donated memorabilia from his illustrious career to the Smithsonian National Museum of American History. If jazz fails to thrive into the next generation, it will not be due to a lack of effort from Ramsey Lewis.

Selected discography

Ramsey Lewis and His Gentlemen of Swing, Argo, 1956.
Lem Winchester and the Ramsey Lewis Trio, Argo, 1958.
An Hour with the Ramsey Lewis Trio, Cadet, 1959.
Stretchin' Out, Cadet, 1960.
Never on Sunday, Cadet, 1961.
Country Meets the Blues, Argo, 1962.
Bach to the Blues, Cadet, 1964.
The In Crowd (live), Chess, 1965.
Wade in the Water (live), Jazz Time, 1966.
Goin' Latin, Cadet, 1967.
Up Pops Ramsey, Cadet, 1968.
Them Changes, Cadet, 1970.
Back to the Roots, Cadet, 1971.
Upendo Ni Pamoja, CBS, 1972.
Funky Serenity, Columbia, 1973.
Groover, Cadet, 1974.
Don't It Feel Good, Columbia, 1975.
Salongo, CBS, 1976.
Love Notes, CBS, 1977.
Ramsey, CBS, 1979.
Solar Wind, Columbia, 1980.
Live at the Savoy, Columbia, 1981.
Chance Encounter, Columbia, 1982.
Les Fleurs, CBS, 1983.
(With Nancy Wilson) *The Two of Us,* Columbia, 1984.
Keys to the City, Columbia, 1987.
A Classic Encounter, Columbia, 1988.
Urban Renewal, Columbia, 1989.
Fantasy, Columbia, 1991.
Ivory Pyramid, GRP, 1992.
Sky Islands, GRP, 1993.
Between the Keys, GRP, 1995.
Dance of the Soul, GRP, 1997.
In Person: 1960–1967 (live), GRP, 1998.
Appassionata, Narada, 1999.
(With Nancy Wilson) *Meant to Be,* Narada, 2002.
20th Century Masters—The Millennium, Chess, 2002.
Urban Knights V, Narada, 2003.

(With Nancy Wilson) *Simple Pleasures,* Narada, 2003.
Time Flies, Narada, 2004.
Urban Knights VI, Narada, 2005.
With One Voice (live), Narada, 2005.
Mother Nature's Son (original recording remastered), Verve, 2007.

Sources

Books

Kernfeld, Barry, editor, *The New Grove Dictionary of Jazz,* Macmillan, 1988.

Periodicals

Billboard, February 12, 1994, p. 19; May 10, 2008, p. 6.
Chicago Sun-Times, June 7, 1998.
Chicago Tribune, February 4, 2007.
Down Beat, February 2000, p. 40; April 2002, p. 60.

Ebony, October 2005, p. 24.
Jet, April 21, 2008, p. 36.
Los Angeles Times, September 24, 1987; January 13, 1997, p. F10.
St. Petersburg Times (*Clearwater Times* edition), October 16, 1991, p. X15.

Online

"Biography" by Scott Janow and album review by Matthew Greenwald, allmusic, http://www.allmusic.com (accessed August 17, 2008).
"Ramsey Lewis," All about Jazz, http://www.allaboutjazz.com/ramseylewis (accessed August 17, 2008).
"Ramsey Lewis Biography," Legends of Jazz with Ramsey Lewis, http://www.legendsofjazz.net/ramseylewis/ (accessed August 17, 2008).
Ramsey Lewis Official Web Site, http://www.ramseylewis.com/ (accessed August 17, 2008).

—James M. Manheim and Bob Jacobson

Marcus Mabry

1967—

Journalist, author

Marcus Mabry is an award-winning journalist and author who recounted his own life story in a 1995 memoir, *White Bucks and Black-Eyed Peas: Growing Up Black in White America.* Twelve years later he profiled then–U.S. Secretary of State Condoleezza Rice in *Twice as Good: Condoleezza Rice and Her Path to Power.* That 2007 biography "works hard to solve the Rice puzzle," noted reviewer Jonathan Freedland in the *New York Times.* "Mabry, himself African-American and sharply alive to even the subtlest distinctions between different black experiences, shows that Rice inherited her father's view of racism: don't deny it, but don't be defined by it."

Mabry was born in 1967 and raised in Trenton, New Jersey, on the edge of the city's predominantly white suburbs. In *White Bucks and Black-Eyed Peas* he chronicled some of those earliest years, when he and his brother were part of a single-parent household led by his maternal grandmother. In addition to himself, his brother, his mother, and his grandmother, two uncles lived there, and "when the gaggle was at home," he wrote, "my grandmother's house brooded with potential conflict…. The underlying theme was always the same: my mother hated having to leave us with her relatives while she worked." He recounted how frequent disagreements between his mother and grandmother usually escalated into shouting matches, and sometimes his mother even took him and his brother to stay at a nearby motel. "It was worse if we had nowhere to go," he wrote. "Then, my mother and my grandmother would yell from one floor to the other for what felt like hours, going to the stairwell to vent their rage."

In that house the most important material possessions in Mabry's young mind were the family's pair of encyclopedia sets—1968 editions of the *World Book* and the *Encyclopedia Britannica,* which he read in his expansive spare time and which instilled in him a deep curiosity about the world beyond Trenton. As a teen, his grades won him a scholarship to the Lawrenceville School, an elite private academy in New Jersey. Though he was not the only African-American student there, he appreciated that most of his classmates had come from a very different world than his own, one marked by privilege and ease. As his memoir recounts, he began to feel divided between the two cultures, but confessed, "I was more comfortable in the White world. It demanded less role-playing of me, so I chose it."

Mabry went on to earn two undergraduate degrees from another prestigious school, Stanford University in Palo Alto, California. The first was in English and French literature, and the second in international relations; he also earned a master's degree in English, studied in Paris at the famed Sorbonne, and landed a nine-month Edward R. Murrow fellowship at the Council on Foreign Relations. His career in journalism included internships at the *Trentonian,* the *Boston Globe,* and *Newsweek,* and he began full time at *Newsweek* in 1989 as an associate editor. In 1991 he became the weekly magazine's Washington correspondent for the U.S. State Department and the Depart-

At a Glance . . .

Born in 1967; raised in Trenton, NJ. *Education:* Stanford University, BA, English and French literature, BA, international relations, MA, English (with distinction); also studied at the Sorbonne, Paris.

Career: *Newsweek,* associate editor, 1989–91, Washington correspondent, 1991–93, Paris correspondent, 1993–96, Johannesburg, South Africa, correspondent, February of 1996–July of 1996, Johannesburg bureau chief, after July of 1996, senior editor and chief of correspondents, until 2007; *New York Times,* editor of Business Day section, 2007—.

Awards: Edward R. Murrow Press Fellowship, Council on Foreign Relations; Morton Frank Award for best business reporting (with Bill Powell), Overseas Press Club, 1996, for the *Newsweek* story "End of the Good Life?"

Addresses: *Agent*—Charlotte Sheedy Literary, 65 Bleecker St., Fl. 12, New York, NY 10012. *Office*—New York Times, 620 Eighth Ave., New York, NY 10018.

ment of Labor, and two years later was sent to Paris as one of *Newsweek*'s European correspondents. Mabry wrote several notable cover stories during this period, including "The Glory That Was France" in 1994, which examined the changing French national identity. In 1995 another cover story, "End of the Good Life?," looked at Western Europe's worsening economic climate and the subsequent cutbacks in the once-generous social-benefit programs that had been hallmarks of French, German, and Dutch life since the end of World War II. That latter story, written with Bill Powell, won Mabry and his colleague the 1996 Morton Frank Award for best business reporting from the Overseas Press Club.

Mabry's autobiography was published during this period of his life. A year after it appeared, he moved on to Johannesburg, South Africa, as *Newsweek*'s correspondent there, and was soon promoted to bureau chief. That job took him all over the African continent, and he reported stories on the AIDS crisis, the retirement of South African President Nelson Mandela, turmoil in Sierra Leone, Nigeria, and Zaire, and the bombings of the U.S. embassies in Nairobi, Kenya, Dar es Salaam, and Tanzania by Islamic fundamentalists. In June of 2007 he left *Newsweek* for the *New York*

Times, where he became an editor of its Business Day section.

Mabry's biography of Condoleezza Rice was published by Modern Times/Rodale that same year. Mabry had known Rice from his time at Stanford in the 1980s, when Rice taught political science and courses on Soviet studies, which was Mabry's field of specialty as an international-relations student. *Twice as Good* recounts Rice's childhood in Birmingham, Alabama, during the civil rights turmoil and takes its title from an oft-repeated saying in her household when she was growing up—that African Americans needed to be "twice as good as whites" in order to succeed in the world. Rice appeared to have followed that dictum closely, first training as a classical pianist but then earning her doctorate in political science by the age of twenty-six and making her name among foreign-policy operatives in Washington, DC. She left her post as provost of Stanford—an executive position responsible for the school's financial and academic affairs—to become national security advisor in the first administration of President George W. Bush in 2000. In 2005 she became secretary of state during Bush's second term in office. Both positions meant that Rice was one of the most influential figures in the lead-up to the 2003 invasion of Iraq. "Mabry dwells at length on ... Rice's inability to admit to error," noted a reviewer for the *Economist.* "The book presents abundant evidence of the warnings repeatedly sent to her by the CIA (one of the agency's untrumpeted successes) and of her failure to take them seriously."

Mabry's bylines appear less frequently in his new post as a *New York Times* business-desk editor. The paper, however, does offer its journalists the opportunity to publish longer op-ed pieces in its Sunday "Week in Review" section. In June of 2008 Mabry wrote about the phenomenon of presumptive Democratic presidential nominee Barack Obama in an article headlined "Color Test: Where Whites Draw the Line." In it he examined the Illinois senator's popularity with white and Hispanic voters, and noted that "social observers say a common hallmark of African-Americans who have achieved the greatest success, whether in business, entertainment or politics—Oprah Winfrey, Magic Johnson and Mr. Obama—is that they do not convey a sense of black grievance." Mabry saw another aspect of Obama's appeal, too, in the fact that the candidate "is genuinely of a different place and time than the generation of black leaders forged in the civil rights struggle." Observed Mabry, "His story is, in part, an immigrant's story, devoid of the particular wounds that descendants of American slaves carry."

Selected works

White Bucks and Black-Eyed Peas: Growing Up Black in White America (memoir), Scribner's, 1995.

Twice as Good: Condoleezza Rice and Her Path to Power (biography), Modern Times/Rodale, 2007.

Sources

Books

Mabry, Marcus, *White Bucks and Black-Eyed Peas: Growing Up Black in White America,* Scribner's, 1995.

Periodicals

Black Collegian, October 1995.
Economist, August 18, 2007, p. 73.
New York Times, July 1, 2007, p. 21; June 8, 2008.
Newsweek, May 7, 2007, p. 42.

Online

"Marcus Mabry, Senior Editor, Newsweek International," MSNBC, http://www.msnbc.com/m/nw/nwinfo_mabry.asp (accessed August 25, 2008).

—Carol Brennan

Julianne Malveaux

1953—

Economist, writer, activist

Julianne Malveaux is a highly respected economist whose works explore some of the most complex issues facing American culture. She has appeared often on radio and television to discuss public policy, labor issues, gender and race relations, and the economy. Known as something of a firebrand, Malveaux has on more than one occasion courted controversy while getting her point across. Following the events of September 11, 2001, and the U.S. invasion of Iraq, Malveaux began exploring more deeply the role of minorities in an imperial nation. In 2005 she took part in the Millions More Movement—along with other black American luminaries, including filmmaker Spike Lee, Nation of Islam leader Louis Farrakhan, and hip-hop music producer Russell Simmons—to commemorate the tenth anniversary of the Million Man March and bring awareness to continuing high rates of poverty among African Americans. In 2007 her career took an unexpected turn when she was offered, and accepted, the position of president of Bennett College for Women in Greensboro, North Carolina.

Malveaux was born September 22, 1953, in San Francisco, California, the oldest of five children of Paul Warren Malveaux, a real estate agent, and Proteone Alexandria Malveaux, a social worker. Malveaux began writing poetry at age sixteen, and her first works were published in the late 1960s in the *Journal of Black Poetry*. After earning bachelor's and master's degrees in economics from Boston College, Malveaux earned a doctorate in the field from Massachusetts Institute of Technology in 1980. She remained in academia, teaching economics, public policy, and African-

American studies at the New School for Social Research in New York City, San Francisco State University, and the University of California at Berkeley.

Malveaux began writing a weekly column for the *San Francisco Sun Reporter* in 1981. The column was syndicated by King Features, and she regularly contributed to *Essence, Ms. Magazine,* and *USA Today,* as well as other newspapers and journals. She hosted *Julianne Malveaux's Capitol Report,* a weekly radio show in New York City, and has been a commentator on such television talk shows as PBS's *To the Contrary* and *Lehrer News Hour,* as well as on CNN, MSNBC, C-SPAN, Fox News, and CNBC. As president and chief executive officer of Last Word Productions, a multimedia production company, Malveaux produced public affairs radio and television programs both nationally and in Washington, DC.

Sex, Lies, and Stereotypes: Perspectives of a Mad Economist, the first of Malveaux's two "Mad Economist" books, was published in 1994. The volume presents a collection of Malveaux's columns investigating the relationships between sex, politics, economics, and race. What set Malveaux's writing apart was her use of real people and real situations to illustrate her criticisms. When she argued that the failure of inner-city schools is the fault of misappropriated fiscal priorities, Malveaux told the story of her own friend, a teacher, who was burned out by a low salary, job instability, and disinterested students. Malveaux tackled such issues as homelessness, NAFTA, conservatism, welfare reform, and multicultural programs. Her ap-

At a Glance . . .

Born Julianne Marie Malveaux on September 22, 1953, in San Francisco, CA; daughter of Paul Warren Malveaux (a real estate agent) and Proteone Alexandria Malveaux (a social worker). *Education:* Boston College, BA, 1974, MA, 1975; Massachusetts Institute of Technology, PhD, 1980.

Career: WFAA-TV, media intern, summer, 1975; White House Council of Economic Advisers, junior staff economist, 1977–78; Rockefeller Foundation, research fellow, 1978–80; New School for Social Research, assistant professor of economics, 1980–81; *San Francisco Sun Reporter,* columnist, 1981–; San Francisco State University, assistant professor of economics, 1981–85; University of California, Berkeley, research associate, 1985–, also visiting professor; president and CEO, Last Word Productions; president, Bennett College for Women, 2007–. Contributor of articles to newspapers and magazines, including and *Black Enterprise, Essence, Ms. Magazine, USA Today,* and *Working Woman.*

Memberships: Board of directors of the Economic Policy Institute, the Recreation Wish List Committee, and the Liberian Education Trust.

Awards: Honorary degrees from Sojourner Douglas College, Baltimore, MD, and Benedict College, Columbia, SC.

Addresses: *Office*—President's Office, Bennett College for Women, 900 East Washington St., Greensboro, NC 27401.

proach to social problems ranging from AIDS to recycling to racial solidarity was from a primarily economic perspective.

Reviewing *Sex, Lies, and Stereotypes* in the *Progressive,* Mary A. Kane noted that Malveaux can be absolutely unpredictable when she takes a stance on an issue. "Woe unto those who get their exercise leaping to conclusions about where Malveaux will come down on an issue," the critic wrote. Malveaux criticized both conservatives and liberals for their lack of understanding that "the real issue is economics": "Too many analysts are caught in the sex, lies, and stereotypes of the media to make public policy."

In 1999 the stock market was high and unemployment was at an all-time low in the United States, but Malveaux was keenly aware that there were still economic losers within the flush economy. In her second collection of columns, those published from 1994 to 1998, titled *Wall Street, Main Street, and the Side Street: A Mad Economist Takes a Stroll,* Malveaux explored the status of women and people of color in foreign policy and in the workplace. In the introduction to the book she wrote, "Some days I want to scream at … the way the rich get richer, the poor, poorer, and the rest of us more complacent." In *Essence* critic Martha Southgate commented that Malveaux "tells it like she sees it" and encourages readers to "think hard about those who have and those who don't."

On occasion Malveaux's views have elicited vehement reactions from political conservatives. When eventual Supreme Court Justice Clarence Thomas was accused of sexual harassment by Anita Hill, Malveaux outraged his supporters by calling him "an absolutely reprehensible person" on a PBS talk show in 1994 and maintaining that she hoped his wife's cooking would lead him to have a diet-induced heart attack. A decade later, in 2005, Malveaux again drew the scorn of the political right when she declared on a politically themed radio program that, regarding the U.S. war in Iraq and accusations of abuse at the Guantanamo Bay prisoner of war camp, the United States is a "terrorist nation" and said of President George W. Bush, "He is a terrorist. He is evil. He is arrogant. And he is out of control."

Some observers were surprised when, in 2007, Malveaux accepted an offer to serve as president of Bennett College for Women, taking over for the departing Dr. Johnnetta Cole, who is credited with bringing the college back into financial solvency after some precarious financial times. Malveaux's lack of administrative experience was considered by some to be a drawback despite her strong background in economics, but Howard University department of economics chair William Spriggs noted, "I think that because she comes from a different background she will approach [the presidency] with a 'let's get it done' attitude. She won't have the patience to do things at a slower pace, and I think this is a plus."

While she is both an analyst and commentator on the issue of economics and how it is affected by gender and race, Malveaux is also an activist who passionately desires change. "Not only is the pace of social change exceedingly slow, but the backlash in terms of the new racism, sexism, and classism are incredibly frustrating," she told *Contemporary Authors.* Because of her impatience with the status quo, Malveaux has been involved with numerous social, civic, and economics groups as a board member and lecturer. As of mid-2008 she had given up the presidency of the multimedia company she founded, Last Word Productions, and was developing a public affairs program for PBS.

Selected writings

Books

(With Phyllis A. Wallace and Linda P. Datcher) *Black Women in the Labor Force,* MIT Press, 1980.

(Coeditor with Margaret Simms) *Slipping through the Cracks: The Status of Black Women,* Transaction Books, 1986.

Sex, Lies, and Stereotypes: Perspectives of a Mad Economist, Pines Ones, 1994.

Wall Street, Main Street, and the Side Street: A Mad Economist Takes a Stroll, Pines Ones, 1999.

(With Deborah Perry) *Unfinished Business: A Democrat and a Republican Take on the 10 Most Important Issues Women Face,* Penguin, 2002.

(Coeditor with Reginna Green) *The Paradox of Loyalty: An African American Response to the War on Terrorism,* Third World Press, 2002.

(Contributor) *Race and Resistance: African Americans in the Twenty-First Century,* South End Press, 2002.

(Contributor) *When Race Becomes Real: Black and White Writers Confront Their Personal Histories,* Chicago Review Press, 2002.

Sources

Books

Malveaux, Julianne, *Wall Street, Main Street, and the Side Street: A Mad Economist Takes a Stroll,* Pines Ones, 1999.

Periodicals

Black Enterprise, April 6, 2007.
Essence, August 1999, p. 66.
Diverse: Issues in Higher Education, March 26, 2007.
Publishers Weekly, August 8, 1994, p. 418.
Progressive, October 1994, p. 52.

Online

Contemporary Authors Online, The Gale Group, 2001 (accessed September 29, 2008).
Dr. Julianne Malveaux, http://www.juliannemalveaux.com (accessed September 29, 2008).
Malveaux Report, http://www.themalveauxreport.com (accessed September 29, 2008).

—Brenna Sanchez and Nancy Dziedzic

Rita Marley

1947—

Reggae artist, record producer, philanthropist

Perhaps best known as the widow of reggae legend Bob Marley and often called the "Queen of Reggae," Rita Marley has spent time and energy as the guardian of her late husband's estate and musical legacy, and, more important, as the keeper of the flame of his ideas. But her role in the history of Jamaican music has not been limited to her relationship with Bob Marley. In the mostly male-dominated field of reggae, she was a solo act of note before she ever joined with her husband musically, and she emerged as a successful artist on her own

Marley, Rita, photograph. Bruno Vincent/Getty Images.

after his death. Moreover, as part of Bob Marley's backing trio of female vocalists, the I-Threes, Rita Marley was an important contributor to the music that made her husband famous worldwide. She has also emerged as an important booster of economic development and self-sufficiency in her adopted home country of Ghana.

Rita Marley was born Alpharita Constantia Anderson in Cuba in 1947. Growing up poor, she was raised in the Trenchtown neighborhood of Kingston, Jamaica, which spawned the careers of many of the musicians who created a rhythmically complex, spiritually inclined

new music called reggae. Three of those musicians, who had formed a trio called the Wailers, often passed by the metal shack where Rita was living with her aunt and small child. The Wailers consisted of Bob Marley, Peter Tosh, and Bunny Wailer; they were among the first acts to record at the influential studio of producer Coxsone Dodd. Bob Marley, already a standout talent, made a special impact. "I remember how I would scream to hear his songs on the radio," Rita Marley told *Interview*.

Received Proposal on Paper

An aspiring singer herself, Rita asked the group to set up an audition with Dodd for her. The eighteen-year-old singer succeeded at the audition and was joined with two other young women in a trio called the Soulettes, with Bob Marley as their producer. The Soulettes scored several hits under Bob's leadership, and what was at first a purely professional relationship took a new turn one day when Wailer delivered to Rita a handwritten love note from Bob. The two married in 1966. Rita Marley had a solo hit of her own, "Pied

At a Glance . . .

Born Alpharita Constantia Anderson in 1947 in Cuba; married Robert Nesta (Bob) Marley (a singer), 1966 (deceased 1981); children: Sharon, Cedella, David (Ziggy), Stephen, Stephanie, and Serita. *Religion:* Rastafarian.

Career: Began performing, mid-1960s; joined trio, the Soulettes, and recorded with Bob Marley as producer; performed in Bob Marley's backing trio, the I-Threes, 1970s; solo artist, 1981—; chair of Bob Marley Foundation and curator of Bob Marley Museum, Kingston, Jamaica; founded Rita Marley Foundation, 1998; produced albums by Ziggy Marley and her other children and other artists; involved in operations of Marley family–owned Tuff Gong record label.

Awards: Personality of the Year in Ghana, 2004.

Addresses: *Home*—Ghana. *Office*—Rita Marley Foundation, PO Box 34, Aburi-Akwapim, Ghana.

Piper," and also sang backup on some of the Wailers' early recordings.

Marley influenced her husband in what became the central spiritual tenet of his music—the Jamaican variant of Christianity known as Rastafarianism. It was she who turned out for a personal appearance by Ethiopian emperor Haile Selassie—thought by Rastafarians to be the returned Jesus Christ—and noticed marks on his hands that she believed were the nail scars left by Christ's crucifixion. Marley, a former Sunday school teacher, converted to Rastafarianism and induced her husband to do the same. One of the recordings that would really launch his fame as a solo artist and bandleader in the early 1970s was "Jah Live," an anthem written after Selassie's death.

For that record, Bob Marley assembled another backing trio, dubbed the I-Threes and consisting of Rita Marley, Judy Mowatt, and Marcia Griffiths—all of whom would go on to important solo careers. The I-Threes evolved into a fundamental component of the reconstituted Bob Marley and the Wailers, which over the course of the 1970s forged an internationally popular music that featured a language of its own that expressed Rastafarian concepts; a distinctive look featuring the twined strands of hair known as dreadlocks; and a political side that looked to the eventual overthrow of the white elites who ruled the peoples of the African diaspora.

Wounded at Home by Gunmen

With Bob Marley and the Wailers, Rita Marley and the I-Threes toured the world, appearing as far afield as newly independent Zimbabwe. In 1976 the Marleys became victims of Jamaica's notoriously violent political culture; they were shot in their home by gunmen two days before performing a benefit concert for a socialist-oriented political party. Wounded, both still performed—Rita in her hospital gown. The I-Threes also appeared on their own, and Rita Marley was making plans to release a solo album when Bob Marley died of brain cancer in 1981, at the age of thirty-six.

After her husband's death, Marley went ahead with plans to release the album, *Who Feels It Knows It.* Far from being a funeral dirge lamenting Bob's death, the album showcased Rita's musical personality. It contained a comic piece about marijuana, "One Draw," which was banned by radio stations due to a passage in which a schoolteacher instructs her students in the enjoyment of the drug.

The controversy fueled sales of the album, and Marley went on to record two more successful albums in the 1980s, released in the United States on the roots-oriented Shanachie label. The 1990 album *We Must Carry On,* which included several previously unknown Bob Marley compositions, was nominated for a Grammy Award. She also contributed backup vocals to albums by other artists ranging from West African reggae star Alpha Blondy to Haitian-American rapper Wyclef Jean.

Rights to Estate Contested

Much of Marley's energy in the 1980s, however, was devoted to the care of her husband's legacy in various ways. Bob Marley died without a will, and associates from several phases of his career came out of the woodwork to contest the Marley family's rights to his estate, valued in the tens of millions of dollars. The resulting litigation went all the way to the Jamaican Supreme Court, which ruled in Rita Marley's favor in 1991. Legal activity continued through the 1990s, however. Marley produced several albums by her son Ziggy Marley and his band, the Melody Makers, and worked successfully to promote the group's career.

She also cared for her husband's other ten children, several of which he had fathered with other women. In 1998 Marley established the Rita Marley Foundation as a sister organization of the Bob Marley Foundation. Both foundations served as the bases for Marley's work to help residents of impoverished areas become more self-sufficient. A few years later Marley moved to Ghana, where she both lives and runs her foundation, as well as a studio outpost of the Marley family's Jamaica-based Tuff Gong empire of recording and production operations. There, through her foundation, she has distributed vaccinations, furnished schools, helped develop community agricultural projects, and delivered needed household goods to remote villages. Meanwhile, she has continued to record and tour extensively, releasing several albums during the first decade of the twenty-first century, and producing albums for other musicians, mostly her own children. In 2004 Marley published a memoir, cowritten with Hettie Jones, called *No Woman No Cry: My Life with Bob Marley.* The book recounted in wrenching detail the story of their relationship, from the streets of Trenchtown to the heights of international stardom.

In 2008 two different movie projects focusing on the life of Bob Marley were launched. Early in the year acclaimed director Martin Scorsese announced plans to make a documentary about Marley, to be coproduced by Tuff Gong, with Rita's blessing. Just a couple months later producer Harvey Weinstein announced that he would produce a film version of Rita Marley's book, *No Woman No Cry,* with Marley as executive producer. Marley expressed her hope that she would be played by award-winning singer/rapper Lauryn Hill in the movie adaptation. The appearance so close together of two competing movies sparked conflict over the rights to use Bob Marley's music, which the Marley family had historically refused to license. Initially, the family refused to license the music to Weinstein, even though Rita was named as an executive producer on the project. The problem was that the family had already granted rights to Scorsese, and they saw the Weinstein film, which was likely to hit the theaters around the same time, as a threat to the Scorsese documentary, in which they were already invested. In May of 2008 Scorsese withdrew from the Marley project and was replaced by fellow award-winning director Jonathan Demme. As of late 2008 neither the Weinstein movie nor the Demme documentary had progressed significantly.

Regardless of what Marley accomplishes during her life, in either the musical or philanthropic realm, her name will always be most closely tied to the work of her late husband, who she concedes had a profound influence in making her the person she has become. Marley is head of the Bob Marley Foundation in Kingston, which operates a museum devoted to the singer's life and work. "He was a good boy, still is, and that's why we have to carry on his mission," Marley explained to the *Guardian* of her work with the foundation. "He was a father figure for me," she continued. "He saved me from being somebody else. I could have been prime minister, I could have been a prostitute on the streets, but I am what I am and Bob has a lot to do with that."

Selected works

Books

(With Hettie Jones) *No Woman No Cry: My Life with Bob Marley,* Hyperion, 2004.

Albums

Who Feels It Knows It, Shanachie, 1981.
Harambe, Shanachie, 1983.
We Must Carry On, Shanachie, 1990.
One Draw: The Best of Rita Marley, Varese Sarabande, 2002.
Sings Bob Marley ... and Friends, Shanachie, 2003.
Sunshine after Rain, Snapper, 2003.
Play Play, Universal International, 2004.
Live in San Francisco, 2B1, 2008.

Sources

Books

Marley, Rita, with Hettie Jones, *No Woman No Cry: My Life with Bob Marley,* Hyperion, 2004.

Periodicals

Billboard, July 6, 1991, p. 8; November 28, 1992, p. 10; March 4, 2008.
Daily News (South Africa), March 7, 2008, p. 10.
Guardian (London), October 30, 1996, p. 13; August 2, 2000, p. 4.
Hollywood Reporter, March 21, 2008, p. 1.
Interview, January 1995, p. 88.
Milwaukee Journal-Sentinel, January 22, 1999.
People, November 19, 1984, p. 221.
Plain Dealer (Cleveland, Ohio), October 20, 2001, p. E1.
Relix, October 25, 2004.
Sunday Tribune (South Africa), February 4, 2007, p. 6.

Online

"Competing Bob Marley Films Fight Over Music Rights," CBCnews, March 23, 2008, http://www.cbc.ca/arts/music/story/2008/03/23/marley-biopic-documentary.html?ref=rss (accessed August 19, 2008).
"The Queen of Reggae," Rita Marley Foundation, http://ritamarleyfoundation.org/about_rita.html (accessed August 19, 2008).
"Rita Marley," allmusic, http://www.allmusic.com/cg/amg.dll (accessed August 19, 2008).
"Rita Marley: A Philanthropist and a Patriot," Public Agenda, February 3, 2006, http://www.ghanaweb.com/public_agenda/article.php?ID=4805 (accessed August 19, 2008).
"The Weinstein Company Acquires Rights to Produce the First Ever Feature Film about Legendary Musician Bob Marley" (Weinstein Company news release), Reuters, March 4, 2008, http://www.reuters.com/article/pressRelease/idUS176364+04-Mar-2008+PRN20080304 (accessed August 19, 2008).

—James M. Manheim and Bob Jacobson

Crystal McCrary Anthony

1969—

Writer, producer, lawyer

McCrary Anthony, Crystal, photograph. Paul Hawthorne/Getty Images.

Crystal McCrary Anthony is no stranger to the high life. During the 1990s, as an up-and-coming entertainment lawyer and wife of National Basketball Association (NBA) star Greg Anthony, she became part of a circle of affluent, influential, upper-crust African Americans living in New York City. Now, after splitting from her celebrity husband, she stands on her own in that world, having left behind a career in law to become a best-selling author twice over and a high-powered television and film producer. In her novels *Homecourt Advantage* (1998) and *Gotham Diaries* (2004), she takes aim at the very social milieu she is a part of, satirizing the glamorous and gaudy lives of basketball wives, back-stabbing socialites, and business tycoons, all the while leaving readers wondering how much is fact and how much is fiction. Leveraging the success of her books, she has gone on to launch yet another career as a television personality and producer, becoming a key player in the entertainment world.

Crystal McCrary was born in October of 1969 in Detroit, Michigan. After attending the University of Michigan and earning a bachelor's degree in English in 1991, her next move seemed clear: She would go on to law school. "There are 10 lawyers in my family," she told *Crain's New York Business* in 2007. "I always knew law was an option." After a stint at American University in Washington, DC, she moved to New York City to attend the New York University School of Law, completing her degree in 1995.

Wrote Draft of Novel While Lawyer

McCrary Anthony began her career as an associate in the New York firm Paul, Weiss, Rifkind, Wharton & Garrison, where she practiced entertainment law, representing authors, playwrights, and directors—Andrew Lloyd Webber was a notable client—in their contract negotiations. But she harbored much more creative ambitions, she told *Crain's,* keeping a draft of an unfinished novel in her desk, working on it in her spare time but telling no one. In 1997 she made the leap and quit her job as an attorney to focus on writing full time.

For her first effort, she teamed up with best friend and fellow NBA wife Rita Ewing, who was then married to New York Knicks center Patrick Ewing, to write *Home-*

At a Glance . . .

Born Crystal McCrary in Detroit, MI, in October of 1969; married Greg Anthony (a sports commentator and former basketball player; divorced); children: Cole, Ella. *Education:* University of Michigan, BA, English, 1991; New York University School of Law, JD, 1995; studied international law at Tulane University and European Community law in Paris.

Career: Paul, Weiss, Rifkind, Wharton & Garrison LLP, entertainment attorney, 1995–97; author of books; legal analyst for Fox News Channel, CNBC, and Court TV; commentator for CNN's *American Morning;* guest host for *The View;* partnered with BET J network on various projects; television and film executive producer.

Memberships: JumpStart, advisory board; New 42nd Street, board of directors; Hyperion Books, Voice Imprint, advisory board.

Awards: Blackboard Fiction Book of the Year, 2005, for *Gotham Diaries;* chosen as one of *Crain's New York Business*'s 40 under 40, 2007.

Addresses: *Office*—c/o BET, 1235 W St. NE, Washington, DC 20018-1101. *Publisher*—c/o Hyperion Books, 77 W. 66th St., 11th Fl., New York, NY 10023-6201. *Web*—http://www.crystalmccraryanthony.com.

court Advantage, a racy novel that lays bare the lives of the fictional "New York Flyers" basketball team and their wives and girlfriends. Writing for the *Washington Post* in 1998, reviewer Kevin Merida described the book as "336 pages of lust and distrust, gossip and innuendo, the trappings of money and the seductions of power. Love and heartache turn in strong performances. So do friendship and betrayal. And, oh yeah, basketball makes a cameo. That's because basketball is just a prop for the narrative, which centers on the dysfunctional off-court lives of multimillionaire athletes and their significant others."

Though some called *Homecourt Advantage* the *Primary Colors* of the basketball world, suggesting it was a thinly veiled exposé of the athletes' lives—the Ewings were then in the midst of a messy and public divorce—McCrary Anthony and Ewing maintained that the work was strictly fiction, with no parallels to real life. The novel became a best seller, perhaps more for its

salaciousness than for its literary merit, and film rights to the book were quickly snapped up.

McCrary Anthony's second work, *Gotham Diaries,* grew out of a collaboration with Tonya Lewis Lee, a lawyer and the wife of filmmaker Spike Lee. With both lawyers seeking a more creative outlet, the two women initially envisioned a television series that would profile upper-class black New Yorkers. When their pitch for the show, however, scheduled for September 12, 2001, was interrupted by the terrorist attacks on the World Trade Center, McCrary Anthony and Lee decided instead to turn their idea into a book.

Once again, McCrary Anthony and her coauthor provide skewering social commentary. The novel centers on Lauren Thomas—the trophy wife of a billionaire who yearns to be so much more—and her backstabbing friends, Tandy, an aging socialite, and Manny, a real estate broker who has moved to New York from Alabama to make it big. *Gotham Diaries* is, McCrary Anthony told the *New York Post* in 2004, "a cautionary tale of coming to New York City and getting chewed up and spit out—and the danger of believing the hype that New York will feed one."

The novel put McCrary Anthony on the best-seller list a second time, but again, readers could not help but wonder how much of the book was really fiction. Reviewer Heidi Singer in the *New York Post* noted, "All that's missing in 'Gotham Diaries' are the real-life boldface names.... A reader can only speculate on whether the flamboyant rapper couple greeted with such distaste by the other characters was based on anyone in real life."

Published in 2004, *Gotham Diaries* contributed to an emerging genre of fiction that some dubbed "black chick-lit"—a sort of African-American answer to such best sellers as *Bergdorf Blondes* and *Sex and the City.* In a 2004 article, Lola Ogunnaike of the *New York Times* described the genre: "Like its white counterpart, black chick-lit often centers on single women with dream jobs, precariously balancing the personal and professional.... Neither racially charged nor didactic, these books seem meant to be read on sandy shores from Sag Harbor to St.-Tropez. The protagonists, educated and decidedly middle to upper class, effortlessly mingle with both black and white characters. Love, not privilege, is the only real speed bump." Sales figures suggested a booming market for such literature.

Parlayed Success into New Career

McCrary Anthony used the success of her two books to channel her career into new ventures in television. She appeared as a legal analyst on the Fox News Channel, CNBC, and Court TV (now truTV) and delivered pop-culture commentary on CNN's *American Morning.* As a guest host on the popular ABC talk show *The View,* she interviewed Senator Hillary Clinton. McCrary Anthony went on to develop a partnership with the BET J (BET Jazz) network, cohosting the program *My Two Cents* and serving as executive producer of *My Model Is Better Than Your Model* (2006), a model reality show, and *Real-Life Divas,* a series profiling prominent African-American women (2006—).

McCrary Anthony made her first foray into Hollywood with the 2007 theatrical release of *Dirty Laundry,* a feature film on which she was an executive producer. When funds for the production fell short, she provided a bridge loan to cover the budget of just under $1 million so that shooting could begin. The film, which deals with homosexuality in African-American families, appealed to McCrary Anthony because of the story's "focus on strong, beautiful, well-rounded black women," she told *Black Enterprise* magazine in 2006. That year the picture took the Best Feature Film Award at the American Black Film Festival.

McCrary Anthony became a member of the advisory board of JumpStart, a national organization that works to increase early childhood literacy in low-income neighborhoods, in 2006. In the fall of that year she joined the Voice Professional Women's Advisory Council for Hyperion Books' Voice imprint, which publishes books focused on women thirty-five and older. In the fall of 2007 McCrary Anthony joined the board of directors of the New 42nd Street, a nonprofit that oversees the redevelopment of historic theaters. In 2008 she resided in New York with her son Cole and daughter Ella.

Selected works

Books

(With Rita Ewing) *Homecourt Advantage,* Avon, 1998.
(With Tonya Lewis Lee) *Gotham Diaries,* Hyperion, 2004.

Television

(Executive producer) *My Model Looks Better Than Your Model,* 2006.
(Executive producer) *Real-Life Divas,* 2006—.
(Cohost) *My Two Cents,* 2006.

Film

(Executive producer) *Dirty Laundry,* 2007.

Sources

Periodicals

Black Enterprise, December 2006.
New York Post, July 6, 2004, p. 33.
New York Times, May 31, 2004.
Washington Post, October 27, 1998.

Online

Crystal McCrary Anthony official Web site, http://www.crystalmccraryanthony.com (accessed July 30, 2008).
"40 Under 40: Crystal McCrary Anthony," *Crain's New York Business,* 2007, http://mycrains.crains newyork.com/40under40/profiles/2007/10003 (accessed July 30, 2008).

—Deborah A. Ring

James Alan McPherson

1943—

Educator, writer, editor

Although the short stories of writer and educator James Alan McPherson often concern African-American characters, the stories transcend racial barriers to confront the universal human problems of ordinary, working-class people. The son of a master electrician and a domestic servant, McPherson was born on September 16, 1943, in the historic port city of Savannah, Georgia, where he attended segregated public schools. As a teenager, he worked as a waiter on passenger trains, an almost exclusively African-American profession that figures prominently in much of his work. The well-known short story "A Solo Song: For Doc" (from his first collection, 1969's *Hue and Cry*), for example, is a character study of two railroad waiters of different generations. McPherson continued to work on the trains of the Great Northern Railroad while attending Morris Brown College, a private, predominately African-American institution in Georgia. In a 1997 interview with Calvin Reid in *Publishers Weekly,* McPherson remembered Morris Brown College with gratitude and affection. "People are surprised that I advanced as far as I have coming from a small private black college," he told Reid. "But I got my start there. I had some teachers who loved literature and they passed that on to me."

After receiving his bachelor's degree from Morris Brown in 1965, McPherson attended Harvard Law School, working as a janitor to support himself. Even while immersed in his law courses, however, he found himself drawn increasingly to writing. In 1968, the same year he received his law degree, he submitted his first manuscript to the *Atlantic Monthly,* a venerable magazine based, like Harvard, in Cambridge, Massa-chusetts. Ed Weeks, the magazine's editor at the time, accepted the submission, a short story titled "Gold Coast," and helped arrange for the publication of McPherson's first book, the short-story collection *Hue and Cry,* which appeared the following year. The *Atlantic Monthly* has continued to play a major role in McPherson's career; he has been a contributing editor there since 1969, and the magazine has been the first publisher of many of the short stories and essays he has written since.

Critics reacted enthusiastically to *Hue and Cry*'s stories, most of which are precisely rendered character studies of African-American workers. Ralph Ellison, for example, whose own character studies of African Americans made him one of the nation's most respected writers, provided a jacket blurb for *Hue and Cry* in which he called McPherson "a writer of insight, sympathy, and humor and one of the most gifted young Americans I've had the privilege to read." *Hue and Cry* also prompted the first of McPherson's many awards, a 1970 Academy Award for literature from the National Institute of Arts and Letters (now known as the American Academy of Arts and Letters). Around the time of the book's publication, McPherson left Massachusetts to study at the University of Iowa's acclaimed Writers' Workshop, the country's oldest and arguably most distinguished creative writing program, which granted him a master's degree in fine arts in 1969. It was also in this period that he began teaching. After serving as an instructor at Iowa (from 1968 to 1969), he moved to the University of California–Santa Cruz, where he lectured in English from 1969 to 1976, taking a leave of absence in his final year to serve as an assistant

At a Glance . . .

Born on September 16, 1943, in Savannah, GA; son of James Allen McPherson (a master electrician) and Mable Smalls McPherson (a domestic servant); married in 1973 (divorced); children: Rachel Alice. *Education:* Morris Brown College, BA, 1965; Harvard Law School, LLB, 1968; University of Iowa, MFA, 1969.

Career: Worked as a waiter on passenger trains, 1960s; University of Iowa, instructor, 1968–69, professor of English, 1981—; University of California–Santa Cruz, lecturer in English, 1969–76; *Atlantic Monthly,* contributing editor, 1969—; Morgan State University, assistant professor of English, 1975–76; University of Virginia, associate professor of English, 1976–81; *Ploughshares,* guest editor, 1985 and 1990.

Awards: Academy Award for literature, National Institute of Arts and Letters (now the American Academy of Arts and Letters), 1970, for *Hue and Cry;* fellowship, Guggenheim Foundation, 1972–73; Pulitzer Prize for fiction, 1978, for *Elbow Room;* fellowship ("genius grant"), MacArthur Foundation, 1981; inducted into the American Academy of Arts and Sciences, 1995.

Addresses: *Office*—c/o Graduate Program in Creative Writing, University of Iowa, 102 Dey House, Iowa City, IA 52242-1408.

professor of English at Baltimore's Morgan State University. From Baltimore, McPherson moved to the University of Virginia, where he held the rank of associate professor from 1976 to 1981. Since 1981 he has been a permanent faculty member of the Writers' Workshop at Iowa, where he holds the rank of full professor.

Helped by a fellowship from the Guggenheim Foundation from 1972 to 1973, McPherson spent much of the first half of the 1970s working on a new collection of stories, which appeared under the title of *Elbow Room* in 1977. Like *Hue and Cry, Elbow Room* is a series of detailed character studies. Unlike the dependable workers featured in the earlier volume, however, *Elbow Room*'s characters, both white and African American, exist on the margins of society. One story, "Elbow Room," for example, features a white draft resister, while another, "The Story of a Dead Man," is a study of an African-American man immersed in violence. *Elbow Room* received the 1978 Pulitzer

Prize for fiction, an award that solidified McPherson's growing reputation as a major new talent. Three years later he would receive yet another prize, one of the so-called genius grants awarded annually by the MacArthur Foundation "to talented individuals," in the words of its Web site, "who have shown extraordinary originality and dedication in their creative pursuits and a marked capacity for self-direction."

Despite this growing recognition, however, the late 1970s and 1980s were a difficult period for McPherson, as he himself has frequently acknowledged. His marriage in 1973 produced a daughter but ended in divorce, and he had increasing trouble with depression and writer's block. Though he continued to teach and to publish individual essays, he would not publish another book for more than twenty years. The volume that broke that silence, 1998's *Crabcakes,* was therefore a personal triumph; it was also a commercial and critical success. An impressionistic, often fragmentary memoir, *Crabcakes,* in the words of Lorenzo Thomas in the *Houston Chronicle,* "re-creates the chaotic quality of memory. The taste of Maryland crabcakes, an old friend's special chair, the timbre of an impatient clerk's or customer's voice all assume symbolic overtones." Thomas concluded that the book was "an unusual—and engaging—virtuoso performance."

McPherson's literary output has increased somewhat since the publication of *Crabcakes.* An essay collection titled *A Region Not Home: Reflections from Exile* appeared in 1999. Less fragmentary than *Crabcakes, A Region Not Home* combines the autobiographical focus of the earlier volume with ruminations on suicide, homelessness, and other social problems. Mary Carroll in *Booklist* noted that this approach yielded "flashes of unexpected insight." Other publications by McPherson include several volumes he edited or coedited, notably two issues in 1985 and 1990 of *Ploughshares,* an influential literary journal, and an essay collection titled *Fathering Daughters: Reflections by Men* in 1998, with DeWitt Henry. While he is generally reticent about work in progress, McPherson has expressed interest in writing what he described to Reid in *Publishers Weekly* as "an experimental novel."

Selected writings

Short-story collections

Hue and Cry (includes "A Solo Song: For Doc"), Little, Brown, 1969.
Elbow Room (includes "Elbow Room" and "The Story of a Dead Man"), Little, Brown, 1977.

Edited works

(With Miller Williams) *Railroad: Trains and Train People in American Culture,* Random House, 1976.
(With DeWitt Henry) *Fathering Daughters: Reflections by Men,* Beacon Press, 1998.

Essay collections

Crabcakes, Simon and Schuster, 1998.
A Region Not Home: Reflections from Exile, Simon and Schuster, 1999.

Sources

Periodicals

Booklist, February 15, 2000.
Houston Chronicle, March 29, 1998.
Publishers Weekly, December 15, 1997.

Online

"James Alan McPherson: Contributor Profile," *Atlantic Online,* 1996, http://www.theatlantic.com/unbound/mcpherso/jambio.htm (accessed July 23, 2008).

"The Kelly Writers House Fellows Program: James Alan McPherson," University of Pennsylvania, April 19–20, 2004, http://writing.upenn.edu/~whfellow/mcpherson.html (accessed July 23, 2008).

—R. Anthony Kugler

Walter Dean Myers

1937—

Writer

Walter Dean Myers is one of the best-known African-American writers of children's and young adult literature. Since the late 1960s, Myers has published dozens of books for young readers seeking realistic stories and recognizable characters. In the pages of his books Myers has tackled such pressing issues as teen pregnancy, crime, imprisonment, drug abuse, school shootings, and gang violence, as well as the ties of family and friendship that exist in black communities. He also frequently addresses historical topics in both fiction and nonfiction books and has written many biographies of notable black Americans. He often collaborates with his son, Christopher Myers, a respected illustrator, and has received numerous awards and honors, including the Coretta Scott King Award. Carmen Subryan noted in the *Dictionary of Literary Biography*: "Whether he is writing about the ghettos of New York, the remote countries of Africa, or social institutions, Myers captures the essence of the developing experiences of youth."

Raised by Foster Parents

Myers was born in Martinsburg, West Virginia, in 1937. Before he turned three years old, his mother died, leaving the family in chaos. Caring for his many children with no mother and little income, Myers's father placed the boy with his first wife and her new husband. With his foster parents, Herbert and Florence Dean, and their biological children, Myers moved to Harlem. His teachers recognized his intelligence and his foster parents encouraged him to read and write—

although Herbert Dean was himself illiterate—but Myers was stigmatized because of a speech impediment. Many years later, in an interview with Juan Williams on National Public Radio, Myers admitted that he had carried another burden as a child: his foster mother's alcoholism. These factors led the young Myers to neglect his studies and get into trouble often.

Although he knew early on that he had a talent for writing poems and stories, Myers was convinced that professional writing was for those from an elite white background. "I was from a family of laborers, and the idea of writing stories or essays was far removed from their experience," Myers clarified in *Something about the Author Autobiography Series.* "Writing had no practical value for a black child… . Minor victories did not bolster my ego. Instead they convinced me that even though I might have some talent, I was still defined by factors other than my ability." Myers was classified as a "bright" student in school and was steered toward college-preparation courses. He won several awards—including a set of encyclopedias—for his essays and poetry, but, as he recounted in his 2001 memoir *Bad Boy,* he was torn between a hypermasculine drive to prove himself on the street and a more private, and, he felt, embarrassing, urge toward "book-smarts."

Although he thought he would never go to college, Myers continued writing. He bought a used typewriter with money he earned at a part-time job, and he read several books each week. At the age of seventeen he joined the army, still convinced that writing would be only a lifetime hobby. After three years of military service he was able to pay part of his college tuition with money from the G.I. Bill. He earned a bachelor's degree, married, and supported a family with a succession of jobs. Occasionally a periodical such as *The Liberator* or *Negro Digest* would publish one of his pieces. By 1970 Myers's marriage had ended. He was, however, beginning to make strides toward his goal of becoming a professional writer. In 1969 he had published his first book, *Where Does the Day Go?* A picture book for children, *Where Does the Day Go?* features a group of children from several ethnic backgrounds who discuss their ideas about night and day

with a sensitive and wise black father during a long walk. The book won a contest sponsored by the Council on Interracial Books for Children. It also established Myers as an author who addressed the needs of a segment of children who had too long been overlooked by the American publishing industry.

Began Writing for Teens

During the 1970s Myers worked as a senior editor for the Bobbs-Merrill publishing house. He also wrote additional picture books and began writing young adult novels. Among his earliest fiction for teens were the books *Fast Sam, Cool Clyde, and Stuff* and *Mojo and the Russians.* Both tales feature, in Subryan's words, adventures depicting "the learning experiences of most youths growing up in a big city where negative influences abound." Central to these and subsequent stories by Myers is the concept of close friendships as a positive, nurturing influence, as well as the healing and strengthening power of humor. Drawing on his own youthful experiences and the stories told him by his foster father, Myers has presented characters for whom urban life is an uplifting experience despite the dangers and disappointments lurking in the streets.

Books such as *The Young Landlords* and *Sweet Illusions* tell stories of teenagers faced with adult responsibilities. *Hoops* and *The Outside Shot* offer realistic treatments of the place of sports in young people's lives. *It Ain't All for Nothin', Won't Know Till I Get There,* and *Scorpions,* among others, show young adult characters who overcome the lure of crime and drugs or the pain of broken families. In 1992 Myers published *The Righteous Revenge of Artemis Bonner,* a humorous adventure-crime novel for young readers that showcased African-American characters in the Wild West. His next book, *Brown Angels: An Album of Pictures and Verse,* was something of a departure for Myers. While his focus was still the black American experience, he told of it in poetry that he had written to describe photographs of black children at the turn of the twentieth century.

A number of Myers's works center on historical or biographical subjects. In the nonfiction book *Now Is Your Time! The African American Struggle for Freedom,* Myers combined historical narrative with biographical accounts of courageous and innovative blacks throughout American history. Similarly, in *Malcolm X: By Any Means Necessary,* Myers wove the story of the civil rights leader's life and work into the larger story of the historical context of the civil rights movement. For *Amistad: A Long Road to Freedom,* Myers included ample archival material—maps, newspaper clippings, illustrations, and photographs—to interpret the story of mutiny on the slave ship *Amistad.* In *The Greatest: The Life of Muhammad Ali,* Myers combined biographical detail with a broader exploration of politics, religion, racism, and the world of professional boxing to illustrate the life of one of the greatest and most controversial American athletes.

Wrote about War, Juvenile Crime

Beginning in the late 1980s war became a recurring topic in Myer's works. *Fallen Angels,* published in 1988, is a fictionalized account of a young black soldier's experiences fighting in the Vietnam War, where he begins to question his own motives for fighting and faces institutional racism in the armed forces. Praised for its unvarnished portrayal of war, *Fallen Angels* won the 1989 Coretta Scott King Award and is still considered a landmark novel in children's literature. In *A Place Called Heartbreak: A Story of Vietnam,* Myers recounted the experiences of Air Force Colonel Fred V. Cherry, the first African-American fighter pilot to become a prisoner of war during the Vietnam War. Myers returned to the subject of Vietnam in *Patrol: An American Soldier in Vietnam,* an illustrated book for grade-school children for which Myers wrote the narrative.

In 2008 Myers wrote about the Iraq war in his novel *Sunrise over Fallujah.* A loose sequel to *Fallen Angels, Sunrise over Fallujah* centers on the nephew of the soldier depicted in the earlier novel. Against his father's wishes, the young man decides to forego college and join the military after witnessing the terrorist attacks of September 11, 2001. When he is sent to Iraq in the early days of the invasion, he learns that the situation is not as clear-cut as he had imagined, and, like his uncle in Vietnam, he finds that fighting in a war raises far more questions than it answers. Reviewing the novel in the *New York Times Book Review,* Leonard S. Marcus wrote simply, "This is an astonishing book."

In *Monster* he explored another complicated topic; the novel recounts a young man's experience in prison awaiting trial after he takes part in a fatal robbery. In 2000 the novel was awarded the first Michael L. Printz Award, an honor bestowed by the American Library Association (ALA) for excellence in young adult literature. In *Shooter,* Myers tackled the related problems of bullying and school shootings. In an interview in *Scholastic News Online,* he explained that he was motivated to write the book after going to speak to young people in juvenile detention centers and found that being bullied was a common experience among them. "[Being bullied] changes a kid. When you have an 11- or 12-year-old kid his or her life is full of potential. I want to show what turns these kids around. Is it the abuse they suffer? Why are kids abusing themselves? Because of the abuse they are already going through."

The author of more than ninety books, Myers was selected by the American Library Association to deliver the May Hill Arbuthnot Honor Lecture for 2009. The selection is an award that is given to "an individual of distinction in the field of children's literature," according to the ALA Web site. Amy Kellman, chairperson of the selection committee explained, "Myers does not shy away from real and serious problems, yet his work offers hope as it stresses connections to others and personal responsibility. ... His themes of the human struggle are universal." In 2008 Myers told Marti Parham in *Jet,* "I'm never going to stop writing. It's my hobby as much as it is my profession. ...I do this because I love it. I'll write until I die."

Selected works

Books

(As Walter M. Myers) *Where Does the Day Go?,* illustrated by Leo Carty, Parents' Magazine Press, 1969.

The Dancers, illustrated by Anne Rockwell, Parents' Magazine Press, 1972.

The Dragon Takes a Wife, illustrated by Ann Grifalconi, Bobbs-Merrill, 1972.

Fly, Jimmy, Fly!, illustrated by Moneta Barnett, Putnam, 1974.

Fast Sam, Cool Clyde, and Stuff, Viking, 1975.

The World of Work: A Guide to Choosing a Career, Bobbs-Merrill, 1975.

Social Welfare, F. Watts, 1976.

Brainstorm, with photographs by Chuck Freedman, F. Watts, 1977.

Victory for Jamie, Scholastic Book Services, 1977.

It Ain't All for Nothin', Viking, 1978.

The Young Landlords, Viking, 1979.

The Black Pearl and the Ghost; or, One Mystery after Another, illustrated by Robert Quackenbush, Viking, 1980.

The Golden Serpent, illustrated by Alice Provensen and Martin Provensen, Viking, 1980.

Hoops, Delacorte, 1981.

The Legend of Tarik, Viking, 1981.

Won't Know Till I Get There, Viking, 1982.

The Nicholas Factor, Viking, 1983.

Tales of a Dead King, Morrow, 1983.

Mr. Monkey and the Gotcha Bird, illustrated by Leslie Morrill, Delacorte, 1984.

Motown and Didi: A Love Story, Viking, 1984.

The Outside Shot, Delacorte, 1984.

Sweet Illusions, Teachers & Writers Collaborative, 1986.

Crystal, Viking, 1987.

Shadow of the Red Moon, Harper, 1987.

Fallen Angels, Scholastic, Inc., 1988.

Me, Mop, and the Moondance Kid, Delacorte, 1988.

Scorpions, Harper, 1988.

The Mouse Rap, Harper & Row, 1990.

Mop, Moondance, and the Nagasaki Knights, Delacorte Press, 1992.

Now Is Your Time!: The African American Struggle for Freedom, HarperCollins, 1992.

A Place Called Heartbreak: A Story of Vietnam,

illustrated by Frederick Porter, Raintree Steck-Vaughn, 1992.

The Righteous Revenge of Artemis Bonner, Harper-Collins, 1992.

Somewhere in the Darkness, Scholastic, 1992.

Malcolm X: By Any Means Necessary, Scholastic, 1993.

Young Martin's Promise, Raintree Steck-Vaughn, 1993.

Darnell Rock Reporting, Delacorte Press, 1994.

The Glory Field, Scholastic, 1994.

The Dragon Takes a Wife, illustrated by Fiona French, Scholastic, 1995.

Glorious Angels: An Album of Pictures and Verse, HarperCollins, 1995.

Shadow of the Red Moon, illustrated by Christopher Myers, Scholastic, 1995.

The Story of the Three Kingdoms, illustrated by Ashley Bryan, HarperCollins, 1995.

How Mr. Monkey Saw the Whole World, illustrated by Synthia Saint James, Doubleday, 1996.

More River to Cross: An African American Photograph Album, Harcourt Brace, 1996.

Smiffy Blue: Ace Crime Detective: Case of the Missing Ruby and Other Stories, Scholastic, 1996.

Toussaint L'overtoure: The Fight for Haiti's Freedom, illustrated by Jacob Lawrence, Simon & Schuster, 1996.

Amistad: A Long Road to Freedom, Dutton, 1997.

Harlem, illustrated by Christopher Myers, Scholastic, 1997.

Angel to Angel, HarperCollins, 1998.

Slam!, Scholastic, 1998.

At Her Majesty's Request, Scholastic, 1999.

The Journal of Joshua Loper: A Black Cowboy, Chisholm Trail, 1871 (My Name Is America), Scholastic, 1999.

The Journal of Scott Pendleton Collins: World War II, Normandy, France (My Name Is America), Scholastic, 1999.

Monster, HarperCollins, 1999.

145th Street: Short Stories, Delacorte, 2000.

The Blues of Flats Brown, illustrated by Nina Laden, Holiday House 2000.

The Greatest: The Life of Muhammad Ali, Scholastic, 2000.

Malcolm X: A Fire Burning Brightly, HarperCollins 2000.

Bad Boy: A Memoir, HarperCollins, 2001.

The Journal of Biddy Owens: The Negro Leagues, 1948 (My Name Is America), Scholastic, 2001.

Handbook for Boys: A Novel, HarperCollins, 2002.

Patrol: An American Soldier in Vietnam, illustrated by Ann Grafalconi, Harper Collins, 2002.

Three Swords for Granada, Holiday House, 2002.

The Beast, Scholastic, 2003.

Blues Journey, illustrated by Christopher Myers, Holiday House, 2003.

The Dream Bearer, HarperCollins, 2003.

A Time to Love: Stories from the Old Testament, illustrated by Christopher Myers, Scholastic, 2003.

Antarctica, Scholastic, 2004.

Constellation, Holiday House, 2004.

Here in Harlem: Poems in Many Voices, Holiday House, 2004.

I've Seen the Promised Land; Martin Luther King, HarperCollins, 2004.

Shooter, HarperCollins, 2004.

Southern Fried, St. Martin's Minotaur, 2004.

Autobiography of My Dead Brother, illustrated by Christopher Myers, HarperCollins, 2005.

The Harlem Hellfighters: When Pride Met Courage, HarperCollins, 2006.

Jazz, illustrated by Christopher Myers, Holiday House, 2006.

Street Love, HarperCollins, 2006.

Game, HarperTeen, 2008.

Sunrise over Fallujah, Scholastic, 2008.

Sources

Books

Bishop, Rudine Sims, *Presenting Walter Dean Myers,* Twayne, 1990.

Dictionary of Literary Biography, Volume 33: Afro-American Fiction Writers after 1955, Gale, 1984, pp. 199–202.

Rush, Theresa G., editor, *Black American Writers: Past and Present,* Scarecrow Press, 1975.

Something about the Author Autobiography Series, Volume 2, Gale, 1986, pp. 143–56.

Periodicals

Booklist, May 1, 2008, p. 97; September 1, 2008, p. 121.

Chicago Tribune, June 1, 1993, section 7, p. 1.

Ebony, September 1975.

Jet, April 28, 2008, p. 37.

New York Times Book Review, November 9, 1986, p. 50; May 11, 2008.

World Literature Today, May-June 2007, p. 63.

Online

American Library Association, "Walter Dean Myers to Deliver 2009 Arbuthnot Honor Lecture," January 14, 2008, http://www.ala.org/ala/newspresscenter/news/pressreleases2008/january2008/arbuthnot08.cfm (accessed October 1, 2008).

Carillo, Donna, "Walter Dean Myers on Stopping the Bullies," *Scholastic News Online,* http://teacher.scholastic.com/scholasticnews/indepth/bullying/bullying_news/index.asp?article=WalterDeanMyers&topic=0#, (accessed October 1, 2008).

Walter Dean Myers, http://www.walterdeanmyers.net/ (accessed October 1, 2008).

Other

Williams, Juan, "Walter Dean Myers: A 'Bad Boy' Makes Good," *National Public Radio,* August 19,

2008, http://www.npr.org/templates/story/story. php?storyId=93699480 (accessed October 1, 2008).

—Anne Janette Johnson and Nancy Dziedzic

Katoucha Niane

1960–2008

Model, human-rights advocate

Niane, Katoucha, photograph. Foc Kan/WireImage.

Katoucha Niane was a fashion model whose exotic, regal West African looks brought her fame and fortune in the 1980s. Often referred to as the first black French supermodel, she worked for some of the country's top fashion designers, including Thierry Mugler, Paco Rabanne, Christian Lacroix, and Yves Saint Laurent. After retiring from the runway in 1994, Niane became a women's rights advocate and campaigned to halt the practice of female genital circumcision, of which she herself had been a victim. Her death in Paris in February of 2008 was ruled an accidental drowning.

Niane was born on December 30, 1960, in Conakry, the capital of Guinea. Her heritage was Fula, the dominant ethnic group in the country. Djibril Tamsir Niane, her father, was a prominent playwright, historian, and professor who had been educated in neighboring Senegal and France. Not long after Niane's birth, her father's translation of an important epic of West African history, *Sundiata,* was published in the West for the first time. The saga, which recounts the founding of the Mali Empire in the thirteenth century, is named after a central figure and nation builder.

At the age of nine, Niane underwent the ritual of female genital cutting that is still practiced in some parts of Africa. The procedure varies from place to place, but usually includes removal of some parts of the female genitalia. Historically, it has been done to prevent women from becoming sexually aroused, to preserve their virginity, to alter their appearance, or some combination of those reasons. In many parts of Africa religious and social customs make it a prerequisite for marriage. Niane later said she was tricked into the procedure by her mother, who had been educated abroad, like her father, but was nevertheless faithful to longstanding Fula traditions. Her mother told Niane she was taking her to the cinema to see the Beatles movie *Help!,* but instead took her to a woman who performed the procedure without anesthetic.

A year later Niane's father provoked the ire of Guinea's president, Ahmed Sékou Touré, and Niane was sent to Mali to live with an uncle to ensure her safety. In her autobiography, *Dans ma chair* (In My Flesh), published in France in 2007, she divulged that she was a victim of sexual abuse in that household. At the age of twelve she was reunited with her immediate family in Dakar, Senegal, where another branch of the family was well connected to the country's elite: Niane's aunt served as executive assistant to Léopold Sédar Senghor, the president of the West African nation. Niane married at age eighteen after becoming pregnant, but the marriage did not last, and she moved to Paris against the wishes of her family.

With her exotic looks, Niane found work in the French capital as a model for some of world's top fashion designers. Saint Laurent, especially, was inspired by her height, strong shoulders, and long neck. The French fashion press dubbed her the "Ebony Princess" or "Peul Princess," a French-language reference to her Fula heritage. In the following years she had two more children. During a period of drug and alcohol abuse, she lost custody of them for a time.

In 1994 Niane retired from modeling and founded the organization *Katoucha pour la lutte contre l'excision* (Katoucha for the Battle against Female Circumcision), which is generally known by its initials, KPLCE. In her autobiography she detailed the psychological damage that the mutilation had caused her and how, combined with the childhood sexual abuse, it had played havoc with her self-image and led to substance abuse. By the time *Dans ma chair* was published in France in 2007, Niane had been reunited with her children—then living

in Senegal—and even traveled with them in Africa to raise awareness for her cause. She also started her own clothing line and served as the television host for *Ebène Top Model*, a French-African version of *America's Next Top Model*. In December of 2007 she started a new career as an actor, beginning production on *Ramata*, a film adaptation of a best-selling novel by Senegalese writer Abbas Ndione.

According to friends, Niane did not know how to swim. Nevertheless, she lived on a houseboat on the River Seine near the Pont Alexandre III, an arched bridge that connects the famous Champs-Élysées with the district that is home to the Eiffel Tower. She was last seen leaving a party on the evening of February 1, 2008. Three days later, she was declared missing by French law-enforcement authorities; her purse had been found near the door of the houseboat, although nothing appeared to be missing from it. On February 28 her body was found in the water some two miles away from the houseboat. The Paris coroner ruled her death an accidental drowning. Authorities speculated that Niane, who had been drinking, struggled to open the door—it reportedly was sometimes difficult to open and was at the end of a gangplank—and fell into the wintry Seine. She was forty-seven years old. "Her triumph in the French fashion scene in the 1980s," noted an obituary in the *Times* of London, "paved the way for black models such as Naomi Campbell to follow in her footsteps."

Selected works

(With Sylvia Deutsch) *Dans ma chair,* Editions Michel Lafon, 2007.

Sources

Periodicals

Daily Record (Glasgow), March 1, 2008, p. 37.
Guardian (London), March 1, 2008, p. 27; March 3, 2008, p. 34.
New York Daily News, March 2, 2008.
Times (London), February 11, 2008, p. 33; March 1, 2008.

—Carol Brennan

Star Parker

1956—

Commentator

Conservative pundit Star Parker chronicled her own life story in the 1997 book *Pimps, Whores, and Welfare Brats: From Welfare Cheat to Conservative Messenger.* In her early twenties, she led a life of drug abuse, sexual promiscuity, and welfare fraud. After a religious conversion, she entered the workforce, became an entrepreneur and then a radio talk-show host. As an author and media commentator, Parker's most passionate argument holds that government-benefits programs designed to help impoverished Americans are a form of subjugation and political control. In her second book, *Uncle Sam's Plantation: How Big Government Enslaves America's Poor and What We Can Do about It,* she asserts that the liberal black politicians who support such aid "are involved in the slave trade, as surely as if they had put the chains on the people themselves. We work the ghettos instead of the fields, dutifully putting 'massa' back in the Senate or House of Representatives, so they'll keep those compassionate benefits coming."

The third of five children, LarStella Irby Parker was born on Thanksgiving Day of 1956 and named after two aunts, Laura and Stella. She later began calling herself Stella, which means *star* in Italian, and then settled on Star. Because her father was a noncommissioned officer in the U.S. Air Force, the family lived on several Air Force bases during her childhood. Both of her parents came from large southern families that were poor but prided themselves on their economic self-sufficiency.

Engaged in Crime and Drug Use

When Parker was about to enter high school, her parents settled in Mount Holly, New Jersey. She later recalled that she ran with a bad crowd and was arrested for shoplifting. During her sixteenth summer, she found a job at a nearby military base, where she was sexually assaulted by an officer. During her final year at Rancocas Valley High School, she and friends committed a number of home burglaries, firebombed a teacher's vehicle, and robbed a liquor store. At age twenty she and a friend moved to Los Angeles, planning to become dancers on the popular television show *Soul Train.* However, Parker instead watched soap operas all afternoon, smoked marijuana, roller-skated on the promenade at Venice Beach, and went to discotheques at night. During those years, she recounted, she was promiscuous and contracted sexually transmitted diseases. When her boyfriend first offered her a pipe to smoke rock cocaine, she declined only because she was feeling ill from her fourth abortion a few hours earlier.

Parker took occasional community-college classes with the help of student aid. She also became skilled at cheating the Los Angeles County health-care system, which provided coverage to low-income residents. Parker would obtain medical vouchers, sell them to others, and then buy drugs with the proceeds. When she became pregnant for a fifth time, she was stunned to learn that if she kept the baby she could receive $465 a month from the county plus $176 in federal food stamps. She later described this period of her

At a Glance . . .

Born LarStella Irby on November 22, 1956; daughter of James (an Air Force officer) and Essie Doris (a beautician) Irby; married Peter Pentecost Parker (a minister), 1985; children: Angel, Rachel. *Politics:* Republican. *Religion:* Christian. *Education:* Woodbury University, BS, marketing.

Career: Receptionist for a restaurant-supply company, 1983?; *Not Forsaking the Assembling,* a Los Angeles–area Christian magazine, founder and publisher, 1984–92; radio talk-show host in Long Beach, San Francisco, and Los Angeles; Coalition on Urban Renewal and Education (CURE), founder, 1995, and president, 1995—; Scripps Howard News Service, syndicated columnist; Clare Boothe Luce Policy Institute, college lecture program.

Addresses: *Office*—Coalition on Urban Renewal and Education (CURE), 1300 Pennsylvania Ave. NW, Ste. 700, Washington, DC 20004.

life—a young woman with a baby, few job skills, and no family support structure—as being "marooned." "The system makes you believe you can't do any better," she told Ira J. Hadnot in the *Albany Times Union.* "You lose your self-worth being constantly told that you can't make it on your own."

Parker's conversion to Christianity began when two brothers who ran their own advertising agency invited her to attend services at their church. They also chastised her for taking government aid. Parker began to realize that she and her daughter might be reliant upon government support for the rest of their lives, so she removed herself from the county aid system, found a job with a restaurant-supply company, and returned to school. In 1984 she launched a magazine for Los Angeles–area Christians that grew into a successful publication known for its singles ads. A year later she married Peter Pentecost Parker, a white pastor of a charismatic Episcopal parish in Orange County. They had a daughter.

Advocated Conservative Reforms

Parker's magazine was decimated in April of 1992 when riots broke out in Los Angeles following the acquittal of white police officers who had been videotaped beating black motorist Rodney King. During the turmoil, many of the small, black-owned businesses that had been her main advertisers were burned down.

Angry that "criminals," as she called the rioters, had forced her to lay off her employees, she embarked on a new career as co-host of a radio talk show on a Christian station in Long Beach. That led to an offer from an ABC network affiliate to host her own evening call-in show. Her personal story of welfare dependency, along with her vehement opposition to government-aid programs and affirmative-action policies, usually ignited a firestorm of angry calls. She was eventually fired for insubordination because she refused to stay on safer topics during her show.

In 1995 Parker founded the Coalition on Urban Renewal and Education, or CURE, a nonprofit think tank that explored political allegiances of African-American voters. She gained national attention for *Pimps, Whores, and Welfare Brats* in 1997, which was published just as the U.S. federal government was replacing the decades-old state-administered welfare program with "workfare," or Temporary Assistance for Needy Families (TANF). New regulations placed a time limit on aid and forced participants to either find part-time work or participate in a job-training program while receiving benefits. Parker was booked frequently on news programs and talk shows to deliver the viewpoint of someone who had once relied on aid but then refused it and became a successful entrepreneur. She argued strenuously in favor of the welfare-reform efforts.

Conservative radio talk-show host Rush Limbaugh wrote an introduction to *Pimps, Whores and Welfare Brats,* which Parker coauthored with Lorenzo Benet, a writer for *People* magazine. In its first chapters she recounts her own story, and then in part 2 excoriates liberal ideology. Liberal Democrats who push government aid are the "pimps" of the title—a term generally used for men who profit from their female partners' prostitution—while the "whores" are the African-American community leaders who champion government aid and lend their political support to such candidates. By "welfare brats," Parker refers to a generation of children raised by nonworking parents.

Parker also started writing a column syndicated by the Scripps Howard News Service. She presented herself as at war with the African-American political establishment, which generally supports the Democratic Party. Her detractors pointed out that she was an excellent example of how the original welfare program was supposed to work—to provide temporary aid until people could find steady work and support their families on their own—and that not everyone cheated the system, as she admitted doing. Parker recognized that hers was a lone voice. As she wrote in *Uncle Sam's Plantation.* "I know the social problems afflicting black America are great. I know that confronting black anger is exhausting. But I also know the dreams of my ancestors did not include enslavement on the government's plantation of poverty."

Selected works

(With Lorenzo Benet) *Pimps, Whores, and Welfare Brats: From Welfare Cheat to Conservative Messenger,*, Atria, 1997; also published as *Pimps, Whores and Welfare Brats: The Stunning Conservative Transformation of a Former Welfare Queen*, Pocket Books, 1997.

Uncle Sam's Plantation: How Big Government Enslaves America's Poor and What We Can Do about It, WND Books, 2003.

White Ghetto: How Middle Class America Reflects Inner City Decay, Nelson Current, 2006.

Sources

Books

Parker, Star, *Uncle Sam's Plantation: How Big Government Enslaves America's Poor and What We Can Do about It*, WND Books, 2003.

Periodicals

Albany Times Union, April 21, 1997, p. C3.
New York Times, April 15, 2005.

—Carol Brennan

Pinetop Perkins

1913—

Musician

Perkins, Pinetop, photograph. Tim Mosenfelder/Getty Images.

Legendary piano player Pinetop Perkins came into his solo career relatively late in life, after playing with nearly every other famous name in blues, the raw, sorrowful musical form that came out of the Mississippi Delta. For years he played with such artists as John Lee Hooker and Muddy Waters, developing a piano-playing style that was a "mixture of boogie-woogie and blues, by turns elegant and sly and blunt," wrote Jon Pareles in the *New York Times.* "Playing solos, or meshing with a stomping Chicago blues band … Perkins can sling big, churchy chords and riffle off barrelhouse tremolos; he can also sprinkle quick, deftly placed trills and runs that cap suspense with satisfaction."

Perkins was born in 1913 in Honey Island, Mississippi, a town where racism was so entrenched that forty years later it was still one of the most dangerous places in the South for civil-rights activists. Cotton was the primary crop, and most African Americans worked as sharecroppers, though in many cases their parents or grandparents had cleared the land for farming and received ownership as part of a settlement program—and then lost the property to wealthier white neighbors when the market price for cotton dipped. Perkins, who went by

the name Joe Willie as a youngster, grew up working on a piece of farmland known locally as the Honey Plantation. His education ended at the third grade, but he was a skilled tractor driver by his teens. He met other blues musicians when he moved farther north to Clarksdale, where both Hooker and Waters had roots. Like them, Perkins played in bars to supplement his farmhand income of a dollar per day, which covered a weekly rent of $6.

Perkins joined the Great Migration north "after the landlord killed my dog in Clarksdale," he recalled in an interview with Richard Skelly on PinetopPerkins.com. "I was thinkin', 'I might be next!' I loved that dog. So I took off." He worked in Chicago for a time, but eventually returned to the Delta region and worked with slide guitarist Robert Nighthawk, who had a regular gig on radio station KFFA in nearby Helena, Arkansas. One of Nighthawk's musical rivals, Sonny Boy Williamson, became a frequent guest on the station's daily broadcast, *King Biscuit Time,* in 1941. Named after its sponsor, a local flour company, the fifteen-minute live blues show became one of the longest-running radio programs in U.S. history. Perkins played guitar with Williamson for three years.

At a Glance . . .

Born Joe Willie Perkins on July 7, 1913, in Honey Island, MS; married (his wife died in the mid-1990s).

Career: Farmhand in Belzoni and Clarksdale, MS, 1920s–1930s; guitarist with Robert Nighthawk's band, early 1940s; pianist for B. B. King, Earl Hooker, and others, 1940s–early 1950s; blues musician in Chicago after 1954; mechanic, late 1960s; pianist for the Muddy Waters Band, 1969–81; formed the Legendary Blues Band, 1980.

Awards: National Heritage Fellowship, National Endowment for the Arts, 2000; Grammy Award for Lifetime Achievement, National Academy of Recording Arts and Sciences, 2005; Grammy Award, Best Traditional Blues Album, *Last of the Great Mississippi Delta Bluesmen: Live in Dallas*, 2007.

Addresses: *Management*—Blue Mountain Artists, 810 Tyvola Rd., Ste. 114, Charlotte, NC 28217.

Then the tendons of Perkins's left arm got slashed in a bar brawl. "The doctors told me the only way they could save my arm was to sew the tendons back too short," he explained to Stephen Kinzer in the *New York Times*. "Couldn't play guitar after that."

Perkins took up the piano instead, teaching himself by playing along with records. After becoming proficient, he joined blues guitarist B. B. King's band in Memphis. It was there that Perkins and Earl Hooker—cousin of John Lee Hooker—made a recording of "Pinetop's Boogie Woogie," a song Clarence "Pinetop" Smith had recorded in 1928. Following the release of the new version in 1953, Perkins became known as "Pinetop" himself. Soon after that, he moved back to Chicago and played in blues clubs for a number of years before retiring from music. He was working as a mechanic in 1968 when Earl Hooker urged him to reconsider, and Perkins's return to the stage brought an offer from Muddy Waters to join his band as replacement for Otis Spann, another legendary keyboard artist. Perkins spent the next twelve years with Waters, who had an impressive following among rock-and-roll fans because of his influence on a generation of British rock acts, including the Rolling Stones (who took their name from a Waters song). The touring provided a steady, substantial income for Perkins, but it also brought new challenges. "I had to learn to play all over again," he told

Pareles. "Muddy didn't play on the meter. You had to wait on him when he sang, and then get with him."

In 1980 Perkins cofounded the Legendary Blues Band with a few members of Waters's group: Willie "Big Eyes" Smith, on drums; Louis Myers on harmonica and guitar; Calvin Jones, on bass; and Jerry Portnoy, also on harmonica. Perkins, Smith, and Jones all appeared as members of John Lee Hooker's band in the 1980 film *The Blues Brothers,* one of the most successful musical comedies in movie history. For the rest of the decade Perkins played with the Legendary Blues Band and as a solo artist. Some of the live sessions were recorded, and Perkins began to visit the studio with more frequency, too. His releases include *On Top* in 1992; *Portrait of a Delta Bluesman* in 1993; *Down in Mississippi,* in 1998; the Grammy Award–winning *Last of the Great Mississippi Delta Bluesmen: Live in Dallas* in 2007; and *Pinetop Perkins and Friends,* in 2008. Eric Clapton, B. B. King, and a host of blues artists joined him for that recording, which celebrated his ninety-fifth birthday.

After his wife died in the mid-1990s, Perkins experienced serious depression, which was exacerbated by drinking. He gave up alcohol at age eighty-four, but was still driving at age ninety when his car collided with a freight train in La Porte, Indiana, where he had lived for a number of years. "I broke my arm and nearly busted my brains out, but I could've been gone," he told Paul Liberatore in the *Marin Independent Journal.* He left the Midwest and its cold winters permanently after that, settling in Austin, Texas. His management company received many offers from venues that wanted to host Perkins's 100th birthday concert. "I remember the days when I played at chicken fights, and your only pay was the dead chicken," he told Kinzer in the *New York Times.* "But now I can't retire even if I want to. Everybody's calling me."

Selected discography

On Top, Deluge Records, 1992.
Portrait of a Delta Bluesman, Omega Records, 1993.
Down in Mississippi, Hightone Records, 1998.
(With Hubert Sumlin) *Legends,* Telarc, 1998.
Back on Top, Telarc, 2000.
Ladies Man, M.C. Records, 2004.
(With David "Honeyboy" Edwards, Robert Lockwood Jr., and Henry James Townsend) *Last of the Great Mississippi Delta Bluesmen: Live in Dallas,* Blue Shoe Project, 2007.
Pinetop Perkins and Friends, Telarc, 2008.

Sources

Periodicals

Billboard, August 21, 2004, p. 37.
Marin Independent Journal (Marin County, CA), May 9, 2008.

New York Times, May 15, 1987, p. C19; July 12, 2001, p. B2.

Toronto Star, June 26, 2008, p. E7.

Online

PinetopPerkins.com, http://www.pinetopperkins.com /papress.htm (accessed July 12, 2008).

—Carol Brennan

Wayne Rhoden

1966—

Musician

Wayne Rhoden is a professional musician best known for his work as Father Goose, a persona he adopted when he started to perform for children about 2000. A native of Jamaica, Rhoden's career began as a rapper and disc jockey in that country's "reggae dancehall" tradition. His work for children, however, has encompassed a wider variety of Caribbean musical traditions, including ska, a precursor to reggae; calypso, a style most closely associated with the islands of Trinidad and Tobago; and traditional folk songs from across the region.

Relatively few details are available regarding Rhoden's early life. Born in Jamaica in 1966, Rhoden developed an interest in music as early as the age of four. In a 2007 interview with Billy Heller in the *New York Post,* he recalled that his older sisters were not allowed to turn on the family's stereo. "House rules," he told Heller. "So they dared me to do it." Intrigued both by the stereo's electronics and by the music it produced, he soon obtained the job of playing records when his parents entertained. "They'd get up and dance and sort of forget I was supposed to go to bed."

In 1981 Rhoden moved with his family to New York City, settling in Brooklyn's East Flatbush neighborhood, where there was a large and vibrant West Indian community. While a student at Brooklyn's Erasmus High School, he played music for friends and neighbors at parties and organized a band, the JJ Crew, to provide entertainment at dances and other school events. Rhoden's high school career coincided with the explosive growth of dancehall, a variety of reggae that,

like American hip-hop, featured rhyming lyrics, a heavy bass beat, and vocalists who combined their lyrical duties with the astute management of turntables, synthesizers, and other electronic equipment. While still in high school, Rhoden built up a formidable sound system and, under the name of Rankin Don, performed with the swagger and bravado considered indispensable for dancehall performers. At his first major gig, at Brooklyn's Biltmore Ballroom, he turned his speakers up so much that, according to Rob Kenner in the *New York Times* in a 2008 article, "some of the Biltmore's ceiling tiles fell down."

As Rhoden's popularity increased, he began recording singles for release in Jamaica and the United States. In the late 1980s and 1990s he had a series of hits, including "Baddest DJ" and "Real McCoy"; the latter, according to Heller in the *Post,* sold more than 250,000 copies, a remarkable number for a single produced without the marketing and distribution resources of a major label. It was also in this period that Rhoden began a series of fruitful collaborations with some of reggae's best-known artists, including Grammy winners Shabba Ranks and Beenie Man. Then, in 1999, Rhoden met Dan Zanes, the man who would lead him into children's music. Zanes, who had risen to prominence in the 1980s as the lead singer of the Del Fuegos, a pop group, was a friend of Joyce Rhoden, Wayne's mother. The two men quickly bonded over their love of Jamaican music. As the father of a five-year-old daughter, Zanes in 2000 began recording some music for children and asked Rhoden to contribute. "On the spur of the moment," wrote Kenner in the

At a Glance . . .

Born in Jamaica in 1966; son of Joyce Rhoden; immigrated to the United States, 1981; children: one daughter.

Career: Has performed as a disc jockey and vocalist since the 1980s; member of musical group Dan Zanes and Friends, 2000—; known professionally by the names Rankin Don and Father Goose.

Awards: Prominently featured on Dan Zanes and Friends' *Catch That Train!*, which won a Grammy Award, 2007, for best musical album for children.

Addresses: *Office*—c/o Festival Five Records, 323 Dean St., Ste. 2, Brooklyn, NY 11217-1906. *Web*— http://www.fathergoose.net.

Times, "they came up with a skit about a Jamaican Mother Goose who sends her cake-loving husband to the studio as a last-minute replacement. They called the song 'Father Goose,' and Rankin Don was soon reborn."

The transition from dancehall to children's music was difficult in some ways. The lyrics Rhoden composed and sang as Rankin Don, for example, were not what most people would consider appropriate for young children. Though his songs were often less explicit than those of his rivals in the dancehall world, references to sexuality and violence were still frequent. While the lyrics proved relatively easy to change, there were other, more serious challenges; Rhoden was initially intimidated, in particular, by the thought of performing in front of children. Unlike dancehall performances, which feature elaborate, highly ritualized call-and-answer exchanges between vocalists and audience members, concerts for youngsters tend to be extremely informal, even free-form. It is perhaps not surprising, therefore, that, as Rhoden told interviewer Michele Norris for National Public Radio's *All Things Considered* in 2008, "I didn't know what to say or how to act" when performing for children. As he overcame this hesitation, however, he found that they responded enthusiastically to the call-and-answer technique, and it has become a prominent feature of his Father Goose performances.

Between 2000 and 2006 Rhoden recorded five albums of children's music with Zanes and a number of other musicians. Released under the name Dan Zanes and Friends, the albums offered an eclectic mix of acoustic folk songs, rock and roll, and Rhoden's Caribbean rhythms, which Zanes considered essential to the music's multicultural appeal. As Zanes remarked to Kenner in the *Times*, "I always wanted music that sounded like my neighborhood, and my neighborhood had a lot of West Indian people in it." Discernible in Rhoden's contributions are elements of dancehall; ska, dancehall's quieter, more traditional precursor; and calypso, a style most closely associated in the United States with the singer Harry Belafonte.

All five albums did well critically and commercially, particularly the fifth, 2006's *Catch That Train!*, which won a Grammy Award as the year's best album for children. Several months later Zanes produced Rhoden's first full-length solo album for children. Titled *It's a Bam Bam Diddly!*, it reached number seven on *Billboard* magazine's reggae chart, an unprecedented achievement for a children's album. Rhoden followed the album's release with an extended concert tour that included shows at New York's famed Lincoln Center, the Sylvan Theater in Washington, DC, and MacArthur Park in Los Angeles. While he performed in these shows exclusively as Father Goose, Rhoden has not abandoned the Rankin Don persona; indeed, he released an album, *It's Time*, under that name as recently as 2004. As of the summer of 2008, however, it seemed clear that children's music—and the Father Goose character—would be dominating his time, talent, and energy for some years to come. As he told Heller in the *Post*, "When you see those kids and you bring joy to their lives, it's a beautiful thing in the world."

Selected discography

With Dan Zanes and Friends (as Father Goose)

Rocket Ship Beach, Festival Five Records, 2000.
Family Dance, Festival Five Records, 2001.
Night Time!, Festival Five Records, 2002.
House Party, Festival Five Records, 2003.
Catch That Train!, Festival Five Records, 2006.

Solo/bandleader

Color with Father Goose (as Father Goose), Goose Hut, 2004.
It's Time (as Rankin Don), Goose Hut, 2004.
It's a Bam Bam Diddly! (as Father Goose), Festival Five Records, 2007.

Sources

Periodicals

New York Post, October 20, 2007.
New York Times, February 17, 2008.

Online

"About Father Goose," Father Goose, http://www.fathergoose.net (accessed July 26, 2008).

"Father Goose Entertainment," myspace.com, http://www.myspace.com/fathergooseent (accessed July 26, 2008).

Norris, Michele, "Father Goose: 'It's a Bam Bam Diddly,'" *All Things Considered,* National Public Radio, January 1, 2008, http://www.npr.org/templates/player/mediaPlayer.html?action=1&t=1&islist=false&id=17765006&m=17764940 (accessed July 26, 2008).

—R. Anthony Kugler

Sidney Ribeau

1947(?)—

University administrator, educator

Sidney Ribeau is one of the most respected university administrators in the United States. After nearly twenty years as a professor and administrator in the California State University system, Ribeau became president of Ohio's Bowling Green State University in 1995. Over the course of his thirteen-year tenure there, he overhauled the school's academic programs, revitalized its aging campus, attracted more than $100 million in donations, and raised enrollment to record levels. In May of 2008 Ribeau announced that he was leaving Bowling Green to become the sixteenth president of Howard University in Washington, DC.

Born Sidney Allen Ribeau in Detroit, Michigan, he graduated from that city's Mackenzie High School in 1965. He then entered Wayne State University, also in Detroit. After receiving a bachelor's degree in English and speech education from that institution in 1971, he began graduate studies in interpersonal and group communications at the University of Illinois, which granted him a master's degree in 1973 and a PhD six years later. His doctoral dissertation, titled "Rhetorical Vision—Black Social Reality," was a comparison of the rhetorical strategies employed during the civil rights struggle by Dr. Martin Luther King Jr., on the one hand, and the more militant Malcolm X, on the other.

Ribeau began his academic career in 1976, while he was still working on his dissertation, with a post at California State University–Los Angeles. After teaching there for eleven years as a professor of communication studies, he moved to California State University–San Bernardino, where he served for three years, from 1987 to 1990, as the dean of undergraduate studies. He then became dean of the College of Liberal Arts at California State Polytechnic University–San Luis Obispo, where he remained until 1992, when he became vice president for academic affairs at the university's branch campus in Pomona. As Ribeau moved upward through the administrative ranks of the California State system, he began to acquire a national reputation for administrative efficiency. By the 1990s, he was receiving employment offers from schools across the country. When one of these, Bowling Green State University (BGSU) in Ohio, offered him the position of president and chief executive officer in 1995, he accepted. The thirteen years—from 1995 to 2008—he would spend at BGSU solidified his reputation and established him as one of the country's most talented university administrators.

There is no question that Ribeau succeeded in transforming nearly every aspect of academic life at BGSU. Under his tenure, for example, an ambitious campaign to raise $120 million for capital improvements exceeded this goal by a wide margin, thanks in part to a single gift of $8 million, the largest in the school's history. Ribeau was also instrumental in allocating those funds to an array of badly needed infrastructure improvements on the school's aging campus, including renovations to the student union, a new performing arts center, and a new sports arena. These upgrades helped to boost the school's enrollment in 2006–07 to more than twenty-one thousand students—a record.

Ribeau also pursued less tangible improvements, revamping the school's curriculum to reflect a new emphasis on ethics, personal character, and civic involvement. Two programs designed by Ribeau became cornerstones of the new curriculum. One was a new class called BGeXperience. Required of all incoming students, the class aims to promote critical thinking about ethics and values. The second program, known as the President's Leadership Academy, encourages civic involvement and volunteerism. Ribeau has repeatedly stated that one of his major goals as an educator is to give students the resources they need to build and sustain a sense of community, both on campus and after graduation. These two programs can be seen as

part of that larger effort, as can Ribeau's decision to establish innovative "learning communities" in dormitories across campus. According to the BGSU Web site, learning communities offer students with similar interests an opportunity to live together and "work closely with outstanding faculty members who teach classes and have offices right in the residence hall." *America's Best Colleges 2008*, an influential guide published by *U.S. News & World Report*, highlighted BGSU's learning communities as one of the school's major strengths.

Ribeau's tenure at BGSU was not without occasional controversy. In October of 2004, for example, the *Chronicle of Higher Education* reported that a position in the BGSU student-affairs office had been given to Ribeau's wife, Paula Whetsel-Ribeau, without the usual preliminaries of soliciting applications and screening applicants. Whetsel-Ribeau, wrote Piper Fogg and John Gravois in the *Chronicle,* "was invited to apply and did not have to compete with other job applicants" for the $66,000-per-year position. The controversy over this possible conflict of interest soon dissipated, however, after Ribeau emphasized that he had no direct oversight of the student-affairs division.

On May 7, 2008, Ribeau announced that he was leaving BGSU to become president of Howard University, arguably the nation's leading black-majority institution. Reaction on the Bowling Green campus, according to Meghan Gilbert in the *Toledo Blade,* was a mixture of pride and sadness. On the one hand, Kerm Stroh, a former trustee and a major donor, told Gilbert that Ribeau was an "exceptional leader" whose departure represented "a big loss" for the school. Faculty member Patrick Pauken, on the other hand, remarked to Gilbert, "I'm thrilled for him [Ribeau]," adding that the Howard presidency was "a huge gig." Howard, for its part, issued a press release praising Ribeau's efforts at Bowling Green to create "an academic environment that develops culturally literate, technologically sophisticated, productive citizens." The release went on to quote search committee cochair (and former U.S. Secretary of State) Colin L. Powell's characterization of Ribeau as "a charismatic executive who works effectively inside and outside the institution he heads."

Ribeau's predecessor at Howard, H. Patrick Swygert, had announced in April of 2007—after the faculty senate council criticized what it called, according to the *Washington Post,* "an intolerable condition of incompetence and dysfunction at the highest level"—that he would retire the next year. At the start of his new position in 2008, Ribeau faced a variety of new challenges at Howard, an urban institution of approximately 10,500 students. After several years of funding problems and low morale at the historic institution, Ribeau's administrative talents would likely be put to good use.

Selected writings

(With Michael L. Hecht and Ronald L. Jackson) *African American Communication: Exploring Identity and Culture,* second edition, Erlbaum Associates, 2003.

Sources

Periodicals

Chronicle of Higher Education, October 8, 2004.
Toledo Blade, May 8, 2008.
Washington Post, April 28, 2007, p. B1.

Online

"Biography of Dr. Ribeau," Bowling Green State University, June 5, 2006, http://www.bgsu.edu/offices/president/page542.html (accessed July 15, 2008).

"Dr. Sidney A. Ribeau—Biography," Howard University, May 7, 2008, http://www.howard.edu/newsroom/releases/2008/080507president-bio.htm (accessed July 15, 2008).

"Dr. Sidney A. Ribeau Named 16th President of Howard University," May 7, 2008, http://www.howard.edu/newsroom/releases/2008/080507president.htm (accessed July 15, 2008).

"Learning Communities At-a-Glance," Bowling Green State University, http://www.bgsu.edu/offices/mc/communities/index.html (accessed July 16, 2008).

"Rhetoric and Public Address: Abstracts of Doctoral Dissertations Published in *Dissertation Abstracts International,* January through June 1980," *Education Resources Information Center,* http://eric.ed.gov/ERICDocs/data/ericdocs2sql/content_storage_01/0000019b/80/34/4e/4d.pdf (accessed July 16, 2008).

—R. Anthony Kugler

Darryl Roberts

1962(?)—

Filmmaker

Darryl Roberts is a filmmaker whose documentary *America the Beautiful: Is America Obsessed with Beauty?* examined how popular culture and the media shape self-image and standards of attractiveness. In making the film, Roberts interviewed editors of fashion magazines, medical professionals who specialize in plastic surgery and other image-enhancement procedures, and even followed a teenage model as she tried to break into the fashion industry. "I think for a lot of my life I was a victim of falling only for beautiful women without realizing I was a victim," Roberts admitted in an interview with Richard Knight Jr. in the *Windy City Times*. "I think that kind of ruminated under the surface and came out in this documentary."

Roberts grew up on Chicago's predominantly African-American South Side. He studied marketing and accounting, and then, as he told Patrick McDonald on the Web site HollywoodChicago.com, "in 1986, I was in Los Angeles for the first time. I was driving down Sunset Boulevard, and out of the blue, I turned to my girlfriend at the time and said: 'I'm going to make a movie.'" His first job in entertainment was as an

Roberts, Darryl, photograph. Amy Sussman/Getty Images.

announcer for WKKC-FM, a radio station run by Kennedy King College in Chicago, but he went on to a job with Seagram's, the liquor distiller and alcoholic-beverage distributor, as a wine salesperson. The income from that job provided the start-up costs for Roberts's local-access cable television show about the entertainment industry, *Backstage with Darryl Roberts*. It was such a hit that he was hired by the NBC television affiliate in Chicago, WMAQ, to host his own show, *Hollywood Hype*.

However, Roberts was still determined to make a film, and at one point took his computer to a pawnshop to finance production of a script he had written. The owner of the pawnshop took sympathy on him and contributed several thousand dollars of his own money so that Roberts could make *How U Like Me Now,* a comedy about a group of African-American professionals with intertwining careers and romances. Roberts wrote, directed, and acted in the film, which was released in 1993. It received few reviews. In *Variety* Emanuel Levy said that "Roberts shows a keen, witty eye for the small, telling detail" and concluded that the movie's "strong qualities are sociological rather than cinematic. But featuring the talent of

At a Glance . . .

Born in Chicago, IL in 1962(?). *Education:* Studied marketing and accounting at Kennedy King College.

Career: WKKC-FM, Chicago, announcer; Seagram's, wine salesperson; *Backstage with Darryl Roberts,* a local-access cable television show, host; *Hollywood Hype,* WMAQ-TV, Chicago, host; commercial and video director; Sensory Overload Productions, founder.

Awards: Best Director Award for *America the Beautiful,* 2007 Chicago International Film Festival.

Addresses: *Home*—Chicago, IL. *Office*—c/o First Independent Pictures, 2999 Overland Ave., Ste. 218, Los Angeles, CA 90064.

a young helmer with a novel point of view, the film should serve as a calling card."

Roberts spent several years as a director of television commercials and music videos before embarking on the documentary that became *America the Beautiful.* The inspiration for it was a romance doomed by his own ego: He was dating an attractive woman, but was unable to commit fully to the relationship because he thought he could find someone even more attractive. When the woman married another man, a chastened Roberts began to question his values.

Though *America the Beautiful* examines messages in media that affect all Americans, Roberts notably focused on a few African-American voices. One of them was Gerren Taylor, a fashion model who was just twelve years old when Roberts discovered her on a runway during Los Angeles Fashion Week. Stunned to learn that the mature-looking Taylor was still an adolescent, he asked her and her mother if he could follow her with his camera as she tried to break into the industry's upper echelons in New York and Paris. They agreed. Taylor was a sensation for several months. Roberts told Roger Ebert of the *Chicago Sun-Times* that, according to New York State law, "no model should be on that runway unless they're fourteen years old. All of them bent the rules. Gerren brought publicity to their shows." By thirteen Taylor's career prospects had dwindled—partly because she could not remain as thin as French modeling agencies required. The film shows the tall, slim teenager being told that she is overweight.

The documentary also examines the constant flow of celebrity images on television, the Internet, and news-

stands. Roberts interviewed an editor at *Us Weekly* about the glut of stories featuring young, glamorous starlets. She explained to him, he later told McDonald, that "the average American's life is very mundane. The more excitement and repetition [the magazines] generate regarding a beautiful celebrity means the reader will live vicariously through that life and absorb any information they can get about it."

At first Roberts had a difficult time finding a distributor for the documentary, but when it was shown at the American Film Institute festival in Dallas, it became the talk of the event, playing to full houses. He entered it in other film festivals as well; at the Chicago International Film Festival in 2007 he was named best director. First Independent Pictures agreed to distribute the film and gave it a slow rollout during the summer of 2008. In interviews he gave to promote the film, Roberts freely admitted that making *America the Beautiful* had proved a learning experience for him personally. When asked by Kathleen Stebbins in the *Reno Gazette-Journal* about his current views on beauty, he said, "My personal definition of beauty is a person that is confident, assured, kind and compassionate. Basically a person that cares about more than themselves, that when faced with choices concerning others will do the right thing the majority of the time."

Selected works

How U Like Me Now, 1993.
America the Beautiful: Is America Obsessed with Beauty?, 2007.

Sources

Periodicals

Chicago Sun-Times, June 9, 2008.
Chicago Tribune, May 9, 2008.
Entertainment Weekly, August 20, 1993, p. 66.
Los Angeles Times, April 22, 2007.
Reno Gazette-Journal, October 28, 2007.
Variety, April 27, 1993, p. 41.

Online

HollywoodChicago.com, March 30, 2008, http://www.hollywoodchicago.com/news/1963/chicago-filmmaker-darryl-roberts-to-screen-america-the-beautiful-at-midwest-independent-fi (accessed July 15, 2008).
Windy City Times, online edition, May 7, 2008, http://www.windycitymediagroup.com/gay/lesbian/news/ARTICLE.php?AID=18253 (accessed July 15, 2008).

—Carol Brennan

Jimmy Rollins

1978—

Professional baseball player

Rollins, Jimmy, photograph. Mitchell Layton/Getty Images.

As starting shortstop for the Philadelphia Phillies, Jimmy Rollins plays ball with a style and swagger that might seem outsized for a 5-foot, 8-inch, 175-pound infielder. But Rollins, a switch-hitter who goes by the nickname "J-Roll," has the skills and talent to back up his bravado. For his accomplishments on the diamond, Rollins earned the 2007 National League Most Valuable Player (MVP) title, edging out Matt Holliday of the Colorado Rockies and Prince Fielder of the Milwaukee Brewers. A true five-tool player, Rollins racked up impressive stats in 2007, becoming the first player in major league history to have at least 200 hits, 30 home runs, 15 triples, and 25 steals in a single season. His 139 runs scored and 88 extra-base hits set National League records, and his 716 at-bats for the season set another league high. All this capped off a season that had begun with Rollins boasting that the Phillies were the "team to beat" in the National League East. Rollins made good on his claim, powering the Phillies in a late-season drive to the postseason and putting himself among baseball's top players.

James Calvin Rollins III was born on November 27, 1978, in Oakland, California, the oldest child of Jimmy and Gigi Rollins. From an early age Rollins displayed an unmistakable talent on the baseball field. As a boy, he played Babe Ruth Little League and Amateur Athletic Union Junior Olympics baseball. Then, as an infielder for Encinal High School in Alameda, California—the same school that turned out pitcher Dontrelle Willis and Hall of Fame outfielder Willie Stargell—he broke ten school records, including steals (99) and batting average (.484). In 1996, his senior year, Rollins was selected for the All-USA High School Baseball team by *USA Today,* was rated the top high school infielder in northern California, and was named a Baseball America First Team All-American.

While many major leaguers started out tossing the ball around with their fathers, for Rollins it is his mother who deserves the credit for teaching him the finer points of the game. Gigi Rollins, a former middle infielder with the Allen Temple Baptist Church women's fast-pitch softball team, made a name for herself in the 1980s as a star player, one with a style all her own. In a 2008 interview with the *New York Times,* Rollins recalled, "I don't remember my mom ever missing a ball…. Her hitting was good, too. She'd gap some balls

league debut on September 17, 2000, starting at shortstop. In his first major league at-bat, he hit a triple against Florida Marlins pitcher Chuck Smith, and scored his first run batted in (RBI) the following day. In 14 games, he made 11 starts, hitting .321 and scoring 5 runs.

Rollins proved himself in his rookie season, 2001, leading the National League in triples (12) and stolen bases (46), the first player to do so since Lou Brock in 1968. Rollins set a Phillies franchise record of 35 consecutive stolen bases, set a team single-season record for steals by a shortstop (passing Larry Bowa's record of 39 in 1974), and shined with two 10-game hitting streaks in April and June and another 12-game streak the following month. That July, he was the only Phillies player named to the National League All-Star Team, and he assumed the team's leadoff spot in the lineup at the end of the month. At the end of the season, Rollins received the National League Cool Papa Award given by the Negro League Hall of Fame and was selected by the MLB managers for the Topps Major League Rookie All-Star Team.

Over the next five seasons, Rollins became a mainstay on the Phillies, playing in no fewer than 154 games each year and making the All-Star Team again in 2002 and 2005. Rollins ended the 2005 season with a 36-game hitting streak, breaking the franchise record set by Ed Delahanty in 1899, and then extended his run to 38 in early 2006. The race to break Joe DiMaggio's 56-game streak ended on April 5, 2006, when Rollins went 0-for-4 against the St. Louis Cardinals. He batted .379 during the streak, hitting 22 doubles, 4 triples, and 4 home runs.

Had Star Season in 2007

It was 2007, though, that would be Rollins's star season—and the year that would mark the Phillies' first postseason appearance in fifteen years. During the preseason, Rollins made the bold claim that the Phillies were the "team to beat" in the National League East, not the favored New York Mets or Atlanta Braves. Rollins did his part to make that prediction come true, stepping up with his bat and glove when teammates Chase Utley and Ryan Howard were sidelined with injuries.

In a key series against the Mets in September—with the Phillies in shouting distance of the postseason—Rollins hit .346 with 6 home runs and 15 RBIs. Rallying in the final days of the season, the Phillies clinched the National League East division title and their first playoff berth since 1993. Unfortunately, they went on to lose three straight games to the Colorado Rockies in the first round of the playoffs, ending their year.

Rollins ended the season on a high note, though, earning the National League's MVP Award, as well as

and drop it in gear, kind of like myself. She'd always take the extra base; she was far more aggressive than I am." For years, Rollins and his mother argued about who was the better ball player—until 2006, when Gigi finally conceded to her son. "That was the moment for me," Jimmy Rollins told the *Times.*

Began Pro Career with the Phillies

Rollins was picked by the Philadelphia Phillies in the second round of the 1996 Major League Baseball (MLB) Amateur Draft, and the team signed him to a minor league contract just twenty days later, on June 24. He began playing rookie ball with the Martinsville Phillies, a minor league franchise in the Appalachian League, appearing in forty-nine games that season. Over the next four years Rollins worked his way up in the Phillies farm system, starting the 2000 season with the AAA Scranton/Wilkes-Barre Red Barons of the International League.

Rollins was called up from the minor leagues by the Phillies late in the 2000 season and made his major

Gold Glove and Silver Slugger awards. He became the first major leaguer to have at least 200 hits, 30 home runs, 15 triples, and 25 steals in a single season. Overall, he finished the year with a .296 batting average, putting in a major-league record of 716 at-bats and collecting 212 hits, 38 doubles, 20 triples, 30 home runs, 94 RBIs, 139 runs scored, and 41 stolen bases.

Rollins reflected on winning the MVP: "It's exciting. I've always said that I never thought about being an MVP player," he told reporter Ken Mandel for MLB. com in November of 2007. "Winning the Gold Glove to me was winning the MVP for shortstop, and that's as far as I went. But to be blessed with the 2007 MVP...."

Envisioned Life after Baseball

A year before becoming the National League MVP, Rollins had made another bold prediction, announcing his intention to become the "black Donald Trump" in his life after baseball. In an interview with *USA Today* in 2007, Rollins said, "[Baseball] is what I do.... It's what I've always done. But I know I can't do it forever. I intend to be part of something great, not just in sports but in life." To that end, Rollins put his energies into the music business, presiding over his own entertainment company, Rollins Entertainment, and music label, Bay Sluggas, Inc. He was also an early investor in the A&E television show *Flip This House.*

Rollins has maintained an active civic life as well. In 2003 he served as honorary chair of the Negro Leagues Baseball Memorial Fund, and in 2004 he was an honorary chair for the Easter Seals in Philadelphia. He also participated in the Philadelphia Action Team, an initiative of the Major League Baseball Players Association that promotes voluntarism in the commu-

nity, and hosted the annual Celebrity BaseBOWL Tournament benefiting the Arthritis Foundation. Plans were under way in 2008 for the launch of the Jimmy Rollins Foundation, which will work with inner-city youth in Philadelphia and encourage African-American boys to participate in baseball.

Sources

Books

Spatz, Lyle, ed., *The SABR Baseball List and Record Book: Baseball's Most Fascinating Records and Unusual Statistics,* Scribner, 2007.

Periodicals

New York Times, April 13, 2008.
Sports Illustrated, September 10, 2007, p. 50.
USA Today, August 24, 2007, p. 6C.

Online

"Jimmy Rollins," Baseball-Reference, http://www.baseball-reference.com/r/rolliji01.shtml (accessed July 9, 2008).
Jimmy Rollins Official Web Site, http://www.jimmyrollins.com (accessed July 9, 2008).
Mandel, Ken, "Rollins Nabs NL MVP Award," MLB, November 20, 2007, http://mlb.mlb.com/news/article.jsp?ymd=20071120&content_id=2304717&vkey=news_mlb&fext=.jsp&c_id=mlb (accessed July 9, 2008).
"Player File: Jimmy Rollins," Philadelphia Phillies Official Web Site, http://philadelphia.phillies.mlb.com/team/player.jsp?player_id=276519 (accessed July 9, 2008).

—Deborah A. Ring

Anika Noni Rose

1972—

Actress, singer

Rose, Anika Noni, photograph. Vince Bucci/Getty Images.

Actress and singer Anika Noni Rose is living her dream. After struggling to make her big break on the stage, Rose found success on Broadway in 2003 in the critically acclaimed Tony Kushner musical *Caroline, or Change,* earning her first Tony Award only four years after debuting on the "Great White Way," as New York's legendary theater district is known. Following up with starring roles in the Academy Award–winning film *Dreamgirls* (2006) and the all-star Broadway revival of *Cat on a Hot Tin Roof* (2008)—not to mention making history as Disney's first black princess (2009)—it seems the sky's the limit for the talented Rose.

Rose was born on September 6, 1972, in Bloomfield, Connecticut, the daughter of John Rose Jr., corporate counsel for the city of Hartford, and Claudia Rose. Her name (pronounced a-NEEK-a no-NEE), is Swahili in origin, *Anika* meaning "goodness" and *Noni* "gift of God." As a girl, Rose and her brother often went to New York City with their parents to see theater, dance, and opera performances. Although she was enthralled by the theater early on, it was not until she was cast in the musical *Fame* during her freshman year of high school that she considered treading the boards herself.

In fact, her first love was music—in addition to singing, she also played the saxophone and trumpet in school bands—and she initially thought of pursuing a career as a recording artist.

Rose studied theater at Florida A&M University, earning a bachelor's degree in 1994. She went on to study acting at the prestigious American Conservatory Theater (ACT) in San Francisco, completing a master of fine arts in 1998. At the Berkeley Repertory Theater she appeared in productions of Kushner's *Hydriotaphia, or the Death of Dr. Browne* and Athol Fugard's *Valley Song.* For the latter work she received the Garland/Drama-Logue Award and the Dean Goodman Choice Award. At the ACT she appeared in stagings of Robert O'Hara's *Insurrection: Holding History,* Bertolt Brecht's *Threepenny Opera,* and Molière's *Tartuffe.* In 1999 she garnered the San Francisco Bay Guardian Upstage/Downstage Award for her performances as Veronica Jonkers in *Valley Song* and as Polly Peachum in *The Threepenny Opera.*

Rose moved to New York City in late 1999 with big hopes of making it on Broadway. Within three months she had done just that, landing a job as a replacement in the role of Rusty in the musical *Footloose* at the Richard Rodgers Theatre in 2000. The following year she appeared in the musicals *Me and Mrs. Jones,* with Lou Rawls at the Prince Music Theater in Philadelphia, and *Eli's Comin',* an off-Broadway revue at the Vineyard Theatre. Her performance in *Eli's Comin'* brought her an Obie Award, given by the *Village Voice* for off-Broadway performances.

Although Rose was working steadily during this time—at her dream job, no less—she still struggled to pay the bills, often lacking money even for groceries. In an interview with the *Hartford Courant,* she recalled, "Here I was working six days a week, and I found myself having to jump [subway] turnstiles for a week while I waited for that check to come in. So no, it's never been easy."

Rose's fortunes—both professional and financial—took a turn for the better in 2003, when she was cast in the musical *Caroline, or Change,* by Kushner and Jeanine Tesori. Rose originated the role of the headstrong Emmie Thibodeaux, daughter of the title character, a black woman who is a maid for a well-off white family in pre–civil rights Louisiana. After a successful off-Broadway run, the production was transferred to the Eugene O'Neill Theatre on Broadway for 136 performances and then to the Ahmanson Theatre in Los Angeles. Though the show had a short run, it was critically acclaimed and earned a number of Tony

Award nominations. For her standout performance in *Caroline,* Rose took home the 2004 Tony Award for best featured actress in a musical, as well as the Theater World Award, Lucille Lortel Award, Clarence Derwent Award, Los Angeles Critics Circle Award, and a Drama Desk Award nomination.

Winning the Tony opened up new avenues for Rose. Hollywood director Bill Condon, who had seen her in *Caroline,* asked Rose to audition for his upcoming film *Dreamgirls,* and she scored the part of Lorrell Robinson, the third "Dreamette," starring alongside Jennifer Hudson and Beyoncé. Though Rose already had several films to her credit—including the *American Idol* spin-off *From Justin to Kelly* (2003), *Temptation* (2004), and *Surviving Christmas* (2004)—her role in the Oscar-winning *Dreamgirls* marked her arrival as a star, bringing new and even more exciting roles.

For her next project Rose starred as the seductive Maggie in the 2008 Broadway revival of Tennessee Williams's *Cat on a Hot Tin Roof,* the story of a dysfunctional Southern family caught up in a web of lies. The production, which opened at the Broadhurst Theater, was directed by Debbie Allen and featured an all-black, star-studded cast: James Earl Jones as Big Daddy, Phylicia Rashad as Big Mama, and Terence Howard as Brick, in addition to Rose, a relative newcomer in the veteran ensemble. Though reviews of the production were tepid, Ben Brantley, writing for the *New York Times,* noted Rose as a bright spot: "Ms. Rose more than holds her own. She pretty much runs the show whenever she's onstage, and when she's not, the show misses her management." Comparing Rose to Elizabeth Taylor, who portrayed Maggie in the 1958 film version of the play, Brantley wrote, "It's her take-charge energy and unembarrassed directness that make this Maggie such a stimulating presence. When she exclaims, 'Maggie the cat is alive!' you can only nod in admiring agreement."

Rose received nominations for the Drama League Award and the Broadway.com Audience Award for her role in *Cat on a Hot Tin Roof.* More gratifying, perhaps, the production also proved a hit with audiences, especially among African Americans. Remembering an encounter with an elderly woman who had made her first-ever trip to the theater, Rose in 2008 told the *Hollywood Reporter,* "It is wonderful to have a black audience feel like there is a reason for them to come to Broadway and that their money is wanted, desired and appreciated. For so long, the subliminal message has been, 'We don't even want your money because we're not talking about you.'"

Rose followed up her Broadway run with several films, including *The No. 1 Ladies Detective Agency* (2008), starring singer Jill Scott. In the animated film *The Princess and the Frog,* due for release in 2009, Rose gives voice to the role of Tiana, the first black Disney princess.

Selected works

Stage

Valley Song, 1998.
Hydriotaphia, or the Death of Dr. Browne, 1998.
Tartuffe, 1999.
Threepenny Opera, 1999.
Footloose, 2000.
Carmen Jones, 2001.
Eli's Comin', 2001.
Me and Mrs. Jones, 2001.
Caroline, or Change, 2003–04.
Cat on a Hot Tin Roof, 2008.

Films

King of the Bingo Game, 1999.
From Justin to Kelly, 2003.
Temptation, 2004.
Surviving Christmas, 2004.
Dreamgirls, 2006.
Just Add Water, 2007.
The No. 1 Ladies Detective Agency, 2008.
Razor, 2008.

The Princess and the Frog, 2009.

Television

The Starter Wife (miniseries), 2007.

Sources

Periodicals

Hartford Courant, March 2, 2008.
Hollywood Reporter, March 5, 2008, p. 4.
New York Times, March 7, 2008.
San Francisco Chronicle, December 10, 2006.

Online

Cat on a Hot Tin Roof on Broadway, http://www.cat2008onbroadway.com (accessed July 24, 2008).
"Star Files: Anika Noni Rose," Broadway.com, http://www.broadway.com/gen/Buzz_Star_File.aspx?ci=36512 (accessed July 24, 2008).

—Deborah A. Ring

Jimmy Slyde

1927–2008

Tap dancer

There is no mistaking Jimmy Slyde's signature move—that cool, smooth, seemingly effortless slide across the floor from which he took his name. Over an impressive career spanning more than six decades, legendary tap dancer Slyde, also known as the "King of Slides," became synonymous with the style of dance known as rhythm tap. He performed alongside the great big bands of the 1940s during the golden age of tap, and later he starred on Broadway and film in the 1980s when the art made a resurgence. The late tap great Gregory Hines, quoted in *Dance Magazine* in 2005, summed up Slyde's importance: "I can't decide if it's Jimmy Slyde, Fred Astaire, Gene Kelly—or Jimmy Slyde, Gene Kelly, Fred Astaire." Either way, Jimmy Slyde stands among the legends of tap.

The dancer known as Jimmy Slyde was born James Titus Godbolt on October 27, 1927, in Atlanta, Georgia. When he was two years old his family moved to Boston, where he spent his childhood. His mother enrolled him in the New England Conservatory of Music as a youth, hoping to make a concert violinist of him. During his lessons, though, Jimmy could hear the sound of tapping coming from Stanley Brown's dance studio across the street, and soon he was hanging out there, watching such tap greats as Bill "Bojangles" Robinson, John W. Bubbles, Charles "Honi" Coles, and Derby Wilson. At the age of twelve he began taking classes at the studio, and it was there that he learned the slide, which would become his trademark, from teacher Eddie "Schoolboy" Ford.

Godbolt also met another student there, Jimmy Mitchell, who was then going by the name "Sir Slyde." The

two paired up, calling themselves the Slyde Brothers, and later Godbolt adopted the moniker "Jimmy Slyde," the name he would use for the rest of his career. The Slyde Brothers began performing in nightclubs and burlesque and vaudeville theaters around New England, developing a popular following. Before long, they were touring with Duke Ellington, Count Basie, Louis Armstrong, and other celebrated bandleaders. During this era tap dancers proved a popular accompaniment for big bands. As Slyde recalled in the book *Tap! The Greatest Tap Dance Stars and Their Stories,* "During a song, I would tap about three choruses up front. And then the band would come back in, and I'd do another two and a half, three choruses. Then I'd close it up and whip it out."

The timing of Slyde's career, however, was less than fortuitous. Just as he made a name for himself, the big-band music and tap dance acts of the 1940s were declining in popularity as they were supplanted by rock and roll in the 1950s. As work dried up, many tap dancers hung up their shoes or took on menial jobs to pay the bills. Slyde made some television and film appearances and worked during the 1960s as a choreographer for the Crosby Brothers. In 1966 he appeared at the historic Berlin Jazz Festival.

With little work available in the United States, Slyde moved to Paris in 1973. There he performed and taught with Sarah Petronio, who was then leading a revival of tap culture in the city. He became known for a style of dance called "rhythm tap," marked by rapid, intense, and complicated footwork—and, of course, that incredible slide. In this way, the dancer becomes a

At a Glance . . .

Born James Titus Godbolt on October 27, 1927, in Atlanta, GA; died on May 16, 2008, in Hanson, MA; married Donna; children: Daryl.

Career: Tap performer with the Slyde Brothers, 1940s–50s; choreographer for the Crosby Brothers, 1960s; dance instructor and performer in Paris, 1970s; appeared in stage and screen productions.

Awards: Choreographers Fellowship, National Endowment for the Arts, 1984–86, 1988, and 1993; National Heritage Fellowship, National Endowment for the Arts, 1999; Charles "Honi" Coles Award, New York Committee to Celebrate National Tap Dance Day, 2001; Hoofer Award, American Tap Dance Foundation, 2002; Honorary Doctorate in Performing Arts, Oklahoma City University, 2002; Guggenheim Fellowship, 2003; Dance Magazine Award, 2005.

percussive instrument, creating his own music and rhythm. Slyde explained in *Tap!* that "dancing is a translating thing, especially if you're tapping. You're making sounds yourself…. Different dancers have different sounds. Some dance heavy, some dance light. I'm *strictly* sound-oriented…. I'm a musical dancer."

Slyde was a featured performer in the 1985 Paris revue *Black and Blue,* a celebration of black musicians and dancers that recalled the elegance of earlier music-hall days. The show transferred to New York City in 1989, running for 829 performances at the Minskoff Theater on Broadway. Reviewing *Black and Blue* for the *New York Times,* critic Anna Kisselgoff wrote, "It is the dancers … who make up the show's fabric. The variety of styles that tap can but does not always contain is telegraphed in the first dance number, which combines the veterans Bunny Briggs, Jimmy Slyde, Ralph Brown and Lon Chaney with two younger soloists, Ted Levy and Bernard Manners, and the teen-age prodigy Savion Glover. This challenge competition, traditional to hoofers, is a testament of faith in tap as a creative idiom." Slyde earned a Tony Award nomination for his performance, and in 1993 the production was made into a television movie by Robert Altman.

The success of *Black and Blue* marked a reversal of fortune for Slyde, and the beginning of a resurgence of tap dance. Slyde also made several appearances in popular films during the 1980s, portraying Jimmy

Slide in the 1984 Francis Ford Coppola picture *The Cotton Club* and appearing in Bertrand Tavernier's *Round Midnight* in 1986. Slyde followed up with *Tap* in 1989, dancing alongside tappers Sammy Davis Jr. and Hines.

Although his obituary in the *New York Times* described him as a "reluctant teacher," Slyde was keen to act as a mentor to younger artists and stood as an important figure in the tight-knit dance community. He originated and hosted a weekly "jam session" at La Cave, a nightclub in Manhattan, where Slyde and other veterans would trade taps with younger hoofers such as Savion Glover, Van Porter, Ira Bernstein, and Roxane Butterfly. Glover, who performed with Slyde on many occasions, felt a particular affinity for Slyde, whom he called, as quoted in the November 2005 issue of *Dance Magazine,* the "grandfather of tap."

Slyde garnered many accolades during his long career. In 1993 he was honored with a tribute performance at the Miller Theatre in New York celebrating his "45 Years of Foot Poetry-in-Motion." Slyde received the coveted Choreographers' Fellowship from the National Endowment for the Arts in 1984–86, 1988, and 1993, in addition to a National Heritage Fellowship from that organization in 1999. Other honors include the Charles "Honi" Coles Award (2001), the Hoofer Award of the American Tap Dance Federation (2002), a Guggenheim Fellowship (2003), and a Dance Magazine Award (2005).

Praising Slyde in *Dance Magazine* on the occasion of his 2005 award, Sali Ann Kriegsman described the dancer's art: "Slyde's dancing is at once poetry, music, storytelling, philosophy. He has an uncommon lyricism, a lucid, inventive, and immaculate rhythmic sensibility. His tonation is nuanced, his sound mellow, his demeanor elegant, and his taps clear as glass. His virtuosity, spiced with those famous slides and an occasional pirouette or double tour, is always in service to the art."

Though his health declined in later years, Slyde remained a fixture in the tap community—in spirit, if not always in person—well into his seventies. He died at his home in Hanson, Massachusetts, at the age of eighty.

Selected works

Theater

Black and Blue, Paris and New York, 1985–89.

Films

The Cotton Club, 1984.
Round Midnight, 1986.
Tap, 1989.

Sources

Books

Frank, Rusty E., *Tap! The Greatest Tap Dance Stars and Their Stories, 1900–1955,* revised edition, Da Capo Press, 1994.

Periodicals

Guardian (London) June 5, 2008.
Dance Magazine, November 2005.

New York Times, May 21, 1989; May 17, 2008.
Playbill, May 19, 2008.

Online

"Dr. Jimmy Slyde, 2002 Hoofer Award Recipient," American Tap Dance Foundation, http://www.atdf.org/awards/slyde.html (accessed July 25, 2008).
"Jimmy 'Slyde' Godbolt," National Endowment for the Arts, National Heritage Fellowships, http://www.nea.gov/honors/heritage/fellows/fellow.php?id=1999_06 (accessed July 25, 2008).

—Deborah A. Ring

Kemba Smith

1971—

Social-justice activist

Kemba Smith, who spent six years in federal prison in the 1990s, is an advocate for reform of mandatory-sentencing laws. Her conviction stemmed from a romantic relationship with a drug trafficker. Although federal prosecutors acknowledged they had no evidence that Smith had either used cocaine or sold it, she was sentenced to more than twenty-four years in prison for carrying cash related to drug trafficking and for lying to federal authorities, among other charges. Her prison sentence, which was based on mandatory-sentencing guidelines, was commuted by President Bill Clinton in 2000.

Smith was born in 1971 and grew up in suburban Richmond, Virginia. The only child of an accountant and a schoolteacher, she led a relatively idyllic and sheltered life: Smith attended predominantly white schools; was a Girl Scout; took ballet, gymnastics, and piano lessons; and participated in a debutante event staged by her mother's sorority. After graduating from Hermitage High School, she entered Hampton University in the fall of 1989, where, she later told a reporter, she struggled to fit in. She said her circle of friends grew to include those who had chosen Hampton because of its reputation as a party school, and as she joined in with the drinking and marijuana use, her grades slid downward.

Caught in an Abusive Relationship

Smith began dating Peter Hall during her sophomore year after meeting him at a party. The Jamaican immigrant was eight years her senior and appeared to be well-off financially. "I had seen the other girls Peter had been involved with before," she told Reginald Stuart, a writer who profiled her in *Emerge*. "They were smart, pretty, dean's list, and I just couldn't believe he went out with me. I had heard he was dealing drugs, but hadn't seen it. I didn't question how he had all these things because it seemed like it was accepted by everybody."

In private, she recounted later, Hall soon revealed himself to be controlling and physically violent. He struck her and even tried to choke her, but then he would beg for her forgiveness and promise never to hit her again. They were living together in September of 1991 when Hall was arrested on state drug charges and for possession of false identification. It was at that point she discovered the full scope of his criminal activity. His brother gave her money to hire a lawyer, who got Hall out of jail. Prosecutors would later allege that the money came from profits the two brothers had earned as part of a multistate cocaine-trafficking ring.

Hall began to elude law-enforcement authorities, which by that time included federal drug agents. When he moved to Charlotte, North Carolina, in 1992, Smith followed him and enrolled at another college. In early 1993 Hall was arrested in New York City with crack cocaine in his possession. According to Smith's account, Hall's associates asked her to take $75,000 in cash to an address in Brooklyn so that he could make bail, and she complied. At her sentencing hearing that action would be introduced as evidence that she had participated in the laundering of drug money.

At a Glance . . .

Born Kemba Naimi Smith on August 28, 1971, in Virginia; daughter of Gus (an accountant) and Odessa (a teacher) Smith; child: William Armani Smith. *Education:* Attended Hampton University, 1989–91, Johnson C. Smith University, 1992, and Central Piedmont Community College, 1993; Virginia Union University, BSW, 2002; completed one year at Howard University School of Law.

Career: Worked for a housing agency, 1993, and a law firm after 2001; founder of Kemba Smith Foundation; lecturer and public speaker to schools and community groups, 2001—.

Addresses: *Office*—Kemba Smith Foundation, PO Box 2455, Richmond, VA 23218.

Drawn into Illegal Activities

Smith later told Stuart that she had attempted to leave Hall on several occasions, but he always persuaded her to stay. At one point, she said, he told her that he and his two partners were going away on a business trip, but he returned with only one of the partners. He asked Smith to meet him Atlanta, where he borrowed her car. He also divulged that he and his partner had killed their third partner because he was talking to the police. Allowing him to use her car would later be used as evidence against her in court.

In the summer of 1993, when she was living at home with her parents, law-enforcement authorities arrived in the middle of the night and took her into custody as a material witness. She said later that because Hall had admitted killing a partner who talked to the police, she thought he or his associates would murder her or her parents, so she deliberately gave authorities false information about Hall's whereabouts. She continued to speak with him by phone, however, and even wired him money. In December of 1993, without telling her parents, she boarded a train to meet Hall in New Orleans. He failed to pick her up at the train station as planned, but later contacted her and told her to meet him in Houston. Thus began an eight-month odyssey that took them to Arizona, California, and finally Seattle, Washington, living on the run and sleeping in bus stations or seedy motels. Smith became pregnant. Exhausted and broke, she persuaded Hall to let her return home.

When she got back to Richmond, Smith's parents informed her there was a federal warrant out for her arrest. She turned herself in on September 1, 1994,

and was held without bond. When federal agents questioned her, she again deliberately lied about Hall's whereabouts. Then one night, she recounted later, she had a dream in which Hall had died in her arms. The next morning she asked her attorney to arrange a meeting with prosecutors so she could end the "nightmare." At that meeting federal agents divulged that Hall's body had just been discovered in Seattle; he had been shot in the head before U.S. marshals found him.

Received Long Prison Sentence

Smith pleaded guilty to charges of conspiracy to distribute cocaine, lying to federal authorities, and conspiracy to launder drug money. While she was awaiting sentencing, she gave birth to a son. "I had two days with him before giving him to my parents," Smith told *People.* "I didn't sleep, because I did not want to miss any time with him."

At the sentencing hearing, experts testified that Smith's behavior was characteristic of those afflicted by so-called battered-woman syndrome, a condition in which women are unable to free themselves from abusive relationships because of psychological manipulation. However, the charges brought against Smith were covered by mandatory-sentencing laws, which allow little room for judicial discretion. An advocate for Smith pointed out that her actions had been taken "under coercion and duress," factors that, according to the law, would allow the judge to apply a lower mandatory sentence. U.S. District Judge Richard B. Kellam was not persuaded. "The law is the law," he told the packed courtroom, adding "I am not willing to say that her actions and conduct were controlled by her love for Peter Hall or her fear of Peter Hall. It went on for too long a period of time for that to have existed." Even though she had no prior criminal record, he sentenced her to twenty-four years and six months in federal prison.

The mandatory-sentencing guidelines were enacted in the 1980s as part of the U.S. government's highly publicized war on drugs. They were intended to ensure fairness in the justice system, but have been criticized for creating wide disparities instead. Statistics show, for example, that under the mandatory-sentencing law those convicted of using or selling crack cocaine—a cheaper form of the drug that is favored by users in impoverished urban areas—get harsher sentences than those convicted of possession of or selling powder cocaine, the choice of more affluent drug users. In Smith's case, her sentence was actually longer than the average time served by convicted murderers in Virginia.

Pardoned by President Clinton

In the spring of 1996 *Emerge* magazine ran a cover story, titled "Kemba's Nightmare." It led to an offer by the NAACP Legal Defense and Educational Fund to provide legal aid to Smith and her parents. When their efforts to free Smith failed, they petitioned President Bill Clinton for clemency, which he granted in December of 2000.

Following her release from prison Smith earned a bachelor's degree in social work from Virginia Union University and established the Kemba Smith Foundation, which advocates reform of sentencing laws and works with teens to keep them away from illegal drugs and crime. Although she wanted to forget that part of her life, she decided to use her notoriety to help others. "It took me empowering myself because I didn't really particularly care for the reason people know me," she told Margena A. Christian in *Jet*. "But I've been able to embrace that part of my life as a part of me. I've become a strong woman. I've recognized what God has done for me and He's used me as a vessel."

Sources

Periodicals

Black Issues in Higher Education, June 6, 2002, p. 18.
Emerge, May 1996.
Jet, May 26, 2008, p. 56.
People, September 30, 2002, p. 123.
USA Today, November 17, 2004, p. 11A.
Virginian Pilot, June 10, 2001, p. A1.

—Carol Brennan

Marie F. Smith

1939—

Association executive

Marie F. Smith served as national president of AARP, formerly the American Association of Retired Persons, between 2004 and 2006. During her tenure she worked to raise awareness on several issues championed by the thirty-five-million member organization, including Social Security reform and age discrimination. "I think one misperception is that once you reach a certain age, maybe 60, you're no longer useful," she told Joy Bennett Kinnon in *Ebony*. "This image of a sickly, useless individual has been prevalent as far back as I can remember, and we know that this is not true—we know this from our members."

Smith cited her grandmother as an important role model for her when she was growing up in Illinois. Her grandmother enjoyed a long career as a probation officer and was also politically active for much of her adult life. As a young woman, Smith entered the University of Illinois, but as she divulged in an interview with the Newark *Star-Ledger* in 2005, the school "wasn't well integrated. You couldn't join a sorority except for black sororities. I wanted to be on the cheering squad, and that was out." She transferred to Nashville's Fisk University, a historically black college, where she worked toward her bachelor of science degree in biology and premed while a member of the cheerleading squad. She also met her first husband there, who went on to medical school in Chicago. Eager to begin work full time when they arrived in the city, Smith took the federal civil service exam and was hired as a claims representative at the local Social Security office. She recalled her first day of work, when a single mother who was newly widowed sat at her

desk. "She had just lost her husband and was beside herself," Smith said in the *Star-Ledger* interview. "I was able to tell her how much she would get, how much her children would get. I watched her change. We literally saved her life."

Smith went on to spend the next twenty-five years with the Social Security Administration, relocating several times for either promotions or for her husband's job. She earned a certificate in public affairs from Stanford University and rose to become a director of manpower management and organizational planning at the agency, which administers the nation's social insurance programs. It assigns Social Security numbers to individuals, and then keeps track of earnings over the person's work years. Payroll deductions from workers fund their individual pension accounts, which a person may start collecting at age sixty-two. The agency also administers a Supplemental Security Income (SSI) benefits program, which aids the visually impaired, disabled, or elderly with no lifetime earnings record.

Smith spent part of her career managing the Social Security office on the Hawaiian island of Maui, where she and her second husband created a tropical garden on their property that they rented out for weddings and other festive events. Her work with AARP began when she volunteered for its Women's Initiative Program, and she eventually became the program's spokesperson. She moved on to a seat on the AARP National Legislative Council, and became its chair before an appointment to the AARP board of directors.

At a Glance . . .

Born on March 12, 1939, in East St. Louis, IL; daughter of David and Christina Ford; married first husband (marriage ended); married Richard Stanley Smith, December 13, 1986; stepchildren: Jeffrey, Reginald, Laurie Debrotz. *Education:* Attended the University of Illinois; Fisk University, BS, biology and premedical studies, 1961; earned a certificate in public affairs from Stanford University.

Career: U.S. Social Security Administration, began as claims representative, became office manager, management analyst, and director of manpower management and organizational planning; real estate consultant and freelance writer; Women's Initiative Program, AARP, began as volunteer, became spokesperson; joined the AARP National Legislative Council, became chair; named to AARP board of directors; AARP, national president and spokesperson, 2004–06; certified hypnotherapist.

Memberships: Zonta International; National Association of Retired Federal Employees; African American Heritage Foundation of Maui.

Awards: Woman of Excellence Award, Commission on the Status of Women; Commissioner's Citation, Social Security Administration; Named one of America's 100 Most Influential African-American Leaders, *Ebony* magazine, 2004; named one of 25 Influential Black Women in Business, *Network Journal*, 2006.

Addresses: *Office*—c/o AARP, 601 E St. NW, Washington, DC 20049.

AARP is a nonprofit organization that advocates on behalf of Americans over the age of fifty. It was founded in 1958 as an offshoot of the National Retired Teachers Association, and as the baby-boomer population began nearing retirement age in the 1990s, its ranks swelled to become the world's largest nonprofit group. Its name change to "AARP" in 1999 reflected its new focus on Americans aged fifty and above, not just retirees.

Smith was voted AARP's president-elect in 2002, and advanced to her own two-year term in April of 2004 as national president and spokesperson. During her first year, AARP launched a historic "Voices of Civil Rights" bus tour along with the U.S. Library of Congress, which collected oral histories of those who had taken part in the civil rights struggles of the 1950s and 1960s. The bus, which featured unique interactive exhibits, followed the Freedom Ride trail, the bus route that brought voting-rights volunteers to parts of the South where racism was deeply entrenched. "The Freedom Rides of the 1960s were historic, and this bus trip will honor and save that memory," Smith told Jason B. Johnson in the *San Francisco Chronicle*. "These powerful recollections will be preserved and passed down to future generations, to both educate and inspire Americans of tomorrow."

One of the most important issues for Smith and the AARP involved Social Security reform. U.S. President George W. Bush had proposed several changes to Social Security benefits. The changes would disproportionately affect older African Americans, an estimated 40 percent of whom rely solely on Social Security income during their retirement years, compared with 19 percent of whites in the same age group. "Those benefits are all that stand between those beneficiaries and living in poverty," she was quoted by Elizabeth Auster as saying in the *Cleveland Plain Dealer*. The Bush Administration had also argued that its proposed changes could actually help African-American men, who die sooner than their spouses or white counterparts and therefore collect less of their paid-in lifetime earnings on average. On behalf of the AARP, Smith spoke out publicly against many of the ideas put forth by the Bush Administration. "I know Social Security can make a difference," she told writer James Bernstein in *Newsday*. "My mother worked at home, as did many women of her generation. When my father died, because of Social Security, my mother lived with dignity all her life."

Smith was not the first African American to lead AARP: Margaret A. Dixon achieved that milestone back in 1996. In 2006 Smith stepped down as AARP national president and spokesperson. She was uninterested in retirement, however, and returned to her multiple work interests in real estate consulting and freelance writing; she is also a certified hypnotherapist. "When people say they're bored, I think, 'How can you say that?'" she told the *Star-Ledger*. "Everything interests me."

Sources

Periodicals

Ebony, August 2006, p. 124.
Executive Speeches, June–July 2005, p. 28.
Newsday (New York), February 27, 2004, p. A57.
Plain Dealer (Cleveland, OH), April 18, 2005, p. A1.
San Francisco Chronicle, September 4, 2004, p. B1.

Star-Ledger (Newark, NJ), September 26, 2005, p. 25.

Online

"Marie F. Smith—National President, A.A.R.P., Washington, D.C.," *Network Journal,* http://www.tnj.com/events/2006winners/2006msmith.php (accessed August 25, 2008).

Smith, Marie F., "AARP's Commitment to Diversity," AARP.org, July 7, 2004, http://www.aarp.org/aarp /articles/diversitysmith.html (accessed August 25, 2008).

Other

"Marie Smith" (interview), *Tavis Smiley,* PBS, March 28, 2005, http://www.pbs.org/kcet/tavissmiley/archive/200503/20050328_smith.html (accessed August 25, 2008).

—Carol Brennan

Cecil Taylor

1929—

Musician

Pianist Cecil Taylor was one of the pioneers of avant-garde jazz, often called free jazz, along with the saxophonists John Coltrane and Ornette Coleman. Known for masterful leadership of his ensembles, Taylor demonstrated stupendous physical stamina on stage, often playing for more than two hours without a break. "Taylor doesn't play other people's music or lean on a marketing concept. The idea is that he is a once-and-forever new concept," wrote Ben Ratliff in the *New York Times,* adding, "His music is an eruption…. [I]t comes from as broad a consciousness and as deep a commitment to beauty as we have in American culture."

Taylor was born in 1929 in New York City and grew up in Queens, the same borough that was home to the Rivercrest Sanitarium, a mental health facility where his father, Percy, worked as head chef. His mother, Almeida Ragland Taylor, who was a dancer and an actor in some of the earliest black silent films, taught her son a little French and German as well as the piano. Both she and Percy hoped their son would become a professional, perhaps a doctor or lawyer. His mother died before he reached his teens, however, so Taylor's passion for music was stoked at an impressionable age by his uncle, a professional musician who lived with the family. He took the young Taylor to live jazz shows in the city. Although Taylor studied classical music at the New York College of Music and theory and composition at the prestigious New England Conservatory of Music, he was also intrigued by several new currents in jazz music that emerged during the 1940s and the post–World War II years, including bebop. After gradu-

ating in 1953, he moved back to New York and began playing jazz at a variety of venues.

Broke from Bebop Pack

Taylor recorded his debut record, *Jazz Advance,* in Boston. Three other musicians—Steve Lacy on saxophone, Buell Neidlinger on bass, and Dennis Charles on drums—joined Taylor in his first ensemble, whose sound was dubbed post-bebop by puzzled music critics. In an article about jazz trends, *New York Times* writer John S. Wilson called the record "a fascinating, if sometimes unnerving, sampling of a jagged but thoroughly articulate style made up of slivers of Thelonius Monk, Béla Bartók and Jelly Roll Morton, mixed with precise technique by an adamant individualist."

Around that time Taylor began playing regularly at the Five Spot Café, a tiny but legendary jazz venue in the Bowery, then a seedy part of Manhattan. His playing was reportedly so hypnotic that nobody ordered drinks for fear of breaking the spell. During this period Ornette Coleman and John Coltrane were also Five Spot regulars and sometimes played with Taylor. Collectively they were hailed as creators of a new, thoroughly modern sound in jazz. Coltrane and Taylor recorded together once, in 1958; the session was issued under various titles, including *Coltrane Time* and *Hard Driving Jazz.*

After nearly a decade as a professional musician, Taylor began to find his own style as a composer, exemplified by his 1961 recording *Into the Hot.* It included three

more appreciative audiences. Nevertheless, Taylor's works influenced a generation of musical innovators on both sides of the Atlantic.

In the 1970s Taylor began to perform as a solo pianist, and two releases showcased his concert style, *Indent* (1973) and *Silent Tongues* (1974). His occasional collaboration with traditional jazz pianist Mary Lou Williams culminated in a two-piano performance at Carnegie Hall in April of 1977. A year later he performed on the South Lawn of the White House at an event commemorating the twenty-fifth anniversary of the Newport Jazz Festival in Rhode Island. The concert, with its all-star lineup, was considered a pivotal moment in the history of jazz, marking its acceptance into mainstream culture.

Feted in Berlin

Taylor, however, continued to work outside the mainstream. In 1979 he played a series of gigs with Sun Ra, an equally original American jazz artist, whose recording "Arkestra" helped define a new subgenre, otherworldly sounds, that paved the way for electronic-music pioneers. That same year Taylor performed with drummer Max Roach; the events were recorded as *Cecil Taylor & Max Roach: Historic Concerts.* The two performed together on occasion for the next twenty years.

In the 1980s Taylor spent time in what was then West Berlin, which was known for its flourishing arts scene. He made scores of recordings with European and American expatriate free-jazz musicians who had come of age in the 1960s, just as he was releasing his first compositions. In the mid 1990s he played frequently with another member of that generation, Finnish saxophonist Harri Sjöström. Among their joint releases was the two-volume set *Qu'a: Live at the Iridium* (1998). In 2005 Taylor was the subject of a documentary, *Cecil Taylor: All the Notes,* which showed the musician at his favorite piano—a Bösendorfer with ninety-seven keys instead of the standard eighty-eight.

"We can hear more of the world's music than ever before," Taylor reflected in a 1991 interview with Peter Watrous in the *New York Times.* "If Debussy can hear a Balinese gamelon orchestra at a Paris world fair and change his concept, I can learn from [Iannis] Xenakis, Billie Holiday and Duke Ellington.... Literature, theater, it's all important. You want to create the utmost that is possible, to continue the ideas of certain people who have enriched your life."

original compositions in which Taylor "first fully revealed his gifts as a composer," wrote Stanley Crouch in the *New York Times.* "Call-and-response, tension and release, metric shifts and the orchestration of both bluesy and unconventional effects come off marvelously." The record, made with saxophonists Archie Shepp and Jimmy Lyons, marked the beginning of a long collaboration between Taylor and Lyons that endured until Lyons's death in 1986.

Formed the Cecil Taylor Unit

Taylor and Lyons soon joined with Sunny Murray, a jazz drummer whose pioneering percussion willfully departed from the traditional function of keeping time in a piece of music. Often billed as the Cecil Taylor Unit, the combo broke from standard Western musical traditions, creating free-jazz compositions that "featured muscular improvisations of such challenging techniques and structure they bewildered listeners and most fellow musicians alike," Crouch wrote in the *New York Times.*

Releases from this period include *Unit Structures* (1966) and an epic three-volume set, *The Great Concert of Cecil Taylor* (1969), which was recorded live in Paris. For many years Taylor's new style, sometimes referred to as black classical music, seemed to be shunned by the more mainstream jazz music industry. Oftentimes Taylor's releases were issued on independent labels, and gigs took place at private gatherings in New York City. In Europe, however, the sound found

Selected discography

Jazz Advance, Transition, 1956.
Into the Hot, Impulse, 1961.
The World of Cecil Taylor, Candid, 1961.
Coltrane Time (with John Coltrane), United Artists, 1962.

Nefertiti, the Beautiful One Has Come, Arista/Freedom, 1962.
Unit Structures, Blue Note, 1966.
Conquistador! Blue Note, 1966.
The Great Concert of Cecil Taylor, Prestige, 1969.
Indent, Arista/Freedom, 1973.
Silent Tongues, Arista/Freedom, 1974.
Air Above Mountains (Buildings Within), Enja, 1976.
The Cecil Taylor Unit, New World Records, 1978.
3 Phasis, New World Records, 1978.
Mary Lou Williams & Cecil Taylor, Pablo Records, 1978.
Cecil Taylor & Max Roach: Historic Concerts, Soul Note, 1979.
It Is in the Brewing Luminous, Hat Hut, 1980.
Winged Serpent (Sliding Quadrants), Soul Note, 1985.
For Olim, Soul Note, 1986.
Cecil Taylor in Berlin '88, FMP, 1988.
In Florescence, A&M, 1990.

The Tree of Life, FMP, 1998.
Qu'a: Live at the Iridium (with Harri Sjöström), Cadence, 1998.
The Light of Corona (with Harri Sjöström), FMP, 2003.
The Owner of the River Bank, Enja, 2004.
Incarnation, FMP, 2004.
Almeda (with Harri Sjöström), FMP, 2005.

Sources

Periodicals

Daily Variety, June 27, 2002, p. 7.
New York Times, April 21, 1957, p. 100; June 8, 1980, p. D20; May 10, 1991; March 4, 2002, p. B5.
San Francisco Chronicle, May 8, 2005, p. 32.

—Carol Brennan

Jason Taylor

1974—

Athlete, television personality

As one of the best defensive ends in the National Football League (NFL), Jason Taylor was a key element in the improved fortunes of the Miami Dolphins before he was traded to the Washington Redskins in 2008. Though Taylor is considered small for a defensive end at six-foot-six and 255 pounds, his prowess in taking down quarterbacks brought him honors as Defensive Player of the Year. Conversely, his size made him an unlikely candidate for the ABC reality-television competition *Dancing with the Stars*. In the spring of 2008 Taylor and his dance partner placed second in the finals. His unexpected performance was not the first time he had triumphed over detractors—few had expected him to become one of professional football's standout defense players, but Taylor possesses a steely determination and impressive work ethic. "I look at it like this: It doesn't matter what the weather is, whether it is snowing, raining, 10 degrees or 100 degrees," he explained to Damon Hack in the *New York Times* about his athletic career. "It's only three hours. If you can't go out there and play your tail off for three hours in the snow or the heat or whatever it may be, then you're getting paid too much money for not doing your job."

Schooled at Home

Born in 1974, Taylor grew up in Pittsburgh, Pennsylvania. Although he was home-schooled from the tenth through twelfth grades, he was still allowed to participate in the sports program at Woodland Hills High School in Churchill, Pennsylvania. He dreamed of a

career in the National Basketball Association, but before the start of his senior year, he joined Woodland Hills' top-caliber football program, which led to an offer of an athletic scholarship from the University of Akron.

On the second day of his freshman year, however, the National Collegiate Athletic Association (NCAA) declared him academically ineligible because he had been homeschooled. Taylor had finished his high school studies with a 3.85 grade-point average—verified by a homeschool-monitoring association that his mother had used—but he had a relatively weak Scholastic Aptitude Test score, even though it was well above the minimum for scholarship eligibility. His family contacted the Home School Legal Defense Association, which was successful in getting the NCAA to reverse its ruling. He became one of the first homeschooled athletes to win an athletic scholarship at an NCAA Division I school.

Taylor was a linebacker for three years with the Zips, as Akron's athletic teams are called, but switched to defensive end during his senior year. The Zips were never a powerhouse in their Mid-American Conference, but Taylor endured an especially painful losing streak during his time there: Of forty-four games played, the Zips won just twelve. In the 1997 NFL draft, Taylor was a third-round pick by the Miami Dolphins, and few predicted that he would become one of the Dolphins' key players over the next decade. One reason was that he was much smaller than typical NFL defensive ends, many of whom tipped the scales at 300 pounds; at his top weight prior to turning pro, Taylor

lor's fifty-one–yard return on an interception that yielded a touchdown.

That season the South Florida media gave Taylor his fourth Dan Marino MVP Award, which honors the record-setting Dolphins quarterback. Taylor and Marino's professional camaraderie evolved into a solid friendship after Marino's retirement in 2000, and Taylor followed Marino's lead in pursuing community investment and enrichment activities in the off-season. In 2004 he established the Jason Taylor Foundation, which funds after-school programs and college scholarships for at-risk youth in South Florida.

Taylor's wife, Katina, plays an active role in the foundation's work. A former Miss Amarillo, Texas, whose brother Zach Thomas was the Dolphins' longtime linebacker, she and Taylor married in 2001. The have three children. In 2006 highly publicized marital problems nearly brought an unexpected end to Taylor's career when he offered to give up football if it was necessary to save their marriage. In the end, divorce papers were withdrawn, and Taylor promised Dolphins management and fans that he had several more seasons in him.

Those Dolphins fans were disappointed, however: In July of 2008 the Dolphins traded Taylor to the Washington Redskins in exchange for two draft picks. "The [Redskins'] defensive line has really brought me in and made me one of their own" he told Ethan J. Skolnick in the *South Florida Sun-Sentinel.* "They like veterans, and they don't make you feel like an old man."

managed to bulk up to 242 pounds, but was lanky at six-foot-six. During his rookie season, he managed to rack up five sacks, the term for tackling a quarterback behind the line of scrimmage before he is able to throw a forward pass. The following season, in 1999, Taylor had nine sacks. In 2000 he began to gain serious attention for his ability to stop opponents: He ended the season with fourteen and a half sacks. The Dolphins finished first in the East Division of the American Football Conference (AFC) with an 11–5 record.

Two years later Taylor closed out the NFL regular season as the league leader with eighteen and a half sacks. In *Football Digest* he commented on the key to his success: "A lot of people might point to my speed, but at the end of the day, if you don't work hard enough or don't want it bad enough, then all you are is fast." He continued, "[Olympic gold medalist] Carl Lewis was fast, but I don't think he ever hit a quarterback." In the 2003, 2004, and 2005 seasons, Taylor recorded a total of thirty-four and a half sacks.

Named NFL's Defensive MVP

The Dolphins finished the 2006 season with a 6–10 record, but Taylor was still named NFL Defensive Player (MVP) of the Year by Associated Press sportswriters. Game analysts and even fellow players asserted that Taylor was the rare gridiron star who could win a game single-handedly. He was said to have done just that during the 2006 season when the Dolphins defeated the Minnesota Vikings, 24–20, thanks to Tay-

Danced in Television Competition Series

Taylor's off-season activities have included acting classes in the Los Angeles area and representing men's skin-care products made by Neutrogena. Despite his imposing size, he made a surprisingly graceful showing in the reality-television competition *Dancing with the Stars* in March of 2008. Paired with Edyta Sliwinska, a professional ballroom dancer from Poland, Taylor executed some difficult dance moves as the season progressed, including the samba, rumba, foxtrot, and waltz. Their scores kept improving as the weeks progressed, and they wound up in second place behind figure-skating champion Kristi Yamaguchi and her dance partner, Mark Ballas. A writer for *Daily Variety* followed the contestants' training schedule for one week, during which Taylor and Sliwinska logged eight-hour days. "I've never cha-cha'd in my life and I've got a week to make it look like I know what I'm doing. That's tough," he told the trade journal's Jerry Rice. Sliwinska was responsible for teaching him the steps and had the authority to extend practices past the twelve-hour mark. "She's the toughest coach I've been around," Taylor assured Rice.

Sources

Periodicals

Akron Beacon Journal, December 24, 2004.
Daily Variety, May 6, 2008, p. A2.
Football Digest, November 2003, p. 18.

New York Times, December 26, 2002, p. C8.
South Florida Sun-Sentinel (Fort Lauderdale, FL), August 17, 2008.
Sports Illustrated, September 28, 1992, p. 10; June 25, 2007, p. 68.

—Carol Brennan

Viola Vaughn

1947—

Educator, consultant, program administrator

Dr. Viola Vaughn is a U.S.-born educator whose self-sustaining educational program for girls in the West African nation of Senegal has attracted international attention. Known as 10,000 Girls (or, in French, 10,000 Filles), a name reflective of its ambitious agenda, Vaughn's program began in 2001 as an informal tutoring project run out of her home in the Senegalese village of Kaolack. By 2008 it had expanded to include a variety of educational and vocational programs for fifteen hundred girls in six locations.

Viola Marie Vaughn was born on July 29, 1947, in Little Rock, Arkansas. Her father, Wensel Rumble Vaughn, was a Baptist minister and her mother, also named Viola Marie Vaughn, was a schoolteacher. After moving with her family from Little Rock to Niagara Falls, New York, in her teens, the younger Vaughn attended Hampton University, a predominately African-American institution in Virginia. Following an undergraduate career that included a junior year abroad at the University of Poitiers in France, Vaughn received a bachelor's degree in music and French from Hampton in 1969. She spent the first half of the 1970s raising her daughter and attending graduate school at Columbia University Teachers College in New York City, receiving a master's degree in health education in 1976. Her master's thesis was in the field of public health administration, a subject she continued to study as she began work on her doctorate, also at Columbia. Her doctoral dissertation, titled *Planning for Change: The Sine Saloum Rural Health Project, Senegal, West Africa,* was based on her work as project coor-dinator from 1977 to 1979 on a major health care initiative in rural Senegal, where she would spend much of her later career. She received her doctorate in health education, with a specialty in international program planning administration, in 1984.

Vaughn's work as a graduate student in Senegal marked the beginning of a health education career that was remarkable for its geographical and thematic variety. While her interest in international development issues continued, she also found significant need for her expertise in the United States. Throughout the 1980s and 1990s, therefore, she found herself shuttling back and forth between Detroit, Michigan, where she lived for many years, and a number of countries in Africa, notably Senegal. The jobs she took in these locales were intensive but relatively short term; often she would design a health program, oversee its initial implementation, write training manuals for local workers, and then move on to the next project. Among the positions she held in this period, for example, were as the coordinator of consultation for the Michigan Department of Community Mental Health from 1980 to 1983 and as the director of international health for California's Drew Postgraduate Medical School in 1981. In the course of her work for Drew, she supervised public health programs in Kenya, Sierra Leone, Liberia, Togo, Cameroon, and Swaziland.

As the 1980s progressed, she worked increasingly as a consultant, helping small public health programs convey information effectively to the public. These programs included Improved Pregnancy Outcomes, an

At a Glance . . .

Born Viola Marie Vaughn on July 29, 1947, in Little Rock, AR; daughter of Wensel Rumble Vaughn (a Baptist minister) and Viola Marie Vaughn (a schoolteacher); married Sam Sanders (a jazz saxophonist; died October 18, 2000); children: one daughter (deceased). *Religion:* Muslim. *Education:* Hampton University, BA, music and French, 1969; Columbia University Teachers College, MS, health education, 1976, EdD, health education, 1984.

Career: Sine Saloum (Senegal) Rural Health Project, project coordinator, 1977–79; Michigan Department of Community Mental Health, coordinator of consultation, 1980–83; Drew Postgraduate Medical School, director of international health, 1981; worked as a health-information consultant for a variety of public health programs, 1980s–1990s; taught several classes in English as a second language, late 1990s; 10,000 Girls, founder and executive director, 2001—.

Awards: CNN Hero, Cable News Network, 2008.

Addresses: *Office*—c/o 10,000 Filles, BP 2130, Kaolack, Senegal. *Web*—http://www.10000girls.org.

outreach project headquartered at Detroit's Wayne State University, from 1985 to 1986; the continuing education program of the Open Arms shelter for the homeless, also in Michigan, from 1987 to 1988; the National Family Planning Program of Senegal, in the late 1980s and early 1990s; the AIDS research office of Le Dantec Hospital in the Senegalese capital of Dakar, in 1993; and the Family Planning Options Project in the small West African nation of Guinea, from 1994 to 1995. Then, in the late 1990s, she began teaching classes in English as a second language, in both the United States and Senegal, even as she continued her health consultancy work.

Homeschooled Grandchildren in Senegal

In 2000 Vaughn and her husband, well-known jazz saxophonist Sam Sanders, decided to retire to rural Senegal, a setting she had grown to love in the course of her public health work. Accompanying them were five young grandchildren, who had been entrusted to Vaughn's care following the death of their twenty-six-year-old mother (Vaughn's daughter) shortly before. Only a few months after the family had settled in the

town of Kaolack, however, Sanders died of a chronic illness. It was a difficult period for Vaughn, but she resisted despair, choosing to concentrate instead on homeschooling her five grandchildren.

Formal homeschooling, with books and assignments, is rare in West Africa, and Vaughn's activities soon attracted the notice of local residents, notably the neighborhood children who played regularly with her grandchildren. One of these children, a nine-year-old girl, asked Vaughn if she could join the lessons. Though Vaughn had come to Senegal to retire, not to teach, she was touched by the girl's request. Vaughn also knew that, while educational opportunities for both boys and girls are limited in West Africa, the situation is particularly dire for girls, who face intense social pressure to remain at home to help their parents. According to the Senegalese government's own figures (reproduced on the 10,000 Girls Web site), fewer than 40 percent of the nation's age-eligible girls enter the first grade, and fewer than 4 percent enter high school. Alarmed by these statistics, Vaughn decided to act. "I went to see this child's mother," Vaughn recalled to the cable news network CNN in 2008, "and her mother said that she had already failed school once, that she couldn't pass because she wasn't smart enough. Well she was smart enough to come find me. And I said, 'OK, I'll help you.'" Within two weeks, CNN reported, "Vaughn had 20 girls in her house who were failing school and asking her to teach them."

Expanded Schooling

The innovative structure of 10,000 Girls developed gradually. When students continued to appear at her house, she converted spare rooms into classrooms, obtained a small grant, and hired several teachers. Even as late as 2003, however, she wanted to keep the program small, and tried several times to set a limit of one hundred students. Girls kept arriving, however, and those already enrolled prevailed upon her to continue the expansion, urging her not to stop until she had reached "10,000 Girls." To handle the influx and to teach responsibility, Vaughn decided to make each girl responsible for teaching a younger student. "I taught them how to teach each other," Vaughn remarked to CNN.

The same spirit of independence and self-reliance is visible in the program's fund-raising activities. 10,000 Girls receives no funds from the government of Senegal and only limited assistance from aid organizations and individuals. Instead, books, supplies, and teachers' salaries are financed through vocational programs designed and implemented by the students themselves. The most important of these are Celebration Baked Goods, a bakery and catering business, and Celebration Sewing Workshop, which produces dolls for sale and export abroad. The students are allowed to keep 50 percent of the proceeds for themselves, a policy that allows them to contribute significantly to their families' income. The other 50 percent supports school programs.

As of 2008 there were approximately fifteen hundred girls enrolled in Vaughn's program, with another thousand on the waiting list. A 2006 note on the 10,000 Girls Web site indicated that Vaughn that would like to retire again "in about seven years," or around 2013. In the meantime, she continued to find satisfaction in the day-to-day management of a program that has already transformed life for thousands of girls and their families. "Here I am, retired," she remarked to CNN, "and this is the best job I have ever had in my life."

Sources

Periodicals

Detroit News, August 9, 2008.

Online

"The Best Job I Have Ever Had in My Life," CNN.com, April 18, 2008, http://www.cnn.com/2008/LIVING/04/10/heroes.vaughn/index.html?iref=mpstoryview (accessed July 22, 2008).

Leis, Julia, "Sweet Charity," Africa Consultants International, http://www.acibaobab.org/index.php?option=com_content&task=view&id=52&Itemid=82 (accessed July 22, 2008).

Meyer, Amy, "In Her Own Words," 10,000 Girls, April 14, 2006, http://www.10000girls.org/interview.html (accessed July 22, 2008).

"Viola Vaughn, Executive Director," 10,000 Girls, http://www.10000girls.org/violav.html (accessed July 22, 2008).

—R. Anthony Kugler

Gelsy Verna

1961–2008

Artist, educator

Gelsy Verna was an artist and art professor highly regarded by students and peers alike. Born in Haiti, Verna was an experienced, multilingual world traveler before she was in her teens. The richness of her early experiences in Haiti and central Africa, and then Canada—where her family eventually settled—are reflected throughout her work, particularly in her characteristic habit of mixing motifs from a variety of geographical and cultural contexts. The force and originality of her artistic vision, combined with the well-attested warmth of her personality, made her extremely popular among art students at the University of Wisconsin–Madison, where she taught for seven years, and it was with profound grief that that campus greeted the news of her sudden death in March of 2008 at the age of forty-six.

The second of six children born to Joseph Marie Verna, a radiologist, and Clara Lanier Verna, a teacher, Gelsy Verna was born on March 31, 1961, in Port-au-Prince, the capital of Haiti. In a 1999 interview with Jane Robinette of the Iowa Women Artists Oral History Project, Verna said, "I come from a family of eccentrics…. They like an independence of mind and to chart their own path in some ways." The family spent several years in the mid-1960s in Kinshasa, Zaire (now the Democratic Republic of the Congo), an experience often reflected in Verna's art, particularly in her adaptation of traditional African motifs. In 1968, however, the family settled permanently in Montreal, Canada.

For much of her youth, Verna intended to follow her father into medicine, and she excelled in biology. Her interest in art grew gradually. Aware from an early age that she had a good visual memory, her parents encouraged Verna's explorations of shapes, colors, and textures. Her first painting, for example, was a paint-by-numbers kit her mother brought to her during a hospital stay at about the age of ten; Verna would keep the result in her studio throughout her professional career. Her father was similarly encouraging, as an anecdote she told Robinette revealed. "I remember going to the park across from our house [in Montreal]," Verna said, "and there's this piece of root that I found, and I brought it home and I said to my dad, 'I think I want to do something with it.' And he said, 'Okay, well, I'll buy you some sandpaper, and what about if you sand it and then you varnish it with something, or stain it.' The thing that was interesting to me was that it was a root, but it reminded me of a fish. I like shapes that remind you of something else."

Even as they encouraged her artistic explorations, Verna's parents saw to it that she took advantage of more traditional educational opportunities. These included English lessons at a YMCA summer camp, Saturday art classes as a young teenager, and the Paris American Academy, a fine-arts program in the French capital that she attended in the summer of 1985. Her experience in Paris influenced her to apply to art school, and in 1986 she entered the School of the Art Institute of Chicago (SAIC) as an undergraduate. After receiving her BFA degree in the winter of 1988, she remained at the school to enter its graduate program. She would later describe her years in Chicago to Robinette as a "great experience," noting in particular

At a Glance . . .

Born on March 31, 1961, in Port-au-Prince, Haiti; died on March 11, 2008, in Madison, WI; daughter of Clara Lanier Verna (a teacher) and Joseph Marie Verna (a radiologist); children: Clara Alicia Verna. *Education:* School of the Art Institute of Chicago, BFA, 1988, MFA, 1990.

Career: University of Iowa, professor of art, 1995–2001; University of Wisconsin–Madison, professor of art, 2001–08.

Awards: Winter Fellowship (Visual Arts), Fine Arts Work Center, Provincetown, MA, 1997–98.

the help she received from drawing teacher Betsy Rupprecht and the inspiration she drew from the art institute's world-famous collections. She also was able to spend a semester abroad, studying printmaking in Germany.

After receiving her MFA from SAIC in the winter of 1990, Verna spent several years expanding and improving her portfolio before attaining her first major teaching position, at the University of Iowa, in 1995. She would remain there for six years, gaining confidence as a teacher and collaborating with colleagues, notably painter David Dunlap, on several major pieces. In 2001 T. L. Solien, a former colleague who had left Iowa for the University of Wisconsin–Madison, persuaded Verna to make the same move. As at Iowa, Verna carried a full course load in Wisconsin, teaching both introductory and advanced, graduate-level classes in painting and drawing. She was also a sought-after mentor known for her kind but honest appraisals of student work. As graduate student Jose Rodriguez remarked in a tribute posted on the Web site Memory-of.com, Verna "always offered honest and constructive feedback and never failed to bring insightful and enlightening resources and references to the table."

Verna worked in a wide variety of formats, including prints, collage, mixed media, and oil on canvas. In such works as *Untitled—Red Fro* (1999) and *MLK Jr., Reveries/Reverends* (2005–08), she explored issues of personal identity—particularly racial identity—and collective memory. The latter work, for example, juxtaposes a formal photograph of Dr. Martin Luther King Jr. with mundane family snapshots and living-room bric-a-brac. The contrast prompts the viewer to ponder the ways the civil rights struggle has affected the way ordinary people view themselves, their place in society,

and their past. *MLK Jr.* is technically a mixed-media piece, not a collage, but its collage-like juxtaposition of disparate elements is highly characteristic of Verna's work. As she remarked in an artist's statement posted on the Iowa Women Artists Web site, "My images develop through sifting, moving things around."

Verna died suddenly in her sleep on March 11, 2008, at her home in Madison, Wisconsin. The cause was a brain aneurysm. A longtime sufferer of severe headaches, Verna and her doctors knew of the problem; surgery to correct it had been scheduled for the following summer. By prior arrangement, her young daughter, Clara, moved to Canada to live with an aunt. Other survivors included her mother and her five siblings; her father died the same week, and a joint funeral was held in Canada on March 22, 2008.

As the Wisconsin campus struggled to come to terms with the sudden loss of one of its most popular professors, dozens of colleagues and students offered tributes. One of the simplest was given by Elaine Scheer, chair of the art department, who told Amanda Hoffstrom in the *Daily Cardinal,* a student newspaper, that Verna "was just a really wonderful teacher." Her work can be seen in collections across the United States, including at the Princeton University Art Museum in Princeton, New Jersey, and the University of Mississippi's Southern Graphics collection in Oxford, Mississippi.

Selected artwork

Belongings, 1995.
Sketchbook—Dennis & Voodoo, 1996–97.
Untitled—Red Fro, 1999.
Crowd—Salt, 2000.
Untitled (Head), 2001.
MLK Jr., Reveries/Reverends, 2005–08.

Sources

Periodicals

Hoffstrom, Amanda, "'Beloved' U. Wisconsin Art Professor Dies Suddenly," *Daily Cardinal* (Madison, WI), March 13, 2008.

Online

"Art Department to Host Memorial Service for Faculty Member," University of Wisconsin–Madison Art Department, April 29, 2008, http://art.wisc.edu/?folder=news&pagename=details&idNews=172 (accessed July 14, 2008).
"Gelsy Verna (1961–2008)," Memory-of.com, http://gelsy-verna.memory-of.com/Tributes.aspx (accessed July 15, 2008).

Robinette, Jane, "Gelsy Verna" (interview), Iowa Women Artists Oral History Project, August 1, 1999, http://lucidplanet.com/iwa/ArtistPages/vernag. htm (accessed July 14, 2008).

Other

Author's personal acquaintance with Verna, 2006–08.

—R. Anthony Kugler

Thomas Weeks III

1967—

Minister, writer

Weeks, Thomas III, photograph. AP Images.

Followers of preacher Thomas Weeks III, affectionately known among congregants as "Bishop Weeks," believed their leader had a marriage made in heaven. He and his wife, the nationally known televangelist and "prophetess" Juanita Bynum, never seemed to be far from one another's side. Following their much-publicized wedding in 2003 (which had been preceded by a private civil ceremony in 2002), they preached about the sanctity of marriage and offered counsel on relationships in a popular series of books and workshops called Teach Me How to Love You.

Congregants were shocked, to say the least, when in August of 2007 the preacher was accused of domestic violence following an altercation between Weeks and Bynum in an Atlanta, Georgia, hotel parking lot. Weeks, charged with assault, maintained his innocence, while Bynum began speaking publicly about their rocky relationship, calling herself the "new face of domestic violence." The bizarre battle that played out between Weeks and Bynum, both in the courtroom and in the court of public opinion, seemed as if it were straight out of a soap opera. In the aftermath of the couple's divorce, Weeks has tried to rebuild his reputation in the church by telling his side of the story.

Thomas Wesley Weeks III was born in 1967 in Boston, Massachusetts, the eldest son of Thomas W. Weeks and Leona Brown Weeks. After living in New York and Indiana, his family settled in Wilmington, Delaware, where his father was pastor and then bishop of the Greater Bethel Apostolic Temple. Thomas Weeks III attended the University of Delaware, majoring in mass communications. Then, heeding the call of the church, as his father and grandfather had done before him, Weeks went on to study theology and Christian counseling at the Christian International College of Theology. He was ordained as an elder in the Pentecostal Assemblies of the World and served under his father's pastorate, though both men would leave the denomination in 2001.

Established Church in Washington, DC

Thomas Weeks III established the Global Destiny Church, an evangelical church in Washington, DC, in

1997. The enterprise expanded in 2003 to encompass a global outreach ministry for the Internet community, MyGlobalDestiny.com. A second church in Duluth, Georgia, just outside Atlanta, opened in 2006, and a third location in California was planned. As part of his ministry, Weeks lectured widely at churches across the country and wrote several books outlining the relationship between faith and prosperity.

Weeks and Bynum, both of whom had been married previously, wed in a private ceremony in Las Vegas on July 22, 2002, but did not announce their union until October of that year. In the spring of 2003, the couple threw a lavish million-dollar wedding at the Regent Wall Street Hotel in New York City that was attended by nearly one thousand guests and televised on the Trinity Broadcasting Network. At the ceremony Weeks presented Bynum, flanked by a wedding party of eighty people, with a 7.76-carat diamond ring. "This was my once-in-a-lifetime wedding," Bynum famously told *Ebony* magazine in February 2004. "I did it this way because I plan to stay married."

Following their marriage, Weeks and Bynum developed a series of workshops and books called Teach Me How to Love You, in which they counseled Christian congregants on how to build a healthy relationship. In 2006 they moved from Washington, DC, to a new $2.5 million home in Duluth, where they were setting up a second ministry. The couple suffered serious financial problems—Weeks reportedly had left a number of creditors unpaid upon departing Washington—and church members began to suspect that all was not well. According to a report in *Essence* magazine, Weeks removed photographs of his wife at the church

and minimized her presence there. The couple separated in June of 2007.

On the night of August 21, 2007, Weeks and Bynum met at the Renaissance Concourse Hotel in Atlanta to discuss their marital problems. They began arguing in the hotel parking lot around 4:00 a.m. According to police reports, Weeks choked Bynum, pushed her to the ground, and then began kicking her, leaving her with bruises on the neck and upper torso. The altercation ended when a bellman pulled Weeks off his wife. Bynum refused offers of police and ambulance assistance, though she later visited a hospital, and photographs of her bruises soon appeared on the Internet. Weeks fled the scene but, two days later, turned himself in to police at the Fulton County Jail. He was released on a $40,000 bond and ordered to have no contact with Bynum. In court Weeks pleaded not guilty to charges of aggravated assault, terroristic threats, and simple battery.

In the aftermath of the attack, Weeks blamed the devil for the alleged assault, and held to his statement that he had done nothing more than "push" his wife. Later he claimed that, in fact, he was the one who had been abused in the relationship. "I never hit or did anything to physically harm her," Weeks said, according to the *Atlanta Journal-Constitution* on December 19, 2007. "I have been the one that has been physically abused. I kept it quiet for over 90 days. I have been struck on the face and in the head.... I have been choked."

Bynum filed for divorce in September, and soon began speaking publicly about their relationship, which, she said, had been troubled since at least 2005. She appeared on the Tom Joyner radio program and on Fox television's *Divorce Court,* counseling a couple that was considering divorce. In December of 2007 she granted a lengthy interview with *Essence* magazine, in which she aired the couple's dirty laundry. Weeks countered by publishing a tell-all book, *What Love Taught Me,* containing chapters with such provocative titles as "I'd Rather Push You Now Than Punch You Later."

Pleaded Guilty in March of 2008

Though he had steadfastly maintained his innocence for more than six months, even reaffirming his not-guilty plea in February of 2008, Weeks surprised the court in March, when he pleaded guilty to one count of aggravated assault, then turned to Bynum and said, according to the *Atlanta Journal-Constitution* on March 12, 2008, "I want to apologize to my wife for all actions you had to go through. I know it has been difficult. I appreciate you and I thank you." Surprisingly, Bynum asked the court not to send her husband to jail, at the request of Weeks's grandfather. Sentenced as a first offender to three years' probation, Weeks was required to undergo violence and anger counseling and complete two hundred hours of community service outside the church. In statements outside the courtroom, Weeks told reporters that he had changed his plea to spare his wife further embarrassment.

Weeks returned to the pulpit at Global Destiny Church in April, though the congregation, divided in their loyalties to Weeks and Bynum, was much diminished. Although rumors of a possible reconciliation swirled—fueled by images of the couple embracing during depositions—Weeks and Bynum finalized their divorce on June 20, 2008. Weeks retained ownership of Global Destiny Church and his international ministry. He rereleased *What Love Taught Me,* developing the book into a webinar (Web-based seminar) and lecture series, and planned to publish a new book, with the title *Finding Yourself While in Transition: For Singles and Divorcees,* in 2009.

Selected writings

(With Juanita Bynum) *Teach Me How to Love You,* Legacy Publishing, 2003.
Even as Your Soul Prospers: Realize Your Purpose, Release Your Blessings, Harrison House, 2004.
40 Days to a Prosperous Soul Devotional: When You Know Your Purpose, It's Time to Unlock Your Abundance, Harrison House, 2005.

What's on Your Mind? Your Success Begins with Your Thinking, Harrison House, 2006.
Next Level Living: Mastering the Good Life God Has Given You, Harrison House, 2007.
What Love Taught Me, Global Destiny Publishing, 2008.

Sources

Periodicals

Atlanta Journal-Constitution, December 19, 2007; February 26, 2008; March 10, 2008, p. B5; March 12, 2008, p. B1.
Ebony, February 2004.
Essence, November 2007, p. 162.
Jet, September 10, 2007.
New York Times, September 20, 2007.

Online

"About Thomas Weeks III," Harrison House, http://www.harrisonhouse.com/eaysp/index.php?body=about_author (accessed July 31, 2008).
Bishop Weeks Official Web Site, http://www.bishopweeks.com (accessed July 31, 2008).

—Deborah A. Ring

Clarence Williams

1967—

Photojournalist, educator

Clarence Williams is one of the nation's most respected photojournalists. He rose to prominence quickly, winning a Pulitzer Prize for his work in the *Los Angeles Times* by the time he was thirty-one years old. Upon leaving the *Times* in 2003, he embarked on a series of solo projects, most notably an in-depth examination of the devastation of New Orleans, Louisiana, in 2005 by Hurricane Katrina.

Born on January 22, 1967, in Philadelphia, Pennsylvania, Williams attended local schools before entering Temple University, one of the city's leading educational institutions, which granted him a bachelor's degree in mass communication in 1993. While at Temple he worked closely with a highly regarded journalism professor, Ed Trayes, whom Williams has identified as one of his greatest mentors. In his senior year he worked for several months as an intern in the photography department of the *Philadelphia Tribune,* where he gained further experience in the specialized techniques of photojournalism.

Following graduation, Williams obtained a job as a staff photographer for Times Community Newspapers, the publisher of more than a dozen weekly newspapers across northern Virginia. He remained in Virginia for a year, from 1993 to 1994, before moving to Los Angeles, where he won a spot at the *Los Angeles Times,* one of the nation's most influential newspapers, as a trainee in a well-known diversity program known as METPRO. Founded in 1984 by the Times Mirror Group, then the publisher of the *Times,* in an effort to increase the minority presence in its news-

rooms, METPRO offered participants intensive, on-the-job training. Williams completed the program in 1994 and was offered a permanent position as a photographer for the *Times* the following year. In 1996 he received a promotion to staff photographer, a position he held until leaving the *Times* in 2003.

It was while working for the Los Angeles newspaper that Williams established his reputation as a fearless journalist and gifted photographer. His assignments often took him to remote and dangerous regions across the globe, including the West Bank city of Hebron, a focal point of the Israeli-Palestinian conflict, and the war-torn African nation of Angola. It was, however, Williams's detailed depiction of heroin addicts and their children in central Los Angeles that brought him to national prominence. In one widely reproduced photograph from the series, titled *Orphans of Addiction,* a girl of three is shown having her teeth brushed with a toothbrush belonging to her mother, an HIV-positive addict. Another photo depicts an eight-year-old boy cowering in fear from the verbal abuse of his father's girlfriend. In an interview with Vincent Alabiso in the *Nieman Reports,* a publication of Harvard University's Nieman Foundation for Journalism, critic James Dooley cited the series as a prime example of "hard-hitting, provocative, and tender photojournalism." Other critics agreed, and in April of 1998, it was announced that *Orphans of Addiction* had earned Williams the Pulitzer Prize for Feature Photography. It was an extraordinary honor for someone only thirty-

At a Glance . . .

Born Clarence J. Williams III on January 22, 1967, in Philadelphia, PA. *Education:* Temple University, BA, mass communication, 1993.

Career: *Philadelphia Tribune,* photography intern, 1992–93; Times Community Newspapers, Reston, VA, staff photographer, 1993–94; *Los Angeles Times,* MET-PRO trainee, 1994, photographer, 1995, staff photographer, 1996–2003; Iris Photo Collective, cofounder, 1998; University of Southern Mississippi, distinguished visiting lecturer in photojournalism, 2006—.

Memberships: National Association of Black Journalists; National Press Photographers Association.

Awards: Fourth place, *Photographer's Forum* and Nikon Corporation Competition, 1991; first place for issues reporting, Pictures of the Year Contest, National Press Photographers Association, 1996; Pulitzer Prize for Feature Photography, 1998; first prize for domestic photojournalism, Robert F. Kennedy Memorial, 1998; Journalist of the Year, National Association of Black Journalists, 1998; Katrina Media Fellowship, Open Society Institute, 2006—.

Addresses: *Office*—c/o Department of Mass Communication and Journalism, 118 College Dr., #5121, University of Southern Mississippi, Hattiesburg, MS 39406-0001.

one years old, and with only five years of experience as a full-time journalist. As the Pulitzer Web site noted, however, Williams had begun receiving photography awards as early as 1991, when he took fourth place in a contest cosponsored by *Photographer's Forum* magazine and Nikon Corporation. Other notable awards have included first place for issues reporting in the 1996 Pictures of the Year Contest, an annual event sponsored by the National Press Photographers Association; Journalist of the Year honors from the National Association of Black Journalists in 1998; and first prize for domestic photojournalism from the Robert F. Kennedy Memorial, also in 1998.

In 2003 Williams resigned his position at the *Los Angeles Times* to pursue a variety of solo projects. In August of 2005 his career took an unexpected turn when he found himself at the center of one of the worst natural disasters in the nation's history. Williams was

visiting relatives on the east side of New Orleans when Hurricane Katrina struck on August 29, submerging more than 80 percent of the city. Williams spent three days trapped in an attic, along with his family, before escaping. Emerging to face a scene of utter devastation, Williams responded by keeping a journal and by photographing the efforts of the city's mostly African-American population to survive without adequate supplies of food, fresh water, shelter, and electricity. Among Williams's most poignant photos from this period are those featuring members of his own family, including Dominique Williams, the wife of a first cousin, who is shown weeping as she places all that remains of her family's possessions into a few small laundry baskets. In the weeks following the storm, the *Miami Herald* published a large selection of these photos, as well as excerpts from Williams's journal. Though the *Herald*'s series was the first time that Williams's writing had been featured so prominently, it has since become an important facet of his work, and his insightful commentaries on his own photographs have been widely admired.

Williams soon realized that the effects of Hurricane Katrina would not end with the initial recovery efforts he documented so thoroughly. In order to record the slow process of rebuilding, he moved from Los Angeles to New Orleans and obtained a grant from the Open Society Institute (OSI), an organization founded by the philanthropist George Soros, to produce what the institute's Web site calls "a photographic essay of post-Katrina New Orleans, from flood to aftermath to rebuilding, with a visual emphasis on the remnants of the cultural wealth and family ties that make this city unique." Williams's project, one of thirty-one sponsored by OSI in an effort to focus attention on Katrina and its aftermath, is titled *Another Black Blues Story.* "I am documenting the modern, real-life blues story that Hurricane Katrina thrust upon the world's consciousness," Williams wrote on OSI's Web site, adding that he is particularly concerned with "the continuing issues of racism, classism, and poverty that Katrina further unearthed."

In 2006 Williams was appointed distinguished visiting lecturer in photojournalism at the University of Southern Mississippi in Hattiesburg, a small town just over one hundred miles northeast of New Orleans. In addition to his teaching and mentoring duties there, he is heavily involved in the Iris Photo Collective, a group he cofounded with three other photographers in 1998. The purpose of the collective, according to its Website, is "to explore and document the relationships of people of color to the world." As of the summer of 2008, Williams was also reportedly working on his first book.

Sources

Periodicals

Associated Press, April 14, 1998.

Nieman Reports, Summer 1998.
Temple Review, Fall 2003, pp. 28–33.

Online

"About Iris Photo Collective," Iris Photo Collective, http://www.irisphotocollective.com/index2.php?ver=v1 (accessed July 30, 2008).

"Biography: Clarence Williams," Photography at Temple University, http://www.temple.edu/photo/photographers/clarence williams by Sarah Green/bio.htm (accessed July 27, 2008).

"Faculty Biographies," University of Southern Mississippi, http://www.usm.edu/mcj/facultybios.htm (accessed July 27, 2008).

"Fellow: Clarence Williams," Open Society Institute, http://www.soros.org/resources/multimedia/katrina/fellows/williams.php (accessed July 27, 2008).

"The 1998 Pulitzer Prize Winners: Feature Photography," Pulitzer Prizes, http://www.pulitzer.org/biography/1998,Feature+Photography (accessed July 27, 2008).

—R. Anthony Kugler

Russell Williams II

1952—

Sound mixer

Russell Williams II owns a pair of Academy Awards for best sound for his work on the films *Glory* and *Dances with Wolves.* The honors, both awarded in the early 1990s, came after Williams had been in the business nearly twenty years. When he started in Hollywood there were so few African Americans working behind the scenes that everybody knew everybody. "I introduced myself to producers, directors, and anyone who was in a crew position," he told writer Keisha Jackson in the *Washington Post.* "Nowadays they call it networking. Back then we called it hustling."

Born in 1952 in Washington, DC, Williams was raised by his mother's sister and her husband after his mother died when he was still an infant. The piano at his home led him, somewhat inadvertently, to his future vocation. Speaking with Donna Britt in the *Washington Post,* he recalled a childhood outburst of anger at having to do his chores. He began pounding on the keyboard hoping to needle his aunt; but by the time he left the piano he couldn't remember what he'd been angry about. "I said, 'Ahhhhhh—there's an emotional connection here.' So I began to search out music that could make me happy, could calm me." His first musical role model was jazz saxophonist John Coltrane, whose "playing was the first thing that taught me as a black man to go all the way," he told Britt. "Everybody else was telling me to play it safe."

Williams studied film and art history at American University in Washington, and worked at the college radio station for several years. He and a friend even launched WAMU's first black-music program, *Spirits*

Known and Unknown, featuring jazz, blues, and R&B tracks. It proved such a success that they started to host workshops for minority students at other schools who were interested in diversifying their college radio station programming. Williams earned his undergraduate degree from American University in 1974 and also studied at the Recording Institute of America in Silver Spring, Maryland. He spent much of the 1970s as a studio engineer or sound editor at various job sites, including the Library of Congress, Washington's NBC television affiliate station, and the city's ABC radio affiliate. In 1979 he requested and received a three-month leave of absence in order to try his luck in Hollywood. "After 90 days, I had seen enough to convince me to make a go of it," he told Aldore Collier in an interview for *Ebony* magazine.

Launching his own company, Sound Is Ready, Williams landed his first jobs in Southern California on films made by independent producers outside of the studio system, because he had not yet obtained the union card that was required for hiring at the major studios. He worked on a few forgettable B-movies, such as 1980's *Lifepod,* about a spaceship cruise that goes awry, and *Penitentiary 2* in 1982. His first studio production credit came as a boom-mike operator on the set of the popular teen comedy *Valley Girl* in 1983, and steady work as a sound mixer followed over the rest of the decade. He explained the process in the *Ebony* interview, telling Collier that "once my staff and I have met with the director and department heads, we watch a rehearsal of the scenes and determine the best way to

At a Glance . . .

Born on October 14, 1952, in Washington, DC; married Renee Leggett, 1989 (divorced 1994); married Rosalind, 2004; children: two (first marriage). *Education:* American University, BA, 1974; also studied at the Recording Institute of America, Silver Spring, MD, and the University of Sound Arts, Hollywood, CA, 1979.

Career: U.S. Library of Congress, studio engineer, 1971–73; WAMU-FM, engineer and host, 1972–79; WRC/NBC TV, engineer, 1973, 1977; WMAL-TV, documentary sound recordist, transfer engineer, and floor director, 1974–76; WMAL/ABC radio, Washington, engineer and editor, 1978–79; Sound Is Ready, founder and principal, 1979–2002; has taught sound arts in the film-school departments of the University of California–Los Angeles, University of Southern California, and California State University–Northridge; American University, School of Communication, instructor and artist in residence, 2002—.

Memberships: International Alliance of Theatrical Stage Employees, Moving Picture Technicians, Artists and Allied Crafts (IATSE); Academy of Motion Picture Arts and Sciences; Academy of Television Arts and Sciences.

Awards: Emmy Award, Academy of Television Arts and Sciences, outstanding sound mixing, 1988, for *Terrorist on Trial: The United States vs. Salim Ajami* (television movie, CBS); Academy Award, Academy of Motion Picture Arts and Sciences, best sound, 1990, for *Glory* (motion picture); Academy Award, best sound, 1991, for *Dances with Wolves* (motion picture); Emmy Award, outstanding sound mixing, 1998, for *Twelve Angry Men* (television movie, Showtime/ATAS).

Addresses: *Office*—School of Communication, American University, 4400 Massachusetts Ave. NW, Washington, DC 20016.

Terrorist on Trial: The United States vs. Salim Ajami, about a fictional federal prosecution of a man kidnapped in the Middle East and brought to the United States.

Williams worked on the well-received Kevin Costner baseball tale *Field of Dreams,* which was released in 1989, the same year as Williams's most enjoyable project to date, *Glory.* The latter film starred Denzel Washington as one of the soldiers in the historic all-black 54th Massachusetts Volunteer Infantry Regiment that fought in the U.S. Civil War for the Union side. Williams already knew the story of the pioneering infantry soldiers and eagerly accepted the *Glory* job when it was offered to him. "Everybody felt this was going to be an important movie," he told Britt in the *Washington Post* interview. "A lot of films out here are put together strictly for entertainment; it's rare you get a chance to work on a piece of history."

Glory won Williams his first Academy Award in the best sound category, which he shared with colleagues Donald O. Mitchell, Gregg C. Rudloff, and Elliot Tyson. He was not the first African American to win an Oscar for sound—that achievement had gone to Willie Burton a year earlier for *Bird,* the biopic of jazz great Charlie Parker. Williams's second Academy Award came for *Dances with Wolves,* a nineteenth-century epic that starred Costner as a Civil War veteran who falls in with a band of Native Americans and also marked the actor's directorial debut. Williams had hesitated when Costner offered him the job, for it meant long stretches of filming in a remote part of South Dakota. That prairie landscape presented more than the usual challenge for Williams as a sound mixer—often times in period films modern noises like aircraft flying overhead must be masked out of the soundtrack—but in this case the constant high winds common to the plains meant that recording a few lines of dialogue was difficult. The realistic end result on *Dances with Wolves* won Williams his second Oscar, which he shared with colleagues Jeffrey Perkins, Bill W. Benton, and Greg Watkins. It marked a historic moment in the history of the Academy Awards: That year both he and actor Whoopi Goldberg became the first African Americans to win a second Oscar in their categories.

The professional accolades boosted Williams's reputation in Hollywood, and he went on to work on a number of box-office hits. These included *Boomerang, Waiting to Exhale, The Negotiator, Life, Training Day,* and *The Sum of All Fears.* In 2002 he returned to Washington, taking up a position at his alma mater as an instructor and artist in residence at American University's School of Communication. "The only reason I went to L.A. in the first place is because no one would be able to question my credentials once I returned to the area," he told Jackson in the *Washington Post* interview. "I just didn't plan on staying so long."

capture the sound. We either do it with overhead microphones or body mikes." In 1988 he won his first Emmy for sound on the made-for-television drama

Selected works

Sound mixer

Making the Grade, 1984.
Number One with a Bullet, 1986.
Good to Go, 1986.
Invaders from Mars, 1986.
In the Mood (also known as *The Woo Woo Kid*), 1987.
The In Crowd, 1987.
Terrorist on Trial: The United States vs. Salim Ajami (television movie), CBS, 1987.
Field of Dreams, 1989.
Glory, 1989.
The Women of Brewster Place (television movie), ABC, 1989.
Dances with Wolves, 1990.
Jungle Fever, 1991.
The Distinguished Gentleman, 1992.
Boomerang, 1992.
Mo' Money, 1992.
Drop Zone, 1994.
Waiting to Exhale, 1995.
How to Make an American Quilt, 1995.
B*A*P*S, 1997.
The Negotiator, 1998.
The Players Club, 1998.
Life, 1999.
Rules of Engagement, 2000.
Golden Dreams, 2001.
Training Day, 2001.
Martin Lawrence Live: Runteldat, 2002.
The Sum of All Fears, 2002.
Deliver Us from Eva, 2003.

Sources

Periodicals

Ebony, April 1991, p. 86.
Jet, April 15, 1991, p. 79.
Washington Post, April 14, 1991, p. G1; June 25, 2004.

Online

Warren, Mitchell, "The State of Black Film," *theBoxofficereport,* BoxOffice, http://boxoffice.com/report/2007/10/state-of-black-film.php (accessed August 25, 2008).

—Carol Brennan

Rayfield Wright

1945—

Professional football player, business executive

Wright, Rayfield, photograph. Jonathan Daniel/Getty Images.

The life and work of Rayfield Wright focus primarily on two things: his religious faith and football. He is best known for his thirteen seasons in the National Football League (NFL) with the Dallas Cowboys, from 1967 to 1979, appearing in five Super Bowls. Wright was such a superior and versatile athlete that he started out as a basketball player in high school, played both basketball and football in college, and played a variety of positions for the Cowboys during his pro-ball years. Most prominently, however, "Big Cat" Wright played tight end, from 1967 to 1968, and right tackle, from 1969 to 1979. After Wright's retirement from professional football, Dallas Cowboy coach Tom Landry paid homage to this football legend and wrote to the State of Georgia Hall of Fame, as excerpted on Wright's Web site, that Wright was "the most honored offensive lineman in Cowboys history."

Larry Rayfield Wright was born in Griffin, Georgia, in 1945 and was raised by his mother and grandmother. His grandmother was a significant influence in his life, teaching him at a young age about respect, faith, and prayer. Although he had few material things during his childhood years, he had something much more precious to him—a deep love of God and family. The influence that God and family had in Wright's life was made apparent in his speech during his induction into the Pro Football Hall of Fame in 2006. As he reflected on his life and career, Wright described "God's plan" for him and referred to family members as "angels here today that are enshrined in the heavens' Hall of Fame."

As a student at Fairmont High School in Griffin, Georgia, Wright—amazingly—did not make the football team in his first three years at that institution. But the six-foot-seven-inch Wright did make the basketball team. His brother Lamar had taught him the basics of sports, and he practiced on the streets with others in the neighborhood.

Wright played basketball so well, in fact, that Loyola University extended him an invitation to play basketball for them, but Wright declined due to financial hardship. As an alternative, he decided to enter the military and motivated some of his friends do the same. A turn of events, however, changed Wright's decision to enter military service; instead he took an athletic scholarship offered to him by Coach Stan Lomax of Fort Valley

At a Glance . . .

Born Larry Rayfield Wright on August 23, 1945, in Griffin, GA; son of Sam and Opel Wright; raised by his mother and grandmother; children: La Ray, Anisha, Larry, Arial. *Religion:* Christian. *Education:* Graduated from Fort Valley State College, Georgia, 1967.

Career: Dallas Cowboys football team, various positions, 1967–79; Arizona Rattlers (Arena Football League), assistant coach, 1992; Wright's Sports and Nutrition, CEO; PetroSun LLC, president; Rayfield Wright Foundation, president; Kids 4 Tomorrow, cofounder and president; appointed to the Arizona Juvenile Supreme Court; works as a motivational speaker.

Memberships: NFL Alumni, president, mid-1990s; NFL Alumni, Arizona chapter, director.

Awards: All Pro Selection, National Football League, 1971, 1972, 1974, and 1975; Offensive Lineman of the Year, National Football League, 1972 and 1974; Hall of Fame, Griffin GA, 1974; National Football League 1970s All-Decade Team; Hall of Fame, Fort Valley State College, 1983; Hall of Fame, State of Georgia, 1988; All Super Bowl Team, National Football League, 1990; Legends Award, National Football League, 1990; Hall of Faith Award, Athletes International Ministries, 1997; Texas Black Sports Hall of Fame, 2002; Alumni "Ring of Honor," Dallas Chapter, National Football League, 2003; "Ring of Honor" at Texas Stadium, Dallas Cowboys football organization, 2004; Texas Sports Hall of Fame, 2005; Pro Football Hall of Fame, 2006.

Addresses: *Offices*—R. Wright Enterprises and Rayfield Wright Foundation, PO Box 1865, Weatherford, TX 76086; Wright Sports and Nutrition, 2008 E. Randol Mill Rd., Ste. 109, Arlington, TX 76011. *Web*—http://www.rayfieldwright.com.

because he was committed to completing his college degree.

During his senior year, unbeknownst to Wright, Dallas Cowboys' scouts were looking for football talent in historically black colleges and universities. Gil Brandt of the Cowboys noticed Wright and phoned to tell him that the Cowboys were interested in drafting him. In his 2006 Hall of Fame enshrinement speech, Wright refers to this moment as "a God given opportunity," one that he would not turn down. Wright mused that if he did not match the Cowboys' expectations during training camp, he could still capture a slot in the National Basketball Association (NBA) with the Cincinnati Royals. But Wright did not have to worry; he was one of only five players picked by the Cowboys to join the team out of the 137 who had been invited to attend training camp that year.

Wright started his career with the Cowboys as a tight end, but he was also used as a defensive lineman and offensive tackle. In 1969 Dallas Cowboys' right tackle Ralph Neely suffered an injury, and Wright was given his starting position for the 1970 season because of stellar performance on the team. Wright kept that position through 1979 and his retirement from pro football.

During his thirteen seasons with the Dallas Cowboys, Wright was cocaptain for seven seasons and played in 166 games, five Super Bowls, and six NFC (National Football Conference) Championship games. Wright's excellent blocking on the field and his leadership as cocaptain of the team are said to have helped the Dallas Cowboys win ten division titles and six conference crowns. Wright won personal accolades as well, including making All Pro Selection (NFL best players of each position) in 1971, 1972, 1974, and 1975; being named Offensive Lineman of the Year in 1972 and 1974; and being chosen for the All-Decade Team for the 1970s. He was inducted into the Fort Valley State College Hall of Fame in 1983, the State of Georgia Hall of Fame in 1988, the Texas Black Sports Hall of Fame in 2002, the Texas Sports Hall of Fame in 2005, and the Pro Football Hall of Fame in 2006. Wright retired from the Dallas Cowboys and pro football at the age of thirty-four due to a knee injury.

Since his retirement, Rayfield Wright has led an entrepreneurial and philanthropic life. He is president of PetroSun, a company that provides products and services to the oil industry. He is also CEO of Rayfield Wright Sports and Nutrition, a company that sells health-related products such as vitamins, minerals, and skin-care creams.

Wright's philanthropy concentrates on helping children. Wright told E. M. Swift in *Sports Illustrated* in 2006 that he "work[s] with a lot of young kids who feel they don't have the opportunity to make it in this world." Wright's work shows his focus on this goal.

State College, a historically black institution in Georgia. While there, Wright played both basketball and football, but admits he liked playing basketball the most. The Cincinnati Royals recognized Wright's basketball passion and skill and offered him a place on their team. Only a junior, Wright declined the offer to play pro ball,

Shortly after his retirement from football, Wright directed the Arizona chapter of the charitable organization NFL Alumni, which operates by the motto "Caring for Kids." Because of his work with at-risk, inner-city children, Wright was appointed to the Arizona Juvenile Supreme Court. Wright is also the founder—with other retired NFL players—and president of the not-for-profit organization Kids 4 Tomorrow. In this group, retired professional athletes work with school children of all ages. Furthermore, through the Rayfield Wright Foundation, Wright helps students obtain college educations by raising funds for scholarships.

Selected works

Books

(With Jeanette DeVader) *Wright Up Front* (autobiography), EmeraldPress, 2005.

Sources

Periodicals

Sports Illustrated, July 26, 2006, pp. 62–63.

Online

Brandt, Gil, "Hall Recall: Rayfield Wright," Pro Football Hall of Fame, http://www.profootballhof.com/history/release.jsp?release_id=2168&print=yes (accessed September 17, 2008).

"Class of 2006 Will Come from List of Finalists: Rayfield Wright," Pro Football Hall of Fame, January 11, 2006, http://www.profootballhof.com/en shrinement/story.jsp?story_id=1944 (accessed September 15, 2008).

Mosley, Matt, "Rayfield Wright: Hall of Fame Tackle, Respected Voice," ESPN.com, April 18, 2008, http://sports.espn.go.com/espn/print?id=334946 1&type=story (accessed September 14, 2008).

"PetroSun President Rayfield Wright to Be Inducted into the NFL Hall of Fame," *News Blaze,* August 3, 2006, http://newsblaze.com/story/200608030 6582900002.mir/topstory.html (accessed September 15, 2008).

"Rayfield Wright," NationMaster, http://www.nation master.com/encyclopedia/Rayfield-Wright (accessed September 17, 2008).

"Rayfield Wright," Pro Football Hall of Fame, http://www.profootballhof.com/hof/member.jsp?player_id=258&print=yes (accessed September 15, 2008).

"Rayfield Wright," Rayfield Wright Official Web Site, http://www.rayfieldwright.com (accessed September 14, 2008).

"Rayfield Wright's Enshrinement Speech Transcript," Pro Football Hall of Fame, August 5, 2006, http://www.profootballhof.com/history/release.jsp?release_id=2181&print=yes (accessed September 15, 2008).

"Rayfield Wright That Big Cat," Cowboys Pride, http://www.cowboyspride.net/forum/showthread.php?t=27350 (accessed September 17, 2008).

"Six Named to Hall's Class of 2006!" Pro Football Hall of Fame, February 4, 2006, http://www.profoot ball hof.com/history/release.jsp?release_id=1953&print=yes (accessed September 15, 2008).

—Sandra Alters

Cumulative Nationality Index

Volume numbers appear in **bold**

American

Aaliyah **30**
Aaron, Hank **5**
Abbott, Robert Sengstacke **27**
Abdul-Jabbar, Kareem **8**
Abdur-Rahim, Shareef **28**
Abele, Julian **55**
Abernathy, Ralph David **1**
Aberra, Amsale **67**
Abu-Jamal, Mumia **15**
Ace, Johnny **36**
Adams, Eula L. **39**
Adams, Floyd, Jr. **12**
Adams, Jenoyne **60**
Adams, Johnny **39**
Adams, Leslie **39**
Adams, Oleta **18**
Adams, Osceola Macarthy **31**
Adams, Sheila J. **25**
Adams, Yolanda **17, 67**
Adams-Campbell, Lucille L. **60**
Adams Earley, Charity **13, 34**
Adams-Ender, Clara **40**
Adderley, Julian "Cannonball" **30**
Adderley, Nat **29**
Adkins, Rod **41**
Adkins, Rutherford H. **21**
Adu, Freddy **67**
Agyeman, Jaramogi Abebe **10, 63**
Ailey, Alvin **8**
Akil, Mara Brock **60**
Akon **68**
Al-Amin, Jamil Abdullah **6**
Albright, Gerald **23**
Alcorn, George Edward, Jr. **59**
Alert, Kool DJ Red **33**
Alexander, Archie Alphonso **14**
Alexander, Clifford **26**
Alexander, Joyce London **18**
Alexander, Khandi **43**
Alexander, Margaret Walker **22**
Alexander, Sadie Tanner Mossell **22**
Alexander, Shaun **58**
Ali, Hana Yasmeen **52**
Ali, Laila **27, 63**
Ali, Muhammad **2, 16, 52**
Allain, Stephanie **49**
Allen, Byron **3, 24**
Allen, Claude **68**
Allen, Debbie **13, 42**
Allen, Ethel D. **13**
Allen, Marcus **20**
Allen, Robert L. **38**

Allen, Samuel W. **38**
Allen, Tina **22**
Allen-Buillard, Melba **55**
Alston, Charles **33**
Amaker, Norman **63**
Amaker, Tommy **62**
Amerie **52**
Ames, Wilmer **27**
Amos, Emma **63**
Amos, John **8, 62**
Amos, Wally **9**
Anderson, Anthony **51**
Anderson, Carl **48**
Anderson, Charles Edward **37**
Anderson, Eddie "Rochester" **30**
Anderson, Elmer **25**
Anderson, Jamal **22**
Anderson, Marian **2, 33**
Anderson, Michael P. **40**
Anderson, Mike **63**
Anderson, Norman B. **45**
Anderson, William G(ilchrist), D.O. **57**
Andrews, Benny **22, 59**
Andrews, Bert **13**
Andrews, Raymond **4**
Angelou, Maya **1, 15**
Ansa, Tina McElroy **14**
Anthony, Carmelo **46**
Anthony, Wendell **25**
Appiah, Kwame Anthony **67**
Archer, Dennis **7, 36**
Archie-Hudson, Marguerite **44**
Ardoin, Alphonse **65**
Arkadie, Kevin **17**
Armstrong, Louis **2**
Armstrong, Robb **15**
Armstrong, Vanessa Bell **24**
Arnez J **53**
Arnold, Tichina **63**
Arnwine, Barbara **28**
Arrington, Richard **24**
Arroyo, Martina **30**
Artest, Ron **52**
Asante, Molefi Kete **3**
Ashanti **37**
Ashe, Arthur **1, 18**
Ashford, Emmett **22**
Ashford, Evelyn **63**
Ashford, Nickolas **21**
Ashley-Ward, Amelia **23**
Atkins, Cholly **40**
Atkins, Erica **34**
Atkins, Juan **50**

Atkins, Russell **45**
Atkins, Tina **34**
Aubert, Alvin **41**
Auguste, Donna **29**
Austin, Gloria **63**
Austin, Jim **63**
Austin, Junius C. **44**
Austin, Lovie **40**
Austin, Patti **24**
Autrey, Wesley **68**
Avant, Clarence **19**
Avery, Byllye Y. **66**
Ayers, Roy **16**
Babatunde, Obba **35**
Bacon-Bercey, June **38**
Badu, Erykah **22**
Bahati, Wambui **60**
Bailey, Buster **38**
Bailey, Chauncey **68**
Bailey, Clyde **45**
Bailey, DeFord **33**
Bailey, Philip **63**
Bailey, Radcliffe **19**
Bailey, Xenobia **11**
Baines, Harold **32**
Baiocchi, Regina Harris **41**
Baisden, Michael **25, 66**
Baker, Anita **21, 48**
Baker, Augusta **38**
Baker, Dusty **8, 43**
Baker, Ella **5**
Baker, Gwendolyn Calvert **9**
Baker, Houston A., Jr. **6**
Baker, Josephine **3**
Baker, LaVern **26**
Baker, Maxine B. **28**
Baker, Thurbert **22**
Baker, Vernon Joseph **65**
Baldwin, James **1**
Ballance, Frank W. **41**
Ballard, Allen Butler, Jr. **40**
Ballard, Hank **41**
Bambaataa, Afrika **34**
Bambara, Toni Cade **10**
Bandele, Asha **36**
Banks, Ernie **33**
Banks, Jeffrey **17**
Banks, Michelle **59**
Banks, Paula A. **68**
Banks, Tyra **11, 50**
Banks, William **11**
Banner, David **55**
Baquet, Dean **63**
Baraka, Amiri **1, 38**

Barber, Ronde **41**
Barber, Tiki **57**
Barboza, Anthony **10**
Barclay, Paris **37**
Barden, Don H. **9, 20**
Barker, Danny **32**
Barkley, Charles **5, 66**
Barlow, Roosevelt **49**
Barnes, Roosevelt "Booba" **33**
Barnes, Steven **54**
Barnett, Amy Du Bois **46**
Barnett, Etta Moten **56**
Barnett, Marguerite **46**
Barney, Lem **26**
Barnhill, David **30**
Barrax, Gerald William **45**
Barrett, Andrew C. **12**
Barrett, Jacquelyn **28**
Barrino, Fantasia **53**
Barry, Marion S(hepilov, Jr.) **7, 44**
Barthe, Richmond **15**
Basie, Count **23**
Basquiat, Jean-Michel **5**
Bass, Charlotta Spears **40**
Bass, Karen **70**
Bassett, Angela **6, 23, 62**
Bates, Daisy **13**
Bates, Karen Grigsby **40**
Bates, Peg Leg **14**
Bath, Patricia E. **37**
Batiste, Alvin **66**
Battle, Kathleen **70**
Baugh, David **23**
Baylor, Don **6**
Baylor, Helen **36**
Beach, Michael **26**
Beal, Bernard B. **46**
Beals, Jennifer **12**
Beals, Melba Patillo **15**
Bearden, Romare **2, 50**
Beasley, Jamar **29**
Beasley, Phoebe **34**
Beatty, Talley **35**
Bechet, Sidney **18**
Beckford, Tyson **11, 68**
Beckham, Barry **41**
Belafonte, Harry **4, 65**
Bell, Derrick **6**
Bell, James "Cool Papa" **36**
Bell, James A. **50**
Bell, James Madison **40**
Bell, Michael **40**
Bell, Robert Mack **22**
Bellamy, Bill **12**

175

Torres, Gina **52**
Torry, Guy **31**
Touré, Askia (Muhammad Abu Bakr el) **47**
Touré, Faya Ora Rose **56**
Toussaint, Allen **60**
Towns, Edolphus **19**
Townsend, Robert **4, 23**
Tresvant, Ralph **57**
Tribble, Israel, Jr. **8**
Trotter, Donne E. **28**
Trotter, Lloyd G. **56**
Trotter, Monroe **9**
Trueheart, William E. **49**
Tubbs Jones, Stephanie **24**
Tubman, Harriet **9**
Tucker, C. Delores **12, 56**
Tucker, Chris **13, 23, 62**
Tucker, Cynthia **15, 61**
Tucker, Rosina **14**
Tunie, Tamara **63**
Tunnell, Emlen **54**
Turnbull, Charles Wesley **62**
Turnbull, Walter **13, 60**
Turner, Henry McNeal **5**
Turner, Ike **68**
Turner, Tina **6, 27**
Tyler, Aisha N. **36**
Tyree, Omar Rashad **21**
Tyson, Andre **40**
Tyson, Asha **39**
Tyson, Cicely **7, 51**
Tyson, Mike **28, 44**
Tyson, Neil deGrasse **15, 65**
Uggams, Leslie **23**
Underwood, Blair **7, 27**
Union, Gabrielle **31**
Unseld, Wes **23**
Upshaw, Gene **18, 47**
Usher **23, 56**
Usry, James L. **23**
Ussery, Terdema II **29**
Utendahl, John **23**
Valentino, Bobby **62**
Van Lierop, Robert **53**
Van Peebles, Mario **2, 51**
Van Peebles, Melvin **7**
Vance, Courtney B. **15, 60**
VanDerZee, James **6**
Vandross, Luther **13, 48, 59**
Vanzant, Iyanla **17, 47**
Vaughan, Sarah **13**
Vaughn, Countess **53**
Vaughn, Gladys Gary **47**
Vaughn, Mo **16**
Vaughn, Viola **70**
Vaughns, Cleopatra **46**
Vega, Marta Moreno **61**
Velez-Rodriguez, Argelia **56**
Verdelle, A. J. **26**
Vereen, Ben **4**
Verrett, Shirley **66**
Vick, Michael **39, 65**
Vincent, Marjorie Judith **2**
Von Lipsey, Roderick K. **11**
Waddles, Charleszetta "Mother" **10, 49**
Wade, Dwyane **61**
Wade-Gayles, Gloria Jean **41**
Wagner, Annice **22**
Wainwright, Joscelyn **46**
Walker, A'lelia **14**
Walker, Albertina **10, 58**

Walker, Alice **1, 43**
Walker, Bernita Ruth **53**
Walker, Cedric "Ricky" **19**
Walker, Cora T. **68**
Walker, Dianne **57**
Walker, George **37**
Walker, Herschel **1, 69**
Walker, Hezekiah **34**
Walker, John T. **50**
Walker, Madame C. J. **7**
Walker, Maggie Lena **17**
Walker, Margaret **29**
Walker, Rebecca **50**
Walker, T. J. **7**
Wallace, Ben **54**
Wallace, Joaquin **49**
Wallace, Michele Faith **13**
Wallace, Perry E. **47**
Wallace, Phyllis A. **9**
Wallace, Rasheed **56**
Wallace, Sippie **1**
Waller, Fats **29**
Ward, Andre **62**
Ward, Benjamin **68**
Ward, Douglas Turner **42**
Ward, Lloyd **21, 46**
Ware, Andre **37**
Ware, Carl H. **30**
Warfield, Marsha **2**
Warner, Malcolm-Jamal **22, 36**
Warren, Michael **27**
Warwick, Dionne **18**
Washington, Alonzo **29**
Washington, Booker T. **4**
Washington, Denzel **1, 16**
Washington, Dinah **22**
Washington, Fredi **10**
Washington, Gene **63**
Washington, Grover, Jr. **17, 44**
Washington, Harold **6**
Washington, Harriet A. **69**
Washington, Isaiah **62**
Washington, James, Jr. **38**
Washington, James Melvin **50**
Washington, Kenny **50**
Washington, Kerry **46**
Washington, Laura S. **18**
Washington, MaliVai **8**
Washington, Mary T. **57**
Washington, Patrice Clarke **12**
Washington, Regynald G. **44**
Washington, Val **12**
Washington, Walter **45**
Wasow, Omar **15**
Waters, Benny **26**
Waters, Ethel **7**
Waters, Maxine **3, 67**
Waters, Muddy **34**
Watkins, Donald **35**
Watkins, Levi, Jr. **9**
Watkins, Perry **12**
Watkins, Shirley R. **17**
Watkins, Tionne "T-Boz" **34**
Watkins, Walter C. **24**
Watley, Jody **54**
Watson, Bob **25**
Watson, Carlos **50**
Watson, Diane **41**
Watson, Johnny "Guitar" **18**
Watt, Melvin **26**
Wattleton, Faye **9**
Watts, J. C., Jr. **14, 38**
Watts, Reggie **52**

Watts, Rolonda **9**
Wayans, Damon **8, 41**
Wayans, Keenen Ivory **18**
Wayans, Marlon **29**
Wayans, Shawn **29**
Weathers, Carl **10**
Weaver, Afaa Michael **37**
Weaver, Robert C. **8, 46**
Webb, Veronica **10**
Webb, Wellington **3**
Webber, Chris **15, 30, 59**
Webster, Katie **29**
Wedgeworth, Robert W. **42**
Weeks, Thomas, III **70**
Weems, Carrie Mae **63**
Weems, Renita J. **44**
Wein, Joyce **62**
Welburn, Edward T. **50**
Welch, Elisabeth **52**
Wells, Henrietta Bell **69**
Wells, James Lesesne **10**
Wells, Mary **28**
Wells-Barnett, Ida B. **8**
Welsing, Frances Cress **5**
Wesley, Dorothy Porter **19**
Wesley, Valerie Wilson **18**
West, Cornel **5, 33**
West, Dorothy **12, 54**
West, Kanye **52**
West, Togo D., Jr. **16**
Westbrook, Kelvin **50**
Westbrook, Peter **20**
Westbrooks, Bobby **51**
Whack, Rita Coburn **36**
Whalum, Kirk **37, 64**
Wharton, Clifton R., Jr. **7**
Wharton, Clifton Reginald, Sr. **36**
Wheat, Alan **14**
Whitaker, Forest **2, 49, 67**
Whitaker, Mark **21, 47**
Whitaker, Pernell **10**
White, Barry **13, 41**
White, Bill **1, 48**
White, Charles **39**
White, Dondi **34**
White, Jesse **22**
White, John H. **27**
White, Josh, Jr. **52**
White, Linda M. **45**
White, Lois Jean **20**
White, Maurice **29**
White, Michael R. **5**
White, Reggie **6, 50**
White, Walter F. **4**
White, Willye **67**
White-Hammond, Gloria **61**
Whitfield, Fred **23**
Whitfield, Lynn **18**
Whitfield, Mal **60**
Whitfield, Van **34**
Wideman, John Edgar **5**
Wilbekin, Emil **63**
Wilbon, Michael **68**
Wilder, L. Douglas **3, 48**
Wiley, Kehinde **62**
Wiley, Ralph **8**
Wilkens, J. Ernest, Jr. **43**
Wilkens, Lenny **11**
Wilkins, Ray **47**
Wilkins, Roger **2**
Wilkins, Roy **4**
will.i.am **64**
Williams, Anthony **21**

Williams, Armstrong **29**
Williams, Bert **18**
Williams, Billy Dee **8**
Williams, Clarence **33**
Williams, Clarence **70**
Williams, Clarence, III **26**
Williams, Daniel Hale **2**
Williams, David Rudyard **50**
Williams, Deniece **36**
Williams, Doug **22**
Williams, Dudley **60**
Williams, Eddie N. **44**
Williams, Evelyn **10**
Williams, Fannie Barrier **27**
Williams, Frederick (B.) **63**
Williams, George Washington **18**
Williams, Gregory **11**
Williams, Hosea Lorenzo **15, 31**
Williams, Joe **5, 25**
Williams, John A. **27**
Williams, Ken **68**
Williams, Lauryn **58**
Williams, Maggie **7**
Williams, Malinda **57**
Williams, Marco **53**
Williams, Mary Lou **15**
Williams, Montel **4, 57**
Williams, Natalie **31**
Williams, O. S. **13**
Williams, Patricia **11, 54**
Williams, Paul R. **9**
Williams, Pharrell **47**
Williams, Preston Warren, II **64**
Williams, Robert F. **11**
Williams, Ronald A. **57**
Williams, Russell, II **70**
Williams, Samm-Art **21**
Williams, Saul **31**
Williams, Serena **20, 41**
Williams, Sherley Anne **25**
Williams, Stanley "Tookie" **29, 57**
Williams, Terrie M. **35**
Williams, Tony **67**
Williams, Vanessa A. **32, 66**
Williams, Vanessa L. **4, 17**
Williams, Venus **17, 34, 62**
Williams, Walter E. **4**
Williams, Wendy **62**
Williams, William T. **11**
Williams, Willie L. **4**
Williamson, Fred **67**
Williamson, Mykelti **22**
Willie, Louis, Jr. **68**
Willis, Bill **68**
Willis, Dontrelle **55**
Wilson, August **7, 33, 55**
Wilson, Cassandra **16**
Wilson, Chandra **57**
Wilson, Charlie **31**
Wilson, Debra **38**
Wilson, Dorien **55**
Wilson, Ellis **39**
Wilson, Flip **21**
Wilson, Gerald **49**
Wilson, Jackie **60**
Wilson, Jimmy **45**
Wilson, Mary **28**
Wilson, Nancy **10**
Wilson, Natalie **38**
Wilson, Phill **9**
Wilson, Sunnie **7, 55**
Wilson, William Julius **20**

Cumulative Occupation Index

Volume numbers appear in **bold**

Cumulative Subject Index

Volume numbers appear in **bold**

A Better Chance
Lewis, William M., Jr. **40**

A Harvest Biotech Foundation International
Wambugu, Florence **42**

AA
See Alcoholics Anonymous

AAAS
See American Association for the Advancement of Science

Aaron Gunner series
Haywood, Gar Anthony **43**

AARP
Dixon, Margaret **14**
Smith, Marie F. **70**

ABC
See American Broadcasting Company

Abstract expressionism
Lewis, Norman **39**

A. C. Green Youth Foundation
Green, A. C. **32**

Academy awards
Austin, Patti **24**
Freeman, Morgan **2, 20, 62**
Goldberg, Whoopi **4, 33, 69**
Gooding, Cuba, Jr. **16, 62**
Gossett, Louis, Jr. **7**
Jean-Baptiste, Marianne **17, 46**
McDaniel, Hattie **5**
Poitier, Sidney **11, 36**
Prince **18, 65**
Richie, Lionel **27, 65**
Washington, Denzel **1, 16**
Whitaker, Forest **2, 49, 67**
Williams, Russell, II **70**
Wonder, Stevie **11, 53**

Academy of Praise
Kenoly, Ron **45**

A cappella
Cooke, Sam **17**
Reagon, Bernice Johnson **7**

Access Hollywood
Robinson, Shaun **36**

ACDL
See Association for Constitutional Democracy in Liberia

ACLU
See American Civil Liberties Union

Acquired Immune Deficiency Syndrome (AIDS)
Ashe, Arthur **1, 18**
Atim, Julian **66**
Broadbent, Hydeia **36**
Cargill, Victoria A. **43**
Gayle, Helene D. **3, 46**
Hale, Lorraine **8**
Johnson, Earvin "Magic" **3, 39**
Lewis-Thornton, Rae **32**
Mboup, Souleymane **10**
Moutoussamy-Ashe, Jeanne **7**
Norman, Pat **10**
Ojikutu, Bisola **65**
Okaalet, Peter **58**
Pickett, Cecil **39**
Riggs, Marlon **5, 44**
Satcher, David **7, 57**
Seele, Pernessa **46**
Wilson, Phill **9**
Zulu, Princess Kasune **54**

Act*1 Personnel Services
Howroyd, Janice Bryant **42**

ACT-SO
See Afro-Academic Cultural, Technological, and Scientific Olympics

Acting
Aaliyah **30**
Adams, Osceola Macarthy **31**
Ailey, Alvin **8**
Akinnuoye-Agbaje, Adewale **56**
Alexander, Khandi **43**
Allen, Debbie **13, 42**
Amos, John **8, 62**
Anderson, Anthony **51**
Anderson, Carl **48**
Anderson, Eddie "Rochester" **30**
Angelou, Maya **1, 15**
Armstrong, Vanessa Bell **24**
Ashanti **37**
Babatunde, Obba **35**
Bahati, Wambui **60**
Baker, Josephine **3**
Banks, Michelle **59**
Banks, Tyra **11, 50**

Barnett, Etta Moten **56**
Bassett, Angela **6, 23, 62**
Beach, Michael **26**
Beals, Jennifer **12**
Beaton, Norman **14**
Beauvais, Garcelle **29**
Bennett, Louise **69**
Bentley, Lamont **53**
Berry, Fred "Rerun" **48**
Berry, Halle **4, 19, 57**
Beyoncé **39, 70**
Blacque, Taurean **58**
Blanks, Billy **22**
Blige, Mary J. **20, 34, 60**
Bonet, Lisa **58**
Borders, James **9**
Bow Wow **35**
Brady, Wayne **32**
Branch, William Blackwell **39**
Braugher, Andre **13, 58**
Bridges, Todd **37**
Brooks, Avery **9**
Brooks, Golden **62**
Brooks, Mehcad **62**
Brown, Jim **11**
Browne, Roscoe Lee **66**
Byrd, Eugene **64**
Caesar, Shirley **19**
Calloway, Cab **14**
Cameron, Earl **44**
Campbell, Naomi **1, 31**
Campbell-Martin, Tisha **8, 42**
Cannon, Nick **47**
Carroll, Diahann **9**
Carson, Lisa Nicole **21**
Carey, Mariah **32, 53, 69**
Cash, Rosalind **28**
Cedric the Entertainer **29, 60**
Cheadle, Don **19, 52**
Chestnut, Morris **31**
Childress, Alice **15**
Chong, Rae Dawn **62**
Chweneyagae, Presley **63**
Clarke, Hope **14**
Cliff, Jimmy **28**
Cole, Nat King **17**
Cole, Natalie **17, 60**
Coleman, Gary **35**
Combs, Sean "Puffy" **17, 43**
Cosby, Bill **7, 26, 59**
Crothers, Scatman **19**
Curry, Mark **17**
Curtis-Hall, Vondie **17**
Dandridge, Dorothy **3**

David, Keith **27**
Davidson, Jaye **5**
Davis, Eisa **68**
Davis, Guy **36**
Davis, Ossie **5, 50**
Davis, Sammy, Jr. **18**
Davis, Viola **34**
Dee, Ruby **8, 50, 68**
Devine, Loretta **24**
Diesel, Vin **29**
Diggs, Taye **25, 63**
Dixon, Ivan **69**
DMX **28, 64**
Dourdan, Gary **37**
Duke, Bill **3**
Duncan, Michael Clarke **26**
Dungey, Merrin **62**
Dutton, Charles S. **4, 22**
Ejiofor, Chiwetel **67**
Elba, Idris **49**
Elise, Kimberly **32**
Emmanuel, Alphonsia **38**
Epps, Mike **60**
Epps, Omar **23, 59**
Esposito, Giancarlo **9**
Everett, Francine **23**
Faison, Donald **50**
Faison, Frankie **55**
Falana, Lola **42**
Fargas, Antonio **50**
Fields, Felicia P. **60**
Fields, Kim **36**
Fetchit, Stepin **32**
Fishburne, Laurence **4, 22, 70**
Fox, Rick **27**
Fox, Vivica A. **15, 53**
Foxx, Jamie **15, 48**
Foxx, Redd **2**
Freeman, Al, Jr. **11**
Freeman, Morgan **2, 20, 62**
Freeman, Yvette **27**
Gaye, Nona **56**
Gibson, Althea **8, 43**
Gibson, Tyrese **27, 62**
Ginuwine **35**
Givens, Adele **62**
Givens, Robin **4, 25, 58**
Glover, Danny **1, 24**
Goldberg, Whoopi **4, 33, 69**
Gooding, Cuba, Jr. **16, 62**
Gordon, Dexter **25**
Gossett, Louis, Jr. **7**
Greaves, William **38**
Grier, David Alan **28**

Burrell, Tom **21, 51**
Campbell, E. Simms **13**
Chisholm, Samuel J. **32**
Coleman, Donald **24, 62**
Cullers, Vincent T. **49**
Johnson, Beverly **2**
Jones, Caroline R. **29**
Jordan, Montell **23**
Lewis, Byron E. **13**
McKinney Hammond, Michelle **51**
Mingo, Frank **32**
Olden, Georg(e) **44**
Pinderhughes, John **47**
Roche, Joyce M. **17**

Advocates Scene
Seale, Bobby **3**

Aetna
Williams, Ronald A. **57**

AFCEA
See Armed Forces Communications and Electronics Associations

Affirmative action
Arnwine, Barbara **28**
Berry, Mary Frances **7**
Carter, Stephen L. **4**
Edley, Christopher F., Jr. **48**
Higginbotham, A. Leon, Jr. **13, 25**
Maynard, Robert C. **7**
Norton, Eleanor Holmes **7**
Rand, A. Barry **6**
Thompson, Bennie G. **26**
Waters, Maxine **3, 67**

AFL-CIO
See American Federation of Labor and Congress of Industrial Organizations

African/African-American Summit
Sullivan, Leon H. **3, 30**

African American Catholic Congregation
Stallings, George A., Jr. **6**

African American Dance Ensemble
Davis, Chuck **33**

African American folklore
Bailey, Xenobia **11**
Brown, Sterling Allen **10, 64**
Driskell, David C. **7**
Ellison, Ralph **7**
Gaines, Ernest J. **7**
Hamilton, Virginia **10**
Hughes, Langston **4**
Hurston, Zora Neale **3**
Lester, Julius **9**
Morrison, Toni **2, 15**
Primus, Pearl **6**
Tillman, George, Jr. **20**
Williams, Bert **18**
Yarbrough, Camille **40**

African American folk music
Cuney, William Waring **44**
Handy, W. C. **8**
House, Son **8**
Johnson, James Weldon **5**
Lester, Julius **9**

Southern, Eileen **56**

African American history
Angelou, Maya **1, 15**
Appiah, Kwame Anthony **67**
Ashe, Arthur **1, 18**
Benberry, Cuesta **65**
Bennett, Lerone, Jr. **5**
Berry, Mary Frances **7**
Blackshear, Leonard **52**
Blockson, Charles L. **42**
Burroughs, Margaret Taylor **9**
Camp, Kimberly **19**
Chase-Riboud, Barbara **20, 46**
Cheadle, Don **19, 52**
Clarke, John Henrik **20**
Clayton, Mayme Agnew **62**
Cobb, William Jelani **59**
Coombs, Orde M. **44**
Cooper, Anna Julia **20**
Dodson, Howard, Jr. **7, 52**
Douglas, Aaron **7**
Du Bois, W. E. B. **3**
DuBois, Shirley Graham **21**
Dyson, Michael Eric **11, 40**
Feelings, Tom **11, 47**
Franklin, John Hope **5**
Gaines, Ernest J. **7**
Gates, Henry Louis, Jr. **3, 38, 67**
Gill, Gerald **69**
Haley, Alex **4**
Halliburton, Warren J. **49**
Harkless, Necia Desiree **19**
Harris, Richard E. **61**
Hine, Darlene Clark **24**
Hughes, Langston **4**
Johnson, James Weldon **5**
Jones, Edward P. **43, 67**
Lewis, David Levering **9**
Madhubuti, Haki R. **7**
Marable, Manning **10**
Morrison, Toni **2**
Painter, Nell Irvin **24**
Pritchard, Robert Starling **21**
Quarles, Benjamin Arthur **18**
Reagon, Bernice Johnson **7**
Ringgold, Faith **4**
Schomburg, Arthur Alfonso **9**
Southern, Eileen **56**
Tancil, Gladys Quander **59**
Wilson, August **7, 33, 55**
Woodson, Carter G. **2**
Yarbrough, Camille **40**

African American Images
Kunjufu, Jawanza **3, 50**

African American literature
Andrews, Raymond **4**
Angelou, Maya **1, 15**
Appiah, Kwame Anthony **67**
Baisden, Michael **25, 66**
Baker, Houston A., Jr. **6**
Baldwin, James **1**
Bambara, Toni Cade **1**
Baraka, Amiri **1, 38**
Bennett, George Harold "Hal" **45**
Bontemps, Arna **8**
Briscoe, Connie **15**
Brooks, Gwendolyn **1, 28**
Brown, Claude **38**
Brown, Wesley **23**
Burroughs, Margaret Taylor **9**
Campbell, Bebe Moore **6, 24, 59**

Cary, Lorene **3**
Childress, Alice **15**
Cleage, Pearl **17, 64**
Cullen, Countee **8**
Curtis, Christopher Paul **26**
Davis, Arthur P. **41**
Davis, Nolan **45**
Dickey, Eric Jerome **21, 56**
Dove, Rita **6**
Du Bois, W. E. B. **3**
Dunbar, Paul Laurence **8**
Ellison, Ralph **7**
Evans, Mari **26**
Fair, Ronald L. **47**
Fauset, Jessie **7**
Feelings, Tom **11, 47**
Fisher, Rudolph **17**
Ford, Nick Aaron **44**
Fuller, Charles **8**
Gaines, Ernest J. **7**
Gates, Henry Louis, Jr. **3, 38, 67**
Gayle, Addison, Jr. **41**
Gibson, Donald Bernard **40**
Giddings, Paula **11**
Giovanni, Nikki **9, 39**
Goines, Donald **19**
Golden, Marita **19**
Guy, Rosa **5**
Haley, Alex **4**
Hansberry, Lorraine **6**
Harper, Frances Ellen Watkins **11**
Heard, Nathan C. **45**
Himes, Chester **8**
Holland, Endesha Ida Mae **3, 57**
Holmes, Shannon **70**
Hughes, Langston **4**
Hull, Akasha Gloria **45**
Hurston, Zora Neale **3**
Iceberg Slim **11**
Joe, Yolanda **21**
Johnson, Charles **1**
Johnson, James Weldon **5**
Jones, Gayl **37**
Jordan, June **7, 35**
July, William **27**
Kitt, Sandra **23**
Larsen, Nella **10**
Lester, Julius **9**
Little, Benilde **21**
Lorde, Audre **6**
Madhubuti, Haki R. **7**
Major, Clarence **9**
Marshall, Paule **7**
McKay, Claude **6**
McKay, Nellie Yvonne **17, 57**
McKinney-Whetstone, Diane **27**
McMillan, Terry **4, 17, 53**
McPherson, James Alan **70**
Morrison, Toni **2, 15**
Mowry, Jess **7**
Myers, Walter Dean **8, 20**
Naylor, Gloria **10, 42**
Painter, Nell Irvin **24**
Petry, Ann **19**
Pinkney, Jerry **15**
Rahman, Aishah **37**
Randall, Dudley **8, 55**
Redding, J. Saunders **26**
Redmond, Eugene **23**
Reed, Ishmael **8**
Ringgold, Faith **4**
Sanchez, Sonia **17, 51**
Schomburg, Arthur Alfonso **9**

Schuyler, George Samuel **40**
Shange, Ntozake **8**
Smith, Mary Carter **26**
Taylor, Mildred D. **26**
Thomas, Trisha R. **65**
Thurman, Wallace **16**
Toomer, Jean **6**
Tyree, Omar Rashad **21**
Van Peebles, Melvin **7**
Verdelle, A. J. **26**
Walker, Alice **1, 43**
Wesley, Valerie Wilson **18**
Wideman, John Edgar **5**
Williams, John A. **27**
Williams, Sherley Anne **25**
Wilson, August **7, 33, 55**
Wolfe, George C. **6, 43**
Wright, Richard **5**
Yarbrough, Camille **40**

African American Research Library and Cultural Center
Morrison, Sam **50**

African American studies
Brawley, Benjamin **44**
Carby, Hazel **27**
Christian, Barbara T. **44**
De Veaux, Alexis **44**
Ford, Nick Aaron **44**
Hare, Nathan **44**
Henderson, Stephen E. **45**
Huggins, Nathan Irvin **52**
Long, Richard Alexander **65**

African Ancestry Inc.
Kittles, Rick **51**

African Burial Ground Project
Perry, Warren **56**

African Canadian literature
Elliott, Lorris **37**
Foster, Cecil **32**
Senior, Olive **37**

African Continental Telecommunications Ltd.
Sutton, Percy E. **42**

African dance
Acogny, Germaine **55**
Adams, Jenoyne **60**
Ailey, Alvin **8**
Davis, Chuck **33**
Fagan, Garth **18**
Primus, Pearl **6**

African Heritage Network
See The Heritage Network

African history
Appiah, Kwame Anthony **67**
Chase-Riboud, Barbara **20, 46**
Clarke, John Henrik **20**
Diop, Cheikh Anta **4**
Dodson, Howard, Jr. **7, 52**
DuBois, Shirley Graham **21**
Feelings, Muriel **44**
Halliburton, Warren J. **49**
Hansberry, William Leo **11**
Harkless, Necia Desiree **19**
Henries, A. Doris Banks **44**
Hilliard, Asa Grant, III **66**
Jawara, Dawda Kairaba **11**

Music publishing
Combs, Sean "Puffy" **17, 43**
Cooke, Sam **17**
Edmonds, Tracey **16, 64**
Gordy, Berry, Jr. **1**
Handy, W. C. **8**
Holland-Dozier-Holland **36**
Humphrey, Bobbi **20**
Ice Cube **8, 30, 60**
Jackson, George **19**
Jackson, Michael **19, 53**
James, Rick **17**
Knight, Suge **11, 30**
Lewis, Emmanuel **36**
Master P **21**
Mayfield, Curtis **2, 43**
Otis, Clyde **67**
Prince **18, 65**
Redding, Otis **16**
Ross, Diana **8, 27**
Shakur, Afeni **67**
Shorty, Ras I **47**

Music Television (MTV)
Bellamy, Bill **12**
Chideya, Farai **14, 61**
Norman, Christina **47**
Powell, Kevin **31**

Musical composition
Armatrading, Joan **32**
Ashford, Nickolas **21**
Baiocchi, Regina Harris **41**
Ballard, Hank **41**
Bebey, Francis **45**
Blanchard, Terence **43**
Blige, Mary J. **20, 34, 60**
Bonds, Margaret **39**
Bonga, Kuenda **13**
Braxton, Toni **15, 61**
Brown, Patrick "Sleepy" **50**
Brown, Uzee **42**
Burke, Solomon **31**
Burleigh, Henry Thacker **56**
Caesar, Shirley **19**
Carter, Warrick L. **27**
Chapman, Tracy **26**
Charlemagne, Manno **11**
Charles, Ray **16, 48**
Cleveland, James **19**
Cole, Natalie **17, 60**
Coleman, Ornette **39, 69**
Collins, Bootsy **31**
Combs, Sean "Puffy" **17, 43**
Cook, Will Marion **40**
Davis, Anthony **11**
Davis, Miles **4**
Davis, Sammy, Jr. **18**
Dawson, William Levi **39**
Diddley, Bo **39**
Domino, Fats **20**
Ellington, Duke **5**
Elliott, Missy **31**
Europe, James Reese **10**
Evans, Faith **22**
Freeman, Paul **39**
Fuller, Arthur **27**
Garrett, Sean **57**
Gaynor, Gloria **36**
George, Nelson **12**
Gillespie, Dizzy **1**
Golson, Benny **37**
Gordy, Berry, Jr. **1**

Green, Al **13, 47**
Hailey, JoJo **22**
Hailey, K-Ci **22**
Hammer, M. C. **20**
Handy, W. C. **8**
Harris, Corey **39**
Hathaway, Donny **18**
Hayes, Isaac **20, 58**
Hayes, Teddy **40**
Hill, Lauryn **20, 53**
Holland-Dozier-Holland **36**
Holmes, Clint **57**
Holt, Nora **38**
Humphrey, Bobbi **20**
Hutch, Willie **62**
Isley, Ronald **25, 56**
Jackson, Fred James **25**
Jackson, Michael **19, 53**
Jackson, Randy **40**
James, Rick **17**
Jean-Baptiste, Marianne **17, 46**
Jean, Wyclef **20**
Jerkins, Rodney **31**
Jones, Jonah **39**
Jones, Quincy **8, 30**
Jones, Thad **68**
Johnson, Buddy **36**
Johnson, Georgia Douglas **41**
Joplin, Scott **6**
Jordan, Montell **23**
Jordan, Ronny **26**
Kay, Ulysses **37**
Kee, John P. **43**
Kelly, R. **18, 44**
Keys, Alicia **32, 68**
Kidjo, Anjelique **50**
Killings, Debra **57**
King, B. B. **7**
León, Tania **13**
Lincoln, Abbey **3**
Little Milton **36, 54**
Little Walter **36**
Lopes, Lisa "Left Eye" **36**
Mahlasela, Vusi **65**
Majors, Jeff **41**
Marsalis, Delfeayo **41**
Marsalis, Wynton **16**
Martin, Roberta **58**
Master P **21**
Maxwell **20**
Mayfield, Curtis **2, 43**
McClurkin, Donnie **25**
McFerrin, Bobby **68**
Mills, Stephanie **36**
Mitchell, Brian Stokes **21**
Mo', Keb' **36**
Monica **21**
Moore, Chante **26**
Moore, Dorothy Rudd **46**
Moore, Undine Smith **28**
Muse, Clarence Edouard **21**
Nash, Johnny **40**
Ndegéocello, Me'Shell **15**
Osborne, Jeffrey **26**
Otis, Clyde **67**
Pratt, Awadagin **31**
Price, Florence **37**
Prince **18, 65**
Pritchard, Robert Starling **21**
Reagon, Bernice Johnson **7**
Redding, Otis **16**
Reed, A. C. **36**
Reid, Antonio "L.A." **28**

Roach, Max **21, 63**
Robinson, Reginald R. **53**
Run-DMC **31**
Rushen, Patrice **12**
Russell, Brenda **52**
Sangare, Oumou **18**
Shorty, Ras I **47**
Silver, Horace **26**
Simone, Nina **15, 41**
Simpson, Valerie **21**
Sowande, Fela **39**
Still, William Grant **37**
Strayhorn, Billy **31**
Sundiata, Sekou **66**
Sweat, Keith **19**
Tillis, Frederick **40**
Usher **23, 56**
Van Peebles, Melvin **7**
Walker, George **37**
Warwick, Dionne **18**
Washington, Grover, Jr. **17, 44**
Williams, Deniece **36**
Williams, Tony **67**
Winans, Angie **36**
Winans, Debbie **36**
Withers, Bill **61**

Musicology
George, Zelma Watson **42**

Muslim Mosque, Inc.
X, Malcolm **1**

Mysteries
Bland, Eleanor Taylor **39**
Creagh, Milton **27**
DeLoach, Nora **30**
Himes, Chester **8**
Holton, Hugh, Jr. **39**
Mickelbury, Penny **28**
Mosley, Walter **5, 25, 68**
Thomas-Graham **29**
Wesley, Valerie Wilson **18**

The Mystery
Delany, Martin R. **27**

Mystic Seaport Museum
Pinckney, Bill **42**

NAACP
See National Association for the Advancement of Colored People

NAACP Image Awards
Fields, Kim **36**
Lawrence, Martin **6, 27, 60**
Okonedo, Sophie **67**
Rhimes, Shonda Lynn **67**
Warner, Malcolm-Jamal **22, 36**

NAACP Legal Defense and Educational Fund (LDF)
Bell, Derrick **6**
Carter, Robert L. **51**
Chambers, Julius **3**
Edelman, Marian Wright **5, 42**
Guinier, Lani **7, 30**
Jones, Elaine R. **7, 45**
Julian, Percy Lavon **6**
Marshall, Thurgood **1, 44**
Motley, Constance Baker **10, 55**
Rice, Constance LaMay **60**
Smith, Kemba **70**

Smythe Haith, Mabel **61**

NABJ
See National Association of Black Journalists

NAC
See Nyasaland African Congress

NACGN
See National Association of Colored Graduate Nurses

NACW
See National Association of Colored Women

NAG
See Nonviolent Action Group

NASA
See National Aeronautics and Space Administration

NASCAR
See National Association of Stock Car Auto Racing

NASCAR Craftsman Truck series
Lester, Bill **42**

NASCAR Diversity Council
Lester, Bill **42**

Nation
Wilkins, Roger **2**

Nation of Islam
See Lost-Found Nation of Islam

National Academy of Design
White, Charles **39**

National Action Council for Minorities in Engineering
Pierre, Percy Anthony **46**
Slaughter, John Brooks **53**

National Action Network
Sharpton, Al **21**

National Aeronautics and Space Administration (NASA)
Anderson, Michael P. **40**
Bluford, Guy **2, 35**
Bolden, Charles F., Jr. **7**
Campbell, Donald J. **66**
Carruthers, George R. **40**
Drew, Alvin, Jr. **67**
Easley, Annie J. **61**
Gregory, Frederick **8, 51**
Jemison, Mae C. **1, 35**
Johnson, Katherine (Coleman Goble) **61**
McNair, Ronald **3, 58**
Mills, Joseph C. **51**
Nichols, Nichelle **11**
Sigur, Wanda **44**

National Afro-American Council
Fortune, T. Thomas **6**
Mossell, Gertrude Bustill **40**

National Airmen's Association of America
Brown, Willa **40**

North Carolina state government
Ballance, Frank W. **41**

North Carolina State University
Lowe, Sidney **64**

North Pole
Delany, Martin R. **27**
Henson, Matthew **2**
Hillary, Barbara **65**
McLeod, Gus **27**

Notre Dame Univeristy
Willingham, Tyrone **43**

NOW
See National Organization for Women

NPR
See National Public Radio

NRA
See National Resistance Army (Uganda); National Rifle Association

NRL
See Naval Research Laboratory

NSF
See National Science Foundation

Nuclear energy
O'Leary, Hazel **6**
Packer, Daniel **56**
Quarterman, Lloyd Albert **4**

Nuclear Regulatory Commission
Jackson, Shirley Ann **12**

Nucleus
King, Yolanda **6**
Shabazz, Attallah **6**

NUM
See National Union of Mineworkers (South Africa)

Nursing
Adams-Ender, Clara **40**
Auguste, Rose-Anne **13**
Hillary, Barbara **65**
Hughes, Ebony **57**
Hunter, Alberta **42**
Johnson, Eddie Bernice **8**
Johnson, Hazel **22**
Johnson, Mamie "Peanut" **40**
Larsen, Nella **10**
Lyttle, Hulda Margaret **14**
Richards, Hilda **49**
Riley, Helen Caldwell Day **13**
Robinson, Rachel **16**
Robinson, Sharon **22**
Seacole, Mary **54**
Shabazz, Betty **7, 26**
Staupers, Mabel K. **7**
Taylor, Susie King **13**

Nursing agency
Daniels, Lee Louis **36**

Nutrition
Clark, Celeste **15**
Gregory, Dick **1, 54**

Smith, Ian **62**
Watkins, Shirley R. **17**

NWBL
See National Women's Basketball League

NYA
See National Youth Administration

Nyasaland African Congress (NAC)
Banda, Hastings Kamuzu **6, 54**

Oakland Athletics baseball team
Baker, Dusty **8, 43**
Baylor, Don **6**
Henderson, Rickey **28**
Jackson, Reggie **15**
Morgan, Joe Leonard **9**

Oakland Oaks baseball team
Dandridge, Ray **36**

Oakland Raiders football team
Howard, Desmond **16, 58**
Upshaw, Gene **18, 47**

Oakland Tribune
Bailey, Chauncey **68**
Maynard, Robert C. **7**

OAR
See Office of AIDS Research

OAU
See Organization of African Unity

Obie awards
Browne, Roscoe Lee **66**
Carter, Nell **39**
Freeman, Yvette **27**
Orlandersmith, Dael **42**
Thigpen, Lynne **17, 41**

OBSSR
See Office of Behavioral and Social Sciences Research

OECS
See Organization of Eastern Caribbean States

Office of AIDS Research (OAR)
Cargill, Victoria A. **43**

Office of Behavioral and Social Science Research
Anderson, Norman B. **45**

Office of Civil Rights
See U.S. Department of Education

Office of Management and Budget
Raines, Franklin Delano **14**

Office of Public Liaison
Herman, Alexis M. **15**

Ohio House of Representatives
Stokes, Carl B. **10**

Ohio state government
Brown, Les **5**
Ford, Jack **39**

Stokes, Carl B. **10**
Williams, George Washington **18**

Ohio State Senate
White, Michael R. **5**

Ohio Women's Hall of Fame
Craig-Jones, Ellen Walker **44**
Stewart, Ella **39**

OIC
See Opportunities Industrialization Centers of America, Inc.

OKeh record label
Brooks, Hadda **40**
Mo', Keb' **36**

Oklahoma Eagle
Ross, Don **27**

Oklahoma Hall of Fame
Mitchell, Leona **42**

Oklahoma House of Representatives
Ross, Don **27**

Olatunji Center for African Culture
Olatunji, Babatunde **36**

Olympics
Abdur-Rahim, Shareef **28**
Ali, Muhammad **2, 16, 52**
Beamon, Bob **30**
Bonaly, Surya **7**
Bowe, Riddick **6**
Carter, Vince **26**
Cash, Swin **59**
Christie, Linford **8**
Clay, Bryan Ezra **57**
Coachman, Alice **18**
Davis, Shani **58**
Dawes, Dominique **11**
DeFrantz, Anita **37**
Devers, Gail **7**
Edwards, Harry **2**
Edwards, Teresa **14**
Ervin, Anthony **66**
Ewing, Patrick A. **17**
Felix, Allyson **48**
Flowers, Vonetta **35**
Ford, Cheryl **45**
Freeman, Cathy **29**
Garrison, Zina **2**
Gebrselassie, Haile **70**
Gourdine, Meredith **33**
Greene, Maurice **27**
Griffith, Yolanda **25**
Griffith-Joyner, Florence **28**
Hardaway, Anfernee (Penny) **13**
Hardaway, Tim **35**
Harrison, Alvin **28**
Harrison, Calvin **28**
Hill, Grant **13**
Hines, Garrett **35**
Holmes, Kelly **47**
Holyfield, Evander **6**
Howard, Sherri **36**
Iginla, Jarome **35**
Johnson, Ben **1**
Johnson, Michael **13**
Johnson, Rafer **33**
Jones, Lou **64**
Jones, Randy **35**

Joyner-Kersee, Jackie **5**
Keflezighi, Meb **49**
Leslie, Lisa **16**
Lewis, Carl **4**
Malone, Karl **18, 51**
Metcalfe, Ralph **26**
Miller, Cheryl **10**
Montgomery, Tim **41**
Moses, Edwin **8**
Mutola, Maria **12**
Owens, Jesse **2**
Pippen, Scottie **15**
Powell, Mike **7**
Quirot, Ana **13**
Richards, Sanya **66**
Robertson, Oscar **26**
Rudolph, Wilma **4**
Russell, Bill **8**
Scurry, Briana **27**
Swoopes, Sheryl **12, 56**
Thomas, Debi **26**
Thugwane, Josia **21**
Ward, Andre **62**
Ward, Lloyd **21, 46**
Westbrook, Peter **20**
Whitaker, Pernell **10**
White, Willye **67**
Whitfield, Mal **60**
Wilkens, Lenny **11**
Williams, Lauryn **58**
Woodruff, John **68**
Woodward, Lynette **67**

On a Roll Radio
Smith, Greg **28**

Oncology
Leffall, Lasalle **3, 64**

One Church, One Child
Clements, George **2**

100 Black Men of America
Dortch, Thomas W., Jr. **45**

One Way-Productions
Naylor, Gloria **10, 42**

Ontario Legislature
Curling, Alvin **34**

Onyx Opera
Brown, Uzee **42**

Onyx Theater Company
Banks, Michelle **59**

OPC
See Ovambo People's Congress

Opera
Adams, Leslie **39**
Anderson, Marian **2, 33**
Arroyo, Martina **30**
Battle, Kathleen **70**
Brooks, Avery **9**
Brown, Angela M. **54**
Brown, Uzee **42**
Bumbry, Grace **5**
Davis, Anthony **11**
Dobbs, Mattiwilda **34**
Estes, Simon **28**
Freeman, Paul **39**
Graves, Denyce Antoinette **19, 57**
Greely, M. Gasby **27**
Hendricks, Barbara **3, 67**

Davis, Benjamin O., Jr. **2, 43**
Drew, Alvin, Jr. **67**
Dwight, Edward **65**
Gregory, Frederick **8, 51**
Harris, Marcelite Jordan **16**
James, Daniel, Jr. **16**
Johnson, Lonnie **32**
Jones, Wayne **53**
Lyles, Lester **31**

U.S. Armed Forces Nurse Corps
Staupers, Mabel K. **7**

U.S. Army
Adams-Ender, Clara **40**
Baker, Vernon Joseph **65**
Cadoria, Sherian Grace **14**
Clemmons, Reginal G. **41**
Davis, Benjamin O., Sr. **4**
Delany, Martin R. **27**
Flipper, Henry O. **3**
Greenhouse, Bunnatine "Bunny" **57**
Honoré, Russel L. **64**
Jackson, Fred James **25**
Johnson, Hazel **22**
Johnson, Shoshana **47**
Matthews, Mark **59**
Powell, Colin **1, 28**
Stanford, John **20**
Watkins, Perry **12**
West, Togo D., Jr. **16**

U.S. Army Air Corps
Anderson, Charles Edward **37**

U.S. Atomic Energy Commission
Nabrit, Samuel Milton **47**

U.S. Attorney's Office
Lafontant, Jewel Stradford **3, 51**

U.S. Basketball League (USBL)
Lucas, John **7**

USBL
See U.S. Basketball League

U.S. Bureau of Engraving and Printing
Felix, Larry R. **64**

USC
See United Somali Congress

U.S. Cabinet
Brown, Ron **5**
Elders, Joycelyn **6**
Espy, Mike **6**
Harris, Patricia Roberts **2**
Herman, Alexis M. **15**
O'Leary, Hazel **6**
Powell, Colin **1, 28**
Rice, Condoleezza **3, 28**
Slater, Rodney E. **15**
Sullivan, Louis **8**
Weaver, Robert C. **8, 46**

U.S. Circuit Court of Appeals
Hastie, William H. **8**
Keith, Damon J. **16**

U.S. Coast Guard
Brown, Erroll M. **23**

U.S. Commission on Civil Rights
Berry, Mary Frances **7**
Edley, Christopher **2, 48**
Fletcher, Arthur A. **63**

U.S. Conference of Catholic Bishops
Gregory, Wilton D. **37**

U.S. Court of Appeals
Higginbotham, A. Leon, Jr. **13, 25**
Kearse, Amalya Lyle **12**
Ogunlesi, Adebayo **37**

USDA
See U.S. Department of Agriculture

U.S. Department of Agriculture (USDA)
Espy, Mike **6**
Vaughn, Gladys Gary **47**
Watkins, Shirley R. **17**
Williams, Hosea Lorenzo **15, 31**

U.S. Department of Commerce
Brown, Ron **5**
Irving, Larry, Jr. **12**
Person, Waverly **9, 51**
Shavers, Cheryl **31**
Wilkins, Roger **2**

U.S. Department of Defense
Greenhouse, Bunnatine "Bunny" **57**
Tribble, Israel, Jr. **8**

U.S. Department of Education
Hill, Anita **5, 65**
Hill, Bonnie Guiton **20**
Paige, Rod **29**
Purnell, Silas **59**
Thomas, Clarence **2, 39, 65**
Tribble, Israel, Jr. **8**
Velez-Rodriguez, Argelia **56**

U.S. Department of Energy
O'Leary, Hazel **6**

U.S. Department of Health and Human Services (HHS)
See also U.S. Department of Health, Education, and Welfare
Gaston, Marilyn Hughes **60**

U.S. Department of Health, Education, and Welfare (HEW)
Bell, Derrick **6**
Berry, Mary Frances **7**
Harris, Patricia Roberts **2**
Johnson, Eddie Bernice **8**
Randolph, Linda A. **52**
Sullivan, Louis **8**

U.S. Department of Housing and Urban Development (HUD)
Blackwell, J. Kenneth, Sr. **61**
Gaines, Brenda **41**
Harris, Patricia Roberts **2**
Jackson, Alphonso R. **48**
Weaver, Robert C. **8, 46**

U.S. Department of Justice
Bell, Derrick **6**
Campbell, Bill **9**
Days, Drew S., III **10**

Guinier, Lani **7, 30**
Holder, Eric H., Jr. **9**
Lafontant, Jewel Stradford **3, 51**
Lewis, Delano **7**
Patrick, Deval **12, 61**
Payton, John **48**
Thompson, Larry D. **39**
Wilkins, Roger **2**

U.S. Department of Labor
Crockett, George W., Jr. **10, 64**
Fletcher, Arthur A. **63**
Herman, Alexis M. **15**

U.S. Department of Social Services
Little, Robert L. **2**

U.S. Department of State
Bethune, Mary McLeod **4**
Bunche, Ralph J. **5**
Frazer, Jendayi **68**
Keyes, Alan L. **11**
Lafontant, Jewel Stradford **3, 51**
Perkins, Edward **5**
Powell, Colin **1, 28**
Rice, Condoleezza **3, 28**
Wharton, Clifton R., Jr. **7**
Wharton, Clifton Reginald, Sr. **36**

U.S. Department of the Interior
Person, Waverly **9, 51**

U.S. Department of Transportation
Davis, Benjamin O., Jr. **2, 43**

U.S. Department of Veterans Affairs
Brown, Jesse **6, 41**

U.S. Diplomatic Corps
Garrett, Joyce Finley **59**
Grimké, Archibald H. **9**
Haley, George Williford Boyce **21**
Harris, Patricia Roberts **2**
Stokes, Carl B. **10**
Van Lierop, Robert **53**

U.S. District Attorney
Harris, Kamala D. **64**
Lloyd, Reginald **64**

U.S. District Court judge
Bryant, William Benson **61**
Carter, Robert L. **51**
Cooke, Marcia **60**
Diggs-Taylor, Anna **20**
Henderson, Thelton E. **68**
Keith, Damon J. **16**
Parsons, James **14**

U.S. Dream Academy
Phipps, Wintley **59**

USFL
See United States Football League

U.S. Foreign Service
Davis, Ruth **37**
Dougherty, Mary Pearl **47**

U.S. Geological Survey
Person, Waverly **9, 51**

U.S. House of Representatives
Archie-Hudson, Marguerite **44**
Ballance, Frank W. **41**
Bishop, Sanford D., Jr. **24**
Brown, Corrine **24**
Burke, Yvonne Braithwaite **42**
Carson, André **69**
Carson, Julia **23, 69**
Chisholm, Shirley **2, 50**
Clay, William Lacy **8**
Clayton, Eva M. **20**
Cleaver, Emanuel **4, 45, 68**
Clyburn, James **21**
Collins, Barbara-Rose **7**
Collins, Cardiss **10**
Conyers, John, Jr. **4, 45**
Crockett, George W., Jr. **10, 64**
Cummings, Elijah E. **24**
Davis, Artur **41**
Dellums, Ronald **2**
Diggs, Charles C. **21**
Dixon, Julian C. **24**
Dymally, Mervyn **42**
Ellison, Keith **59**
Espy, Mike **6**
Fattah, Chaka **11, 70**
Fauntroy, Walter E. **11**
Fields, Cleo **13**
Flake, Floyd H. **18**
Ford, Harold E(ugene) **42**
Ford, Harold E(ugene), Jr. **16, 70**
Franks, Gary **2**
Gray, William H. III **3**
Hastings, Alcee L. **16**
Hawkins, Augustus F. **68**
Hilliard, Earl F. **24**
Jackson, Jesse, Jr. **14, 45**
Jackson Lee, Sheila **20**
Jefferson, William J. **25**
Jordan, Barbara **4**
Kilpatrick, Carolyn Cheeks **16**
Lee, Barbara **25**
Leland, Mickey **2**
Lewis, John **2, 46**
Majette, Denise **41**
McKinney, Cynthia Ann **11, 52**
Meek, Carrie **6**
Meek, Kendrick **41**
Meeks, Gregory **25**
Metcalfe, Ralph **26**
Mfume, Kweisi **6, 41**
Millender-McDonald, Juanita **21, 61**
Mitchell, Parren J. **42, 66**
Moore, Gwendolynne S. **55**
Norton, Eleanor Holmes **7**
Owens, Major **6**
Payne, Donald M. **2, 57**
Pinchback, P. B. S. **9**
Powell, Adam Clayton, Jr. **3**
Rangel, Charles **3, 52**
Rush, Bobby **26**
Scott, David **41**
Scott, Robert C. **23**
Stokes, Louis **3**
Towns, Edolphus **19**
Tubbs Jones, Stephanie **24**
Washington, Harold **6**
Waters, Maxine **3, 67**
Watson, Diane **41**
Watt, Melvin **26**
Watts, J.C. **14, 38**
Wheat, Alan **14**

Cumulative Name Index

*Volume numbers appear in **bold***

Aaliyah 1979-2001 **30**
Aaron, Hank 1934— **5**
Aaron, Henry Louis *See Aaron, Hank*
Abacha, Sani 1943—1998 **11, 70**
Abbott, Diane (Julie) 1953— **9**
Abbott, Robert Sengstacke 1868-1940 **27**
Abdul-Jabbar, Kareem 1947— **8**
Abdulmajid, Iman Mohamed *See Iman*
Abdur-Rahim, Shareef 1976— **28**
Abele, Julian 1881-1950 **55**
Abernathy, Ralph David 1926-1990 **1**
Aberra, Amsale 1954— **67**
Abiola, Moshood 1937–1998 **70**
Abrahams, Peter 1919— **39**
Abu-Jamal, Mumia 1954— **15**
Abubakar, Abdulsalami 1942— **66**
Ace, Johnny 1929-1954 **36**
Achebe, (Albert) Chinua(lumogu) 1930— **6**
Acogny, Germaine 1944— **55**
Adams Earley, Charity (Edna) 1918— **13, 34**
Adams, Eula L. 1950— **39**
Adams, Floyd, Jr. 1945— **12**
Adams, H. Leslie *See Adams, Leslie*
Adams, Jenoyne (?)— **60**
Adams, Johnny 1932-1998 **39**
Adams, Leslie 1932— **39**
Adams, Oleta 19(?)(?)— **18**
Adams, Osceola Macarthy 1890-1983 **31**
Adams, Paul 1977— **50**
Adams, Sheila J. 1943— **25**
Adams, Yolanda 1961— **17, 67**
Adams-Campbell, Lucille L. 1953— **60**
Adams-Ender, Clara 1939— **40**
Adderley, Julian "Cannonball" 1928-1975 **30**
Adderley, Nat 1931-2000 **29**
Adderley, Nathaniel *See Adderley, Nat*
Ade, Sunny King 1946— **41**
Adeniyi, Sunday *See Ade, Sunny King*
Adichie, Chimamanda Ngozi 1977— **64**
Adjaye, David 1966— **38**
Adkins, Rod 1958— **41**

Adkins, Rutherford H. 1924-1998 **21**
Adu, Freddy 1989— **67**
Adu, Fredua Koranteng *See Adu, Freddy*
Adu, Helen Folasade *See Sade*
Agyeman Rawlings, Nana Konadu 1948— **13**
Agyeman, Jaramogi Abebe 1911-2000 **10, 63**
Aidoo, Ama Ata 1942— **38**
Aiken, Loretta Mary *See Mabley, Jackie "Moms"*
Ailey, Alvin 1931-1989 **8**
Ake, Claude 1939-1996 **30**
Akil, Mara Brock 1970— **60**
Akinnuoye-Agbaje, Adewale 1967— **56**
Akinola, Peter Jasper 1944— **65**
Akomfrah, John 1957— **37**
Akon 1973(?)— **68**
Akpan, Uwem 1971— **70**
Akunyili, Dora Nkem 1954— **58**
Al-Amin, Jamil Abdullah 1943— **6**
Albright, Gerald 1947— **23**
Alcindor, Ferdinand Lewis *See Abdul-Jabbar, Kareem*
Alcorn, George Edward, Jr. 1940— **59**
Alert, Kool DJ Red 19(?)(?)— **33**
Alexander, Archie Alphonso 1888-1958 **14**
Alexander, Clifford 1933— **26**
Alexander, John Marshall *See Ace, Johnny*
Alexander, Joyce London 1949— **18**
Alexander, Khandi 1957— **43**
Alexander, Margaret Walker 1915-1998 **22**
Alexander, Sadie Tanner Mossell 1898-1989 **22**
Alexander, Shaun 1977— **58**
Ali Mahdi Mohamed 1940— **5**
Ali, Ayaan Hirsi 1969— **58**
Ali, Hana Yasmeen 1976— **52**
Ali, Laila 1977— **27, 63**
Ali, Mohammed Naseehu 1971— **60**
Ali, Muhammad 1942— **2, 16, 52**
Allain, Stephanie 1959— **49**
Allen, Byron 1961— **3, 24**
Allen, Claude 1960— **68**
Allen, Debbie 1950— **13, 42**
Allen, Ethel D. 1929-1981 **13**

Allen, Marcus 1960— **20**
Allen, Richard 1760-1831 **14**
Allen, Robert L. 1942— **38**
Allen, Samuel W. 1917— **38**
Allen, Tina 1955— **22**
Allen-Buillard, Melba 1960— **55**
Alston, Charles Henry 1907-1997 **33**
Amadi, Elechi 1934— **40**
Amaker, Harold Tommy, Jr. *See Amaker, Tommy*
Amaker, Norman 1935-2000 **63**
Amaker, Tommy 1965— **62**
Amerie 1980— **52**
Ames, Wilmer 1950-1993 **27**
Amin, Idi 1925-2003 **42**
Amos, Emma 1938— **63**
Amos, John 1941— **8, 62**
Amos, Valerie 1954— **41**
Amos, Wally 1937— **9**
Anderson, Anthony 1970— **51**
Anderson, Carl 1945-2004 **48**
Anderson, Charles Edward 1919-1994 **37**
Anderson, Eddie "Rochester" 1905-1977 **30**
Anderson, Elmer 1941— **25**
Anderson, Ho Che 1969— **54**
Anderson, Jamal 1972— **22**
Anderson, Marian 1902— **2, 33**
Anderson, Michael P. 1959-2003 **40**
Anderson, Mike 1959— **63**
Anderson, Norman B. 1955— **45**
Anderson, Viv 1956— **58**
Anderson, William G(ilchrist), D.O. 1927— **57**
Andre 3000 *See Benjamin, Andre*
Andrews, Benny 1930-2006 **22, 59**
Andrews, Bert 1929-1993 **13**
Andrews, Mark *See Sisqo*
Andrews, Raymond 1934-1991 **4**
Angelou, Maya 1928— **1, 15**
Anna Marie *See Lincoln, Abbey*
Annan, Kofi Atta 1938— **15, 48**
Ansa, Tina McElroy 1949— **14**
Anthony, Carmelo 1984— **46**
Anthony, Crystal *See McCrary Anthony, Crystal*
Anthony, Michael 1930(?)— **29**
Anthony, Trey 1974— **63**
Anthony, Wendell 1950— **25**
Appiah, Kwame Anthony 1954— **67**
Arac de Nyeko, Monica 1979— **66**

Arach, Monica *See Arac de Nyeko, Monica*
Archer, Dennis (Wayne) 1942— **7, 36**
Archer, Michael D'Angelo *See D'Angelo*
Archer, Osceola *See Adams, Osceola Macarthy*
Archie-Hudson, Marguerite 1937— **44**
Ardoin, Alphonse 1915-2007 **65**
Arinze, Francis Cardinal 1932— **19**
Aristide, Jean-Bertrand 1953— **6, 45**
Arkadie, Kevin 1957— **17**
Armah, Ayi Kwei 1939— **49**
Armatrading, Joan 1950— **32**
Armstrong, (Daniel) Louis 1900-1971 **2**
Armstrong, Robb 1962— **15**
Armstrong, Vanessa Bell 1953— **24**
Arnez J, 1966(?)— **53**
Arnold, Monica *See Monica*
Arnold, Tichina 1971— **63**
Arnwine, Barbara 1951(?)— **28**
Arrington, Richard 1934— **24**
Arroyo, Martina 1936— **30**
Artest, Ron 1979— **52**
Arthur, Owen 1949— **33**
Asante, Molefi Kete 1942— **3**
Ashanti 1980— **37**
Ashe, Arthur Robert, Jr. 1943-1993 **1, 18**
Ashford, Emmett 1914-1980 **22**
Ashford, Evelyn 1957— **63**
Ashford, Nickolas 1942— **21**
Ashley, Maurice 1966— **15, 47**
Ashley-Ward, Amelia 1957— **23**
Atim, Julian 1980(?)— **66**
Atkins, Cholly 1930-2003 **40**
Atkins, David *See Sinbad*
Atkins, Erica 1972(?)— *See Mary Mary*
Atkins, Jeffrey *See Ja Rule*
Atkins, Juan 1962— **50**
Atkins, Russell 1926— **45**
Atkins, Tina 1975(?)— *See Mary Mary*
Atyam, Angelina 1946— **55**
Aubert, Alvin 1930— **41**
Auguste, Arnold A. 1946— **47**
Auguste, Donna 1958— **29**
Auguste, (Marie Carmele) Rose-Anne 1963— **13**

Hunter-Gault, Charlayne 1942— **6, 31**
Hurston, Zora Neale 1891-1960 **3**
Hurt, Byron 1970— **61**
Hurtt, Harold 1947(?)— **46**
Hutch, Willie 1944-2005 **62**
Hutcherson, Hilda Yvonne 1955— **54**
Hutchinson, Earl Ofari 1945— **24**
Hutson, Jean Blackwell 1914— **16**
Hyde, Cowan F. "Bubba" 1908-2003 **47**
Hyman, Earle 1926— **25**
Hyman, Phyllis 1949(?)-1995 **19**
Ibrahim, Mo 1946— **67**
Ice Cube 1969— **8, 30, 60**
Iceberg Slim 1918-1992 **11**
Ice-T 1958(?)— **6, 31**
Ifill, Gwen 1955— **28**
Iginla, Jarome 1977— **35**
Ilibagiza, Immaculée 1972(?)— **66**
Iman 1955— **4, 33**
Iman, Chanel 1989— **66**
Imes, Elmer Samuel 1883-1941 **39**
India.Arie 1975— **34**
Ingraham, Hubert A. 1947— **19**
Ingram, Rex 1895-1969 **5**
Innis, Roy (Emile Alfredo) 1934— **5**
Irvin, Michael 1966— **64**
Irvin, (Monford Merrill) Monte 1919— **31**
Irvin, Vernon 1961— **65**
Irving, Clarence (Larry) 1955— **12**
Irvis, K. Leroy 1917(?)-2006 **67**
Isaac, Julius 1928— **34**
Isley, Ronald 1941— **25, 56**
Iverson, Allen 1975— **24, 46**
Ja Rule 1976— **35**
Jackson Lee, Sheila 1950— **20**
Jackson, Alexine Clement 1936— **22**
Jackson, Alphonso R. 1946— **48**
Jackson, Earl 1948— **31**
Jackson, Edison O. 1943(?)— **67**
Jackson, Fred James 1950— **25**
Jackson, George 1960(?)— **19**
Jackson, George Lester 1941-1971 **14**
Jackson, Hal 1915— **41**
Jackson, Isaiah (Allen) 1945— **3**
Jackson, Jamea 1986— **64**
Jackson, Janet 1966— **6, 30, 68**
Jackson, Jesse 1941— **1, 27**
Jackson, Jesse Louis, Jr. 1965— **14, 45**
Jackson, John 1924-2002 **36**
Jackson, Judith D. 1950— **57**
Jackson, Mae 1941-2005 **57**
Jackson, Mahalia 1911-1972 **5**
Jackson, Mannie 1939— **14**
Jackson, Maynard (Holbrook, Jr.) 1938-2003 **2, 41**
Jackson, Michael 1958— **19, 53**
Jackson, Millie 1944— **25**
Jackson, Milt 1923-1999 **26**
Jackson, O'Shea See Ice Cube
Jackson, Randy 1956— **40**
Jackson, Reginald Martinez 1946— **15**
Jackson, Samuel 1948— **8, 19, 63**
Jackson, Sheneska 1970(?)— **18**
Jackson, Shirley Ann 1946— **12**
Jackson, Tom 1951— **70**
Jackson, Vera 1912— **40**

Jaco, Wasalu Muhammad See Fiasco, Lupe
Jacob, John E(dward) 1934— **2**
Jacobs, Marion Walter See Little Walter
Jacobs, Regina 1963— **38**
Jacquet, Illinois 1922(?)-2004 **49**
Jagan, Cheddi 1918-1997 **16**
Jaheim 1978— **58**
Jakes, Thomas "T.D." 1957— **17, 43**
Jam, Jimmy See Jimmy Jam
Jamal, Ahmad 1930— **69**
Jamelia 1981— **51**
Jamerson, James 1936-1983 **59**
James, Charles H., III 1959(?)— **62**
James, Daniel "Chappie," Jr. 1920-1978 **16**
James, Donna A. 1957— **51**
James, Etta 1938— **13, 52**
James, Juanita (Therese) 1952— **13**
James, LeBron 1984— **46**
James, Sharpe 1936— **23, 69**
James, Skip 1902-1969 **38**
Jamison, Judith 1943— **7, 67**
Jammeh, Yahya 1965— **23**
Jarreau, Al 1940— **21, 65**
Jarret, Vernon D. 1921— **42**
Jarvis, Charlene Drew 1941— **21**
Jarvis, Erich 1965— **67**
Jasper, Kenji 1976(?)— **39**
Jawara, Dawda Kairaba 1924— **11**
Jay, Jam Master 1965— **31**
Jay-Z 1970— **27, 69**
Jealous, Benjamin 1973— **70**
Jean, Michaëlle 1957— **70**
Jean, Wyclef 1970— **20**
Jean-Baptiste, Marianne 1967— **17, 46**
Jeffers, Eve Jihan See Eve
Jefferson, William J. 1947— **25**
Jeffries, Leonard 1937— **8**
Jemison, Mae C. 1957— **1, 35**
Jemison, Major L. 1955(?)— **48**
Jenifer, Franklyn G(reen) 1939— **2**
Jenkins, Beverly 1951— **14**
Jenkins, Ella (Louise) 1924— **15**
Jenkins, Fergie 1943— **46**
Jenkins, Jay See Young Jeezy
Jennings, Chester See Jennings, Lyfe
Jennings, Lyfe 1973— **56, 69**
Jerkins, Rodney 1978(?)— **31**
Jeter, Derek 1974— **27**
Jimmy Jam 1959— **13**
Joachim, Paulin 1931— **34**
Joe, Yolanda 19(?)(?)— **21**
John, Daymond 1969(?)— **23**
Johns, Vernon 1892-1965 **38**
Johnson, Angela 1961— **52**
Johnson, Arnez See Arnez J
Johnson, Avery 1965— **62**
Johnson, Ben 1961— **1**
Johnson, Beverly 1952— **2**
Johnson, Buddy 1915-1977 **36**
Johnson, Carol Diann See Carroll, Diahann
Johnson, Caryn E. See Goldberg, Whoopi
Johnson, Charles 1948— **1**
Johnson, Charles Arthur See St. Jacques, Raymond

Johnson, Charles Spurgeon 1893-1956 **12**
Johnson, Clifford "Connie" 1922-2004 **52**
Johnson, Dwayne See Rock, The
Johnson, Earvin "Magic" 1959— **3, 39**
Johnson, Eddie Bernice 1935— **8**
Johnson, George E. 1927— **29**
Johnson, Georgia Douglas 1880-1966 **41**
Johnson, Harry E. 1954— **57**
Johnson, Harvey Jr. 1947(?)— **24**
Johnson, Hazel 1927— **22**
Johnson, J. J. 1924-2001 **37**
Johnson, Jack 1878-1946 **8**
Johnson, James Louis See Johnson, J. J.
Johnson, James Weldon 1871-1938 **5**
Johnson, James William See Johnson, James Weldon
Johnson, Je'Caryous 1977— **63**
Johnson, Jeh Vincent 1931— **44**
Johnson, John Arthur See Johnson, Jack
Johnson, John H. 1918-2005 **3, 54**
Johnson, Johnnie 1924-2005 **56**
Johnson, Katherine (Coleman Goble) 1918— **61**
Johnson, Kevin 1966— **70**
Johnson, Larry 1969— **28**
Johnson, Levi 1950— **48**
Johnson, Linton Kwesi 1952— **37**
Johnson, Lonnie G. 1949— **32**
Johnson, "Magic" See Johnson, Earvin "Magic"
Johnson, Mamie "Peanut" 1932— **40**
Johnson, Marguerite See Angelou, Maya
Johnson, Mat 1971(?)— **31**
Johnson, Michael (Duane) 1967— **13**
Johnson, Norma L. Holloway 1932— **17**
Johnson, R. M. 1968— **36**
Johnson, Rafer 1934— **33**
Johnson, Robert 1911-1938 **2**
Johnson, Robert L. 1946(?)— **3, 39**
Johnson, Robert T. 1948— **17**
Johnson, Rodney Van 19(?)(?)— **28**
Johnson, Sheila Crump 1949(?)— **48**
Johnson, Shoshana 1973— **47**
Johnson, Taalib See Musiq
Johnson, Virginia (Alma Fairfax) 1950— **9**
Johnson, William Henry 1901-1970 **3**
Johnson, Woodrow Wilson See Johnson, Buddy
Johnson-Brown, Hazel W. See Johnson, Hazel
Jolley, Willie 1956— **28**
Jones, Absalom 1746-1818 **52**
Jones, Alex 1941— **64**
Jones, Anthony See Jones, Van
Jones, Bill T. 1952— **1, 46**
Jones, Bobby 1939(?)— **20**
Jones, Carl 1955(?)— **7**
Jones, Caroline R. 1942— **29**
Jones, Clara Stanton 1913— **51**

Jones, Cobi N'Gai 1970— **18**
Jones, Donell 1973— **29**
Jones, Doris W. 1914(?)–2006 **62**
Jones, E. Edward, Sr. 1931— **45**
Jones, Ed "Too Tall" 1951— **46**
Jones, Edith Mae Irby 1927— **65**
Jones, Edward P. 1950— **43, 67**
Jones, Elaine R. 1944— **7, 45**
Jones, Elvin 1927–2004 **14, 68**
Jones, Etta 1928-2001 **35**
Jones, Frederick McKinley 1893–1961 **68**
Jones, Frederick Russell See Jamal, Ahmad
Jones, Gayl 1949— **37**
Jones, Hank 1918— **57**
Jones, Ingrid Saunders 1945— **18**
Jones, James Earl 1931— **3, 49**
Jones, Jonah 1909-2000 **39**
Jones, Kelis See Kelis
Jones, Kimberly Denise See Lil' Kim
Jones, Le Roi See Baraka, Amiri
Jones, Lillie Mae See Carter, Betty
Jones, Lois Mailou 1905— **13**
Jones, Lou 1932-2006 **64**
Jones, Marion 1975— **21, 66**
Jones, Merlakia 1973— **34**
Jones, Monty 1951(?)— **66**
Jones, Nasir See Nas
Jones, Orlando 1968— **30**
Jones, Quincy (Delight) 1933— **8, 30**
Jones, Randy 1969— **35**
Jones, Robert Elliott See Jones, Jonah
Jones, Roy Jr. 1969— **22**
Jones, Russell See Ol' Dirty Bastard
Jones, Ruth Lee See Washington, Dinah
Jones, Sarah 1974— **39**
Jones, Sissieretta See Joyner, Matilda Sissieretta
Jones, Star See Reynolds, Star Jones
Jones, Thad 1923–1986 **68**
Jones, Thomas W. 1949— **41**
Jones, Van 1968— **70**
Jones, Wayne 1952— **53**
Jones, William A., Jr. 1934-2006 **61**
Joplin, Scott 1868-1917 **6**
Jordan, Barbara (Charline) 1936— **4**
Jordan, Eric Benét See Benét, Eric
Jordan, June 1936— **7, 35**
Jordan, Michael (Jeffrey) 1963— **6, 21**
Jordan, Montell 1968(?)— **23**
Jordan, Ronny 1962— **26**
Jordan, Vernon E(ulion, Jr.) 1935— **3, 35**
Joseph, Kathie-Ann 1970(?)— **56**
Josey, E. J. 1924— **10**
Joyner, Jacqueline See Joyner-Kersee, Jackie
Joyner, Marjorie Stewart 1896-1994 **26**
Joyner, Matilda Sissieretta 1869(?)-1933 **15**
Joyner, Tom 1949(?)— **19**
Joyner-Kersee, Jackie 1962— **5**
Julian, Percy Lavon 1899–1975 **6**
Julien, Isaac 1960— **3**